Round the Church in 50 Years

Round the Church in 50 Years

A Personal Journey

Trevor Beeson

scm press

British Library Cataloguing in Publication data

A catalogue record for this book is available
from the British Library

283·42

978 0 334 04148 1

First published in 2007 by SCM Press
13–17 Long Lane,
London EC1A 9PN

www.scm-canterburypress.co.uk

SCM Press is a division of
SCM-Canterbury Press Ltd

Typeset by Regent Typesetting, London
Printed and bound in Great Britain by
William Clowes Ltd, Beccles, Suffolk

Contents

Preface

Fifty years is a short time in the long history of the Church of England but the half century between 1950 and 2000 was a period of turbulence and change on a scale not experienced since the sixteenth and seventeenth centuries. Some of this was energized by the unprecedented changes taking place in British society as a whole but much came from belated recognition by many in the church that the traditional patterns of its life and the inherited expression of its beliefs would no longer assist in the extension of the Kingdom of God in the modern world.

It was my privilege and joy to be called to the full-time service of the church, as a priest, for all but the first year of the half century. I was also fortunate enough to be allowed to serve in a variety of spheres – coalmining and new-housing area parishes in North East England, St Martin-in-the-Fields in Trafalgar Square, a market town in Hertfordshire, Westminster Abbey, with special responsibilities for St Margaret's Church and the chaplaincy of the House of Commons, Winchester Cathedral and finally, in retirement, a group of small rural parishes in Hampshire. All of which, combined with my responsibilities in the Parish and People Movement and Christian Action, enabled me to encounter people and places well beyond the pathway along which I was myself journeying.

I lack the skills of a historian, and in any case the late twentieth century is still too close for anything other than an interim judgement on its extraordinary happenings. So this is not a history book. But for virtually the whole of my ministry as a priest I have also been a journalist and writer, ever seeking to chronicle and interpret current events. This book is therefore a chronicle of the 50 years and I have felt free not only to revisit the highways of my journey but also to linger on the many byways, revelling in the company of remarkable characters, rejoicing in the memory of faithful ministries and new approaches to the Christian mission, and greatly cheered by the rediscovery of a host of zany absurdities.

It is in these byways that the real Church of England is still to be found and where its survival ultimately depends. I have ventured also to include here and there a little biographical material in the hope that this might illuminate particular places and events.

Once again I am grateful to Fiona Mather for help in tracking down long-lost evidence and especially to Kathleen James for dealing efficiently and at breakneck speed with the chaotic writing of an elderly traveller in a breathless hurry.

TB

Easter 2007

An Introduction

1 *A magnificent Norman legacy*

Durham Cathedral, the finest Romanesque church in Europe, standing on an incomparable site high above the River Wear, expresses architecturally and historically the intimate relationship between the Church of England and the English nation over nearly one thousand years. This it shares with Westminster Abbey and Winchester Cathedral, two other great churches with which I was privileged to be associated over the course of a ministry which extended over the second half of the twentieth century.

When, under the direction of William the Conqueror, a cathedral and a castle were built side by side at Durham, he was making a statement about Norman power and at the same time asserting the unity of church and state. It was his intention to bring the English church into the mainstream of continental church life, but not at the expense of submission to the increasing demands of the eleventh-century papacy. His own writ over every part of the nation's life was complete, though he was happy to entrust the day-to-day life of Durham Cathedral, as that of other cathedrals, to a community of Benedictine monks. The bishop, himself a monk, had however other responsibilities, not only within his diocese but also in the administration of government. And as the Middle Ages advanced he was, in the role of a prince bishop, required to rule as court palatine over what amounted to a buffer state between the rest of England and Scotland, with his own army, mint and administrative apparatus.

The cathedral, started in 1090 and completed for the most part in a mere 40 years, is testimony to the zeal and skill of its Anglo-Norman masons. Massive, rugged, powerful and, in comparison with later cathedrals, decidedly austere, it reflects the spirit of the age in which it was built but also the temperament of the Durham people whose lives have been spent within its diocese. And the presence within it of the shrine of St Cuthbert and the tomb of the Venerable Bede are a vivid reminder of the richness of the Celtic Christianity and culture that preceded the Norman invasion.

2 *Hope and a young reformer*

It was before the high altar of this great church that I knelt on Trinity Sunday in 1951 to be admitted by the laying on of episcopal hands to the order of deacon and to which I returned 12 months later to be ordained to the priesthood. Behind me lay a Christian upbringing – my father, a grocer, was a churchwarden – service in the Royal Air Force during the closing stages and immediately after the ending of the 1939–45 war, three years at King's College, London, followed by a further year of pastoral training at St Boniface College, Warminster.

My presence in Durham, rather than any other cathedral, was related directly to a talk given in the chapel of King's College by an archdeacon who set before us the results of research carried out into the distribution of curates. This had revealed a chronic shortage in the North of England and a growing tendency for men to be ordained in the South. It was hoped therefore that some of us would consider very seriously the possibility of helping to correct the imbalance. Having so considered, I concluded, in the pragmatic way that has always tended to influence my decisions, that it would be more reasonable for someone like myself whose home in Nottinghamshire was, as it were, already half way to the North to volunteer, rather than expect dwellers in Devon and Cornwall, or even Surrey, to venture so far from home.

The call to the priesthood had come to me not in some blinding flash of divine illumination demanding the response 'Here am I, send me', but rather in a number of more subtle pointers arising from my involvement in the life of my local church and not least in the influence of Archbishop William Temple whose leadership during the war years had demonstrated the inseparability of Christian faith and social action, and of the need for the church to be deeply involved in the creation of a better world once the war had ended. It also became apparent to me, as to many others, that the church could only fulfil its radical calling it if was itself radically reformed. So I went forward to ordination as a reformer and, as it turned out, there chanced to be in North West Durham the coal-mining parish of Leadgate where a considerable programme of church reform was well under way. My ordination was therefore a moment of high hope and, during the long ministry inaugurated more than half a century ago in Durham Cathedral, that hope has never left me.

3 The dons of Durham and the miners

The senior clergy of the diocese reflected accurately Durham's historic ecclesiastical status and intellectual pre-eminence. The bishop, Alwyn Terrell Petre Williams, had been a notable Headmaster of Winchester College in the 1920s, who then spent a few years as Dean of Christ Church, Oxford, before moving north to succeed the legendary Herbert Hensley Henson in 1937. A former Fellow of All Souls College, Oxford, he was very much an intellectual's intellectual and had apparently read everything. Yet he wrote only one book – a slender volume on *The Anglican Tradition in the Life of England* (1947) – but devoted much time to the chairmanship of the translation committee of the New English Bible. I found him shy, albeit kind, but hardly knew him, since by the time of my ordination he was in poor health and soon to be translated to the more hospitable clime of Winchester. It was a pity that the short biography of so meticulous a scholar should have been full of misprints.

The Dean, Cyril Argentine Alington, was also on the eve of departure – to retirement. Prior to his appointment to the cathedral he had spent all his ministry in public schools – Master in College at Eton, Headmaster of Shrewsbury, then back to Eton as Headmaster. He was a widely cultivated man with some poetic gifts, but I never met him, except at the ordination, or his wife, the Honourable Hester Alington, who was said to be formidable. Much later, however, I did get to know rather well one of their daughters, Elizabeth, who married Alec Douglas-Home, the future Prime Minister and who during my years as chaplain to the House of Commons was a valued mother-figure to MPs' wives.

The Archdeacon of Durham, Egbert de Grey Lucas, was a picaresque figure who had also moved to Durham from Winchester College. He had dirtied his hands as the college's missioner in a Portsmouth high-church slum parish made famous by the devoted but controversial ministry of Father Dolling. Beyond the cathedral he made a splendid sight in an open-top car of great antiquity, which made his visits to parishes specially memorable. He, too, soon departed to retirement.

The Archdeacon of Auckland, John Ramsbotham, was also Suffragan Bishop of Jarrow as well as a canon of the cathedral. He combined intellectual and pastoral gifts and strongly supported my Stockton-on-Tees work before leaving to become Bishop of Wakefield. We remained in touch and were good friends until his death in 1989. The other canons were all scholars. Stanley Greenslade, who held the Van Mildert chair of Divinity in the university, was an early church historian, while H. E. W. (Hughie) Turner, who held the Lightfoot chair, was a patristics specialist. Alan Richardson, a much younger man, had no university appointment but was a well-known biblical scholar and, after holding the chair of Theology at Nottingham University, became Dean of York.

No one could say that this was an undistinguished hierarchy and the replacements – Bishop Michael Ramsey, previously Regius Professor of Divinity at Cambridge, Dean John Wild, previously Master of University College, Oxford, and Archdeacon J. O. C. ('Jock') Cobham, previously Principal of The Queen's College, Birmingham – hardly lowered the standard.

It was very splendid. The only difficulty lay in relating their gifts and experience to a diocese in which coal miners and shipyard and steel workers constituted the overwhelming majority of the population.

4 The road to a Durham mining village

As a mining community Leadgate was scarcely different from the one described by George Orwell in 1937 in *The Road to Wigan Pier,* except that it was a self-contained village of about six thousand people, perched at a thousand feet above sea level in the foothills of the Pennines. On New Year's Eve in 1952 there was a heavy fall of snow, followed by hard frost and further falls, so the ground was not seen again until the end of March. The village served two collieries, each with a board at its entrance proclaiming 'Managed by the National Coal Board on behalf of the people'. Six more collieries were visible from the church, St Ives, located on a hill at the edge of the village. All were hopelessly uneconomic, since the best of the coal had been extracted many years earlier, leaving only thin seams, these requiring the removal of huge quantities of rock before they could be mined. At the coalface the miners lay almost horizontal with mechanical drills which created clouds of choking dust, though overall the mines were wet and smoking was allowed. There were some conveyor belts to move coal to the foot of the mineshaft, but ponies were still used to pull trucks of it and the ponies became almost blind.

The miners were mostly small men, often with curved noses and sometimes showing signs of injured limbs. Their broad Durham accent was, initially, difficult to understand. They were housed in long rows of depressingly grey bungalows, constructed of breeze blocks at the time of the collieries' opening in the nineteenth century. The layout was impersonal in the extreme – 1st Street, 2nd Street, and so on. Addresses were 12/4 Watling Bungalows, 38/5 Pont Bungalows or 20 Front Street. Each bungalow had a long, narrow garden, often neglected, since the men had had more than enough physical toil by the time they returned from the pit. Most were without bathrooms and the collieries lacked pithead baths, so the pale-faced, yet grimy miner's first task on reaching home at the end of a shift was to go into a tin bath that had been prepared by his wife in front of an open fire. Earlier she had prepared his 'bait' – the sandwiches, pies and flask of tea that would sustain him during his eight or more hours underground. Delayed arrival home always created anxiety: had there been an accident? Bobby Packer, in his mid-30s and the father of three, was the admirable superintendent of our mission church Sunday school at Crookhall – a smaller mining community – but soon after my arrival his spine was fractured by an underground roof collapse and he spent the remainder of his life in a wheelchair. I never met a miner who did not vow that none of his own sons would ever work in a pit.

There were alternatives. The Consett Steel Works, about two miles away, was one of the largest in Europe and flourishing. By night the molten steel made a spectacular – some thought hellish – sight, visible for miles around. The pay was good, but its days were also numbered and when closure came in the 1980s, not long after that of the coal mines, the surrounding communities lost their raison d'être and the area recovered much of its pre-industrial beauty.

5 True friendship, true community

This was the community to which ordination took me in a stroke of good fortune – or was it divine providence? – for which I have never ceased to be thankful. The Durham miner was quite special – tough, yet warm-hearted, candid yet kind, never rich yet immensely generous, acquainted with adversity yet rarely downcast, loyal yet not afraid to voice criticism. A community made up of such men and their families had been welded by toil and shared experiences, good and bad, into a rare solidarity of purpose and common concern such as I had never before encountered, neither have I since.

On my arrival in the parish I began, as was customary in the 1950s, to spend every afternoon visiting the people in their homes, but soon there was a complaint to the Vicar that I was unfriendly. The explanation of this was that I knocked on the front door and waited to be admitted, whereas I should have knocked and walked straight in. This was easily remedied and concern for the young curate and his family was soon expressed in a variety of ways – jugs of steaming home-made soup from the large pan permanently stationed on the open-fire range, regular supplies of cheese, surplus to the needs of miners who were allocated a larger ration than the rest of the people, deliveries of coal, again superfluous to requirements, but, since given free to miners, unscreened and, therefore, containing a sometimes explosive mix of coal and rock.

Death evoked intense community solidarity. It was normal for the mortally ill to die in their own homes, or if in hospital for the body to be returned home. During the days before the funeral friends and neighbours called to express their sorrow and usually to see the body. A priest or minister would arrive to conduct prayers, and on the day of the funeral a kindly neighbour would tap on every door of the long street and announce, 'Lifting is at (say) half past one.' Shortly before this hour a bus arrived to convey women and the infirm to church, immediately after the 'screwing down, or lifting, prayers' offered while the undertaker prepared the coffin for removal. The hearse was followed to church by a long procession of men, each wearing his black, flat funeral cap and made a sombre, moving sight as a community accompanied one of its number as he or she went to a resting place in the churchyard.

The parish church, St Ives (so named, it was said, as a gesture to Cornish tin-miners who had migrated to the area to open the coal mines), was Victorian, but free of overmuch ornamentation, and while serviceable rather than beautiful was much loved by those for whom it had become a spiritual home. Sharply contrasting in appearance was the Crookhall mission church, St Barnabas – a former 1914–18 war army hut – immediately adjacent, like the miners' bungalows, to the colliery spoil heap. This towered above the community like a small mountain and on windy days deposited filthy dust on everything within reach. It was a grim place, yet the spirit of it could not have been warmer. There was a lively congregation and the colliery's silver band had a national reputation, winning prizes in competitions in London's Albert Hall, and broadcasting frequently.

The Confident Fifties

When the 1950s arrived the Church of England, in common with the rest of the nation, was still involved in a massive programme of reconstruction following the most devastating war in human history. Church buildings, heavily damaged, sometimes completely destroyed by bombing, required restoration. Large-scale housing developments needed new churches and other meeting places, redeployment of clergy, additional finance and redrawing of parish boundaries. Archbishop Geoffrey Fisher believed that nothing less than a complete revision of canon law was called for.

But the Festival of Britain in 1951 and, most decisively, the Coronation in 1953 signalled the arrival of a new era of confidence in the nation and the church. There was talk of 'a new Elizabethan age'. As the decade advanced, growing affluence suggested that the poverty of the 1930s and the grim days of the 1940s could now be consigned to history, though the Suez debacle in 1956 demonstrated that Britain's place as a major world power had also gone for good.

The Church of England had continued to suffer an erosion of its membership since 1939 and there was now a serious shortage of clergy, but few in the church felt depressed. Most of the population still resorted to their parish churches, if not on a Sunday at least on important occasions in the lives of their families and friends. The post-war intake of clergy – many of whom had been personally matured by battle and all of whom had high ideals – promised the recovery of lost ground and the seizure of new opportunities.

The church retained a prominent place in society. The Archbishop of Canterbury could, if he chose, address leading politicians as if they were delinquent schoolboys. Many of the bishops were men of distinction who, in company with the Lord Lieutenant, stood at the apex of county establishments. The press was still deferential and the Coronation, witnessed by millions for the first time through television, gave the

Church of England massive exposure in a most favourable context. Even the England cricket captain was moving towards ordination and then, as a curate, scored 119 against the Australians at Manchester.

Moreover there soon appeared signs of new life. Christian Action's concern for social and racial justice indicated that the spirit of Archbishop William Temple was still alive. Co-operation with the Free Churches was advancing as never before. The Parish Communion movement was sweeping the country and in some places invigorating the church's mission as well as its worship. Vicars in North London and Leeds wrote widely read books with encouraging titles – The Parish in Action *(1954),* The Parish Comes Alive *(1956). In a remote area of Lincolnshire 12 tiny parishes were formed into what was called a group ministry, with surprisingly encouraging results. In Sheffield a radical new approach to industrial society attracted international interest.*

There was much for Anglicans to cheer and although the Archbishop could not emulate the Prime Minister and tell his flock 'you have never had it so good', he said on the eve of his retirement in 1961, 'I leave the Church of England in good heart.' There were, however, signs that this balloon of confidence and complacency in the church would soon be pricked, and the race riots in London's Notting Hill in 1958 were a clear indication that all was far from well with society as a whole.

1 *The national leadership – the end of an era*

Beyond Durham the Church of England had in its leadership a remarkable number of bishops who were of considerable stature. Geoffrey Fisher was at Canterbury and Cyril Garbett at York. William Wand, a church historian and former Archbishop of Brisbane, was at London. Mervyn Haig, who could well have been an archbishop, was at Winchester, and Leslie Hunter, formidable and prophetic, was an outstanding Bishop of Sheffield. George Bell, internationally famous as a reconciler and ecumenical leader, as well as a courageous opponent of wartime area bombing, was still at Chichester, and Noel Hudson at Newcastle was leading his diocese in the adoption of the Parish Communion as the chief act of Sunday worship.

A. E. J. Rawlinson (Derby), R. C. Mortimer (Exeter), K. E. Kirk (Oxford), J. E. Hunter (Truro), E. W. Barnes (Birmingham) and F. R. Barry (Southwell) were notable scholars, all of whom found time to write serious books. Christopher Chavasse, the founder of St Peter's Hall, Oxford, had led the evangelical opposition to the 1928 Prayer Book, and was now at Rochester, while Edward Woods, one of the twentieth century's great pastoral bishops, was at Lichfield. Neville Gorton, a saintly eccentric and former headmaster of Sedburgh, was edifying and amusing Coventry diocese, and Spencer Leeson, another former headmaster of Winchester College (as a layman) was at Peterborough and the church's authority on schools.

Without realizing it, I had been ordained at the end of an era in which the Church of England had been able to attract to its ranks a good supply of men of this calibre. The occupants of cathedral deaneries were hardly less distinguished. Yet probably no more than two of these leaders, Hunter and Barry, discerned that the world in which they had been born and educated, and in which the greater part of their ministries had been exercised, was gone, never to return.

2 *Another headmaster at Canterbury*

Geoffrey Fisher, who had been at Canterbury for almost seven years by the time I was ordained, was the sixth former public school headmaster among the eight occupants of the Primacy since 1862. After leaving Repton he had become a highly regarded Bishop of Chester and an outstanding wartime Bishop of London, but history has not been kind to his Lambeth years. Donald MacKinnon, whose brilliance as a philosopher was matched by his personal eccentricity, said, famously, 'The history of the Church of England may yet recognise that the worst misfortune to befall its leadership at the end of the war was less the premature death of William Temple than his succession by Fisher of London and not by Bell of Chichester.'

I am less certain about this. Temple evidently thought that Fisher should be his successor and Edward Carpenter, who was a great admirer of Bell and who undertook the official biography of Fisher with much reluctance when no one else would take it on, came to believe, after 16 years of hard labour on the archives, that there was more to be said for Fisher than is commonly recognized. On the negative side he was obviously not in the prophetic tradition exemplified by his predecessor or by George Bell, and he failed to recognize that changes in the intellectual climate and the social order triggered by the war were presenting the Church of England with special new challenges.

Fisher was a top-class pastoral administrator, soaked in the Anglican tradition and deeply conscious of the value of the historic link between church and state in England. His role at the Coronation in 1953, carried out to perfection, expressed everything he stood for. But although deeply conservative, particularly in social matters, he was by no means a backwoodsman. He was the first Archbishop of Canterbury to visit the Pope for over five hundred years and his Cambridge sermon in 1946 set the ball rolling for the unity negotiations of the following decades. His own proposal for federal, rather than organic, union was firmly rejected by most other church leaders at the time, but the failure of the organic approach in the 1960s and 1970s is now leading to more serious consideration of how the churches may retain much of their disparate traditions in a unified Christian community. Fisher, acting on the advice of Max Warren, the General Secretary of the Church Missionary Society, was some way ahead of his time in proposing and facilitating the establishing of autonomous provinces throughout the Anglican Communion in preparation for the granting of independence to the countries of the Commonwealth. He became the most travelled of archbishops.

He was never, however, able to shake off the personal image of the successful public school headmaster he had once been and his management style was tiresome to his episcopal colleagues who did not appreciate being treated as if they were housemasters or even sometimes as prefects.

3 *Twenty-two years of wasted time*

No ecclesiastical person shall wear any Coife or wrought Night-cap but only plain Night-caps of black Silk, Satten or Velvet.

Canon LXXIV of the Canons of the Church of England, 1603

It is hardly surprising that Archbishop Fisher regarded Canons such as this as being out of date. What is most surprising is that he considered it worthwhile for the Convocations of Canterbury and York to devote time, extending over 22 years, 1947–69, to their revision. And on his retirement he declared this task to have been his chief achievement. Faced with the immense challenges of the immediate post-war era, some of the best minds of the church were diverted by an exercise that was totally irrelevant to these challenges. The revised Canons have been ignored no less than those of 1603 soon came to be ignored.

4 *Poor bishops*

The 1939–45 war ended decisively the days when the Church of England's bishops might be considered rich men, and by the 1950s most of those who occupied the many sees created since about 1880 were feeling the pinch. Each had been endowed with an annual stipend of £3,000 and, of course, an official residence. In the pre-war years this was a not unsubstantial income, but even then its value was considerably reduced by the requirement to meet from it all expenses of office as well as the running costs of an overlarge house. Post-war inflation made survival precarious. F. R. Barry, who was bishop of my home diocese of Southwell and whom I came to know well, stated the problem candidly:

> The Bishop's Manor, a dignified and gracious house, had been constructed by Bishop Sir Edwyn Hoskyns out of the 14th century manor, in a quadrangle formed by the ruins. But, like all the pre-war episcopal 'palaces' it was built to be run by a large staff of servants and my predecessor was full of lamentations because the war had left him with only SIX; it pre-supposed unlimited fuel; and it was far too expensive for any bishop who did not possess ample private means.

We had to find everything ourselves, to furnish the house, decorate and maintain it, and cover all our official expenses – secretary, postages, travelling – as well as keeping up an enormous garden out of an income that simply could not bear it. We could never spend on the job what it needed; my devoted secretaries got sweated wages; and I had to go around in an ancient car which was constantly breaking down by the roadside. After a while, a generous, wealthy layman in the diocese gave me the present of a new car, which he then replaced periodically, secretly and strictly 'anonymously' and paid a substantial sum into my account year by year on 1st January. That (bless him) enabled me to carry on. But for that I might well have been forced to resign after only a short time through sheer inability to stand the financial pace.

5 Even poorer priests

If the bishops who lacked a private income were struggling, the plight of many of the parish clergy was on the verge of desperation. A fairly typical stipend in the early 1950s was about £400 a year, plus the collections on Easter Day, which would not amount to all that much, except in the richest parishes, and occupation of a vicarage. As with the bishops, the priest was responsible for the upkeep of the house, the purchase and upkeep of a car (if any) and all his expenses – telephone, postages, stationery, robes and so forth. Bishop Barry again:

> Some of the clergy were desperately poor, and I quickly discovered that inside the vicarages there were families living below the poverty line and who could hardly afford enough to eat. They were, as always, brave and uncomplaining; but they had enough to struggle against without that. There were no Church Commissioners grants then, no official ways of improving stipends. No long-term solution was yet feasible.

Geoffrey Fisher's greatest achievement was to take this situation in hand and secure the basis for a stipend policy that enabled the Church of England to continue with a full-time ordained ministry of substantial size. A national appeal brought in useful new capital, the Church Commissioners were stirred into the adoption of a much more aggressive, and in the end highly successful, investments policy, glebe was centralized and the income from it shared, the laity were urged to give more. The adoption of stipend scales led gradually to the erosion of differentials. By the mid-1960s about half the benefices had been raised to £1,200 or more, with an average approaching £1,000. This was a long way from affluence, and for many more years parochial church councils were unwilling to reimburse housing costs and working expenses, but it represented a significant improvement. By the end of the century the stipends were approaching £20,000, though inflation had taken its toll, expectations were higher and, with the average income of the employed population in the region of £30,000, a working spouse was needed to secure a degree of family comfort in the vicarage.

6 The Lord's people on the Lord's day at the Lord's own service

In much the same way that the First World War provided the impetus for the Life and Liberty movement, which campaigned for greater involvement by both clergy and laity in the governance of the church and greater freedom for the church from the power of parliament, the Second led to the formation of the Parish and People movement, which campaigned for changes in the church's worship. During the inter-war years a few parishes had substituted for Sunday morning Mattins or High Mass what they called a Parish Communion – a celebration of the Eucharist with a simple musical setting, usually Merbecke, in which the congregation could participate, hymns, a sermon and a general Communion of all present who were confirmed. Parish and People, launched at a conference at The Queen's College, Birmingham in 1949, was concerned to extend this change throughout the Church of England and at the same time emphasize that the Parish Communion had a theological basis and missionary implications.

It occupied common ground with the Liturgical Movement which, since the early years of the century, had been gaining ground in continental Roman Catholicism – and would soon result in the massive liturgical reforms decided by the Second Vatican Council. The revival of patristic studies led to a clearer understanding of the character of early Christian worship, in particular its corporate aspect, and this was reinforced by the new biblical theology which emphasized, among other things, the nature of the church as the Body of Christ bound together in faith and love by its participation in the sacred meal instituted by Christ himself. Seminal books by Anglican scholars were Gabriel Hebert's *Liturgy and Society*, Gregory Dix's *The Shape of the Liturgy* and Lionel

Thornton's *The Common Life in the Body of Christ,* and, significantly, the authors were all monks. The title of Hebert's book indicated that the change of liturgical direction was not confined to church sanctuaries but had implications for the ordering of the whole life of the church, for the extension of its mission, and for its involvement in the creation of a society governed by concern for the common good. The pioneers of the Parish Communion in the Church of England tended to be socialists.

7 *Parish and People leads the way*

Once launched, Parish and People soon began to attract a large and enthusiastic membership. Henry de Candole, Suffragan Bishop of Knaresborough and a pioneer liturgical reformer, was a widely trusted chairman and Kenneth Packard, an Oxfordshire country priest with good contacts with the church in France, became General Secretary until I succeeded him in 1963. Conferences were held nationally and regionally, a journal and other literature published, groups were formed in every diocese and the membership grew to about fifteen hundred, including a substantial number of bishops. The number of laity involved was disappointingly small and Ernest Southcott, complaining about this, suggested that 'Parish and Priests' would be a more appropriate name for the organization.

The well-attended annual conferences covered a good deal of ground – The Mission of the People of God, Mission and Communication, The Baptismal Life, Spirituality for Today – with the lectures and a summary of discussion published in book form afterwards. They also provided opportunities for liturgical experiment at the daily Eucharist, though this normally involved no more than reordering of the Book of Common Prayer rite in either its 1662 or 1928 forms. Throughout the 1950s Parish and People remained loyal to these rites, arguing that its aim was to encourage a return to the ideals of the Prayer Book's original compilers.

Other aims included the recovery of baptism as a public event in which the parish church congregation, rather than a handful of parents and godparents gathered around the font on a quiet Sunday afternoon, welcomed new members into the church's life. The parish meeting was also advocated as the point at which Holy Communion on Sunday was translated into Holy Community during the week. But these aims never attracted the same degree of attention as the Parish Communion, which during the 1950s spread like wildfire to the overwhelming majority of

English parishes. Parish and People's leadership now became greatly concerned that in many parishes the change had been motivated by little more than attraction to a 'nice service', and not by theological and liturgical insights. There was not much that could be done to remedy this and by the end of the decade introversion had become a problem. An infusion of new life was urgently needed.

8 *A northern parish in action*

From the moment I arrived at Leadgate I was totally, and happily, immersed in the Parish and People movement. The parish embodied all its ideals and practices – Parish Communion, public baptism, parish meeting, healing ministry, collaboration with other churches and before long house churches. Involvement in the broader community was taken for granted and a newspaper was started to stimulate every aspect of parish life. The response was strong – a large Sunday morning congregation, a good number at Evensong and enthusiastic support for the many weekday activities. Sunday school and youth work was impressive. All this in a wholly working-class parish at a time when churchgoing and support was showing clear signs of decline. It could not have been a better environment for the starting of a new ministry. The prescribed rules for training were not observed. Instead of preaching once a month, I was in the pulpit every Sunday, there was no day off and hardly any time for studying the Greek text of the Letter to the Hebrews and the Fifth Book of Hooker's *Ecclesiastical Polity* on which I was to be examined before ordination to the priesthood. At the end of two years when the Vicar, Bill Portsmouth, fell ill with a serious chest condition, I was in sole charge for nine months. But they were three and a half exhilarating, formative years and, although the second half of my long ministry was spent in situations that could hardly have been more different – Westminster Abbey and Winchester Cathedral – I never ceased to be influenced by them.

9 *Tradition still alive in rural Hampshire*

Deep in rural Hampshire Samuel Boothman was exercising the traditional ministry of a country parson as Rector of Farley Chamberlayne with Braishfield. Born into a substantial farming family south of Dublin, he went to Trinity College, Dublin, became a curate at Enniskillen, moved to another curacy in Winchester, where he married one of the Vicar's daughters, and enlisted as an army chaplain in 1940. He was with an armoured regiment at El Alamein and served in the long struggle through Italy, being Mentioned in Despatches for his sustained, courageous work.

On demobilization in 1946 he returned to Winchester diocese and, desirous of a country living, was appointed to the two linked parishes where he would spend the next 35 years until his retirement. The population was about 600. The small gem of a Norman church at Farley Chamberlayne stands on high ground and is surrounded by fields, the village having disappeared long ago, mostly as a result of plague. The population now numbered about 100 scattered over a wide area and the church drew support from ever further afield.

Braishfield, where Boothman lived, was a fairly compact community and its somewhat austere church, designed by the famous Victorian architect William Butterfield, was erected in 1855. The new rector saw the parish transformed from a largely stable agricultural society to one in which most villagers were employed elsewhere, some travelling as far as Southampton or Winchester. In 1961 the squire of Farley Chamberlayne, Sir George Cooper, died, having been a churchwarden for the last 35 years and a generous benefactor. In the following year the verger and sexton of Braishfield was presented with a pocket watch to mark 30 years of service in those offices and 40 years in the choir. In 1966 the death of a teacher who had given 38 years to the village school was mourned, and two years later the organist at Farley Chamberlayne was given a china tea service in recognition of 50 years on the organ stool.

Although the population was small, the Rector had enough to do. Both churches were well attended, both had choirs. There were four services (Book of Common Prayer) every Sunday between the two churches. A monthly Parish Communion was introduced in the early 1960s and the new experimental services were brought into use in the 1970s. There were two Sunday schools; between six and ten confirmation candidates were presented every year. Holy Communion was celebrated on saints' days and there were monthly meetings of the Mothers' Union, and a Young Wives' Group, which also attended a Pram Service. In Lent there were mid-week study courses and increased activity at Christmas and Easter. Boothman visited every home in the parish and undertook much social as well as pastoral work. He was chairman of the managers of the village school, graced virtually every community event with his presence, enjoyed cordial relations with the minister of the Congregational church and produced an attractive four-page leaflet that was delivered to every house at two-monthly intervals.

Soon after Boothman's arrival a free-will offering scheme was introduced at Braishfield to contribute towards an annual budget of £92.8s.6d., the remainder to be raised from an annual bring-and-buy garden sale and an autumn sale, together with generous assistance from the big houses. But although the parish life was certainly rural and traditional, it was by no means inward-looking. The Rector saw to that. There was strong support for overseas missionary work and sermons by missionary preachers. Parishioners who travelled abroad gave illustrated talks about their experiences and Christian Aid and Shelter were supported. Nearer home the clergy of the rural deanery frequently exchanged places in each other's pulpits and once every year the congregations of the two churches went on Sunday evening to worship in another church in the neighbourhood. This was the Church of England at its traditional best, but Boothman's successor would have three additional neighbouring parishes to serve and church life would never be quite the same again.

10 Straight talking at Eton

Neville Gordon became Bishop of Coventry in 1943, not long after the cathedral had been destroyed by bombing, and stayed until 1958, by which time a new building was rising phoenix-like from the ashes of the old. He had considerable artistic gifts – the arts were his primary means of communication – and was responsible not only for the appointment of Basil Spence as architect, but also for the recruitment of Jacob Epstein to create a dramatic figure of St Michael and Graham Sutherland to design the great tapestry that went behind the main altar.

There was general agreement that preaching was not his *métier*. His mind was filled with so many visionary ideas and his heart with such burning passion that ordered language could not express coherently what he desired to share with others. Thus after a sermon in Eton College chapel, when his struggle with words ended in apparent failure, he stood in the chancel, as the organist was playing over the final hymn, and shouted out, 'What I really meant to say was – you damned well all need to be converted.' Archbishop Temple described him as 'that quaint saint', and someone else said, 'He was a man such as St Francis might have been had he been Balliol trained.' In the end he burnt himself out and died in office. Archbishop Fisher wrote soon afterwards, 'He has gone like a comet, leaving streams of colour, light and exhilaration behind, unto the consuming glory of God and his kingdom.'

11 A short but sweet episcopate

If, when ill health caused Alwyn Williams to leave Durham for the more hospitable climate of Winchester in 1952, the diocese had been allowed to choose his successor, there would have been a unanimous vote in favour of Michael Ramsey. During his time as Van Mildert Professor of Divinity at the university (1940–50) he had not been a remote academic figure but, as a residentiary canon of the cathedral and a devout, albeit eccentric, churchman, had played a considerable part in the life of the diocese. He was already greatly admired and much loved. Moreover he had married the Bishop of Jarrow's secretary who seemed able to organize him and who also had a wide knowledge of the clergy and their partners.

In spite of the fact that he had been Regius Professor at Cambridge for a mere 18 months, Michael Ramsey was appointed. I attended his consecration in York Minster and his enthronement at Durham and there was no mistaking the joy that surrounded him on his return to a place that he, too, greatly loved. He stayed for only four years before he was claimed for the Archbishopric of York, but during that time made a considerable impact. I saw quite a lot of him during his first two years as I, being the only curate in north-west Durham, was roped in to act as his chaplain whenever he visited one of the parishes. He had the advantage of looking every inch a godly bishop, a fatherly figure who brought a certain other-worldliness to the worship and fun to the party afterwards. And he was clever enough to be able to preach sermons that were profound, yet simple enough to be understood by the poorly educated as well as the sophisticated. He often repeated them, but this was only sensible, given the amount of preaching he was required to undertake, and although I heard some several times they were always fresh and illuminating.

The hospitality he and his wife dispensed to the clergy, usually at Durham Castle, was memorable, and even more so was his ability to introduce each guest to his wife by name, even though he had himself probably met them no more than once. The diocesan quarterly magazine *The Bishopric* became an important organ of his teaching ministry, especially for the clergy. It contained his most important sermons and addresses, as well as learned book reviews and recommended reading.

These revealed that Durham had acquired a bishop who was, and always would be, a High Churchman with a marked suspicion of innovation, especially if it seemed to him to be a threat to the central truths of Christian faith or the wisdom of Catholic tradition. After I had gone at his request to start pioneering work on a new housing estate I soon became aware of the pastoral implications of his conservatism, but I was among the Durham multitudes who mourned when his inevitable translation to York was announced.

12 *God save the Queen*

Daniel Jenkins, a Congregationalist scholar, described the Coronation of Queen Elizabeth II as 'perhaps the most universally impressive ceremonial event in history'. This was a large claim but was almost certainly true inasmuch as the ceremony itself – a combination of the religious and the political – was perfectly staged and the whole event was for the first time transmitted worldwide by radio and television.

As to the staging, the success of this owed much to the fact that the experience of George VI's Coronation was still remembered by some of the participants, not least by the Dean of Westminster, Alan Don, who had been a canon of the Abbey at the time. I recall my own amusement when soon after my arrival at Westminster 23 years later I was shown a copy of the order of service for Queen Victoria's Coronation on which the Sub-Dean, Lord John Thynne, had pencilled, 'There must be a rehearsal next time.' Archbishop Geoffrey Fisher's key part was carried out to perfection – well, nearly, for there were I was told a couple of small slips – and he brought to the crowning a sense of both dignity and spirituality. For several weeks the Church of England received massive publicity, reinforcing the impression gained at the time of George VI's funeral, that it was once again at the centre of the nation's life. At Leadgate much use was made of a 'film-strip' which presented pictures of the Coronation service and with which a recorded commentary by the Archbishop had to be carefully matched.

On the day itself, in the pouring rain, a large number came to the church school to watch a television set, kindly loaned by a local dealer. For virtually all of us it was our first experience of television and, no one having the technical know-how, there were sometimes problems when the picture temporarily faded and the splendid ceremony was reduced to silhouette forms. There was, however, no doubting the presence at the Queen's right hand of our own bishop. We did not realize that never again would there be a Coronation quite like it, such would be the extent and pace of social change.

13 A princess's choice

The decision of Princess Margaret, the Queen's sister, not to marry the handsome, but divorced, Group Captain Peter Townsend in 1955 caused much public controversy, not least because her decision was made on religious grounds. She was a High Churchwoman whose views, at least on Church of England matters, were always decidedly conservative. At the time it was widely believed that Archbishop Fisher, whose strict views on marriage and divorce were well known, had encouraged her to say no, but it turned out later that he had not been in touch with her and only knew of the decision after it had been made. Fisher's views were in fact broadly shared throughout the Church of England, but 40 years on, when attitudes to marriage and divorce had changed in the church as well as in society as a whole, it became impossible to doubt that in similar personal circumstances the Princess's decision might well have been different.

14 One wedding and two funerals

My experience as a fledgling priest was greatly, and speedily, enlarged when the parish of Lanchester, a few miles away, fell vacant. As the only curate in the area I was often roped in to conduct services in the beautiful twelfth- to thirteenth-century church of this non-mining village. Two of these proved to be particularly memorable.

Arriving at the church for the funeral of an elderly man who had died in the former workhouse, now converted into some sort of refuge for old people, I was informed that he was without relatives or friends and that there would therefore be no congregation. The undertaker's staff suggested that the service should be shortened and, on learning that I intended to use every word of the Prayer Book provision, elected to carry the coffin into the church, then retire to the porch for a smoke. I did not give an address.

The other event began with a wedding, for which the bridegroom and the congregation had assembled and I was in the vestry completing the register before going to meet the bride at the door. My careful writing was suddenly interrupted by a booming voice from within the church: 'I am the resurrection and the life, saith the Lord, he that believeth in me, though he were dead, yet shall he live . . .' On peering out of the vestry door, I was astonished to see another local parson at the head of a coffin, with a procession of mourners behind. It turned out later that the churchwardens, who were responsible for the parish diary, had double-booked these services. In the meantime the bridegroom and the wedding congregation had to make way for the funeral, and I went to the church gate to comfort a tearful bride. But it was a very happy wedding all the same, and one never to be forgotten by anyone involved.

15 *Childbirth and superstition*

In the parishes of north-west Durham, and possibly further afield, virtually every woman who had given birth to a child came to church to thank God for her safe delivery from 'the great pain and peril of child-birth'. This was expressed in a short service consisting of a psalm, the Lord's Prayer, three versicles and responses, two appropriate prayers and a blessing. A collection bag was conveniently placed for what the Prayer Book called 'the accustomed offering' – normally a florin or a half-crown. The brevity of the service was explained by the further requirement that she should if possible receive Holy Communion soon afterwards, but this seemed rarely possible except for the regular churchgoers.

The laudable custom of 'churching', as it was called, was however surrounded by certain undesirable beliefs and superstitions. The idea that it was an act of purification was probably a reflection of the Virgin Mary's visit to the Jewish Temple after the birth of Jesus to be purified from ceremonial uncleanness. Indeed, the 1549 Prayer Book service following the Sarum use, called the service 'The Order of the Purification of Women'. The suggestion that the act of thanksgiving in church should be a woman's first duty when her confinement was over led to the belief that she would bring bad luck to any house she entered before discharging this duty. I recall a proud Leadgate mother taking her new baby to her parents one Sunday afternoon and being required to have her tea in isolation on the lawn because she had not yet been churched. When I reached a new housing area in Stockton-on-Tees in 1954 the service was unknown, except to a small minority. This was I thought a loss, but it was good to be rid of the superstition.

16 *Muscular Christianity*

During the hearing of a robbery with violence case at York Assizes yesterday, Mr. Gilbert Gray, for the defence, told Mr. Justice Veale: 'Your Lordship may recall in his rugger days being struck on the nose.' Mr. Justice Veale: 'I don't know whom you used to play rugby against, Mr. Gray.' Mr. Gray: 'One or two theological colleges, Mr. Lord. They are notorious for that sort of thing.'

The Times

Mr. Lynd, sentencing Mr. Shaw to six months' imprisonment, said: 'For someone with an evangelical turn of mind it is remarkable that you have 22 previous convictions, including assaulting the police, common assault, malicious damage, disorderly behaviour, larceny, and cruelty to a cat.'

Daily Telegraph

17 *The challenge of historic buildings*

The war years led inevitably to the creation of a huge backlog of essential repairs to the Church of England's buildings. Nearly twelve thousand of its churches were classified as being of 'special architectural or historic interest'. The lack of external pressure also meant that the care of these churches varied considerably from parish to parish, with many glorious buildings in remote rural areas showing signs of neglect extending over many decades. This came to an end in 1955 when the Church Assembly passed an Inspection of Churches Measure. This required every church to be subject to a quinquennial inspection by a qualified architect. His report and recommendations were to be presented to the parochial church council and open to inspection by the archdeacon who was empowered to ask questions about proposed remedial action or lack of it.

None of which provided any of the money – often a very large sum – to carry out the repairs. It did, however, place the matter on every church council agenda and help to create a climate in which proper care of a fine historic building became a matter of pride as well as of necessity. The formation of the Historic Churches Preservation Trust in 1953 had also begun to provide encouragement and some financial support for parishes that were prepared to meet the challenge. With the Queen as patron and a body of distinguished supporters, it gradually began to attract grants from large charitable trusts, as well as legacies, some of them substantial. By the end of the century the Trust was distributing £1.5 million a year to about 300 places of worship. The grants varied in size from £1,000 to £50,000 (in exceptional circumstances more) and, although these represented only a fairly small proportion of the amount required, they provided important encouragement to local effort. About thirty affiliated but independent County Church Trusts also came into being to provide finance locally.

In spite of massive effort, usually involving entire local communities, extending over almost fifty years, the task of fundraising remained formidable and in some places burdensome. But the amount of repair and restoration carried out, to meet rising standards, ensured that England's parish churches were, as a whole, in a better condition than they had been for many years past.

18 A cross Suez-examination

Geoffrey Fisher was the last Archbishop of Canterbury who felt able to cross-examine and rebuke a government minister as if he were a delinquent scholar. This was demonstrated famously at the time of the 1956 Suez Crisis when the Lord Chancellor, Lord Kilmuir, was trying to explain the reason for Britain's invasion of Egypt. The official line was that the army and the RAF had gone to deal with an existing crisis, rather as a fire engine might go in to deal with a blaze. But as the Lord Chancellor proceeded with his defence of the Eden government's policy in the House of Lords, Fisher, who was suspicious of the motives, and in any case believed that Britain was acting contrary to the United Nations Charter, interrupted and subjected him to a relentless cross-examination.

It was most unusual for anyone to interrupt a speech in the House of Lords in this way and it wasn't generally appreciated by the other peers, though Lord Jowett, who had been with him at Marlborough and one day would himself become Lord Chancellor said as they left the chamber together, 'Well, Fisher, that's one of the best pieces of cross-examination I've ever heard.' Lord Hailsham wrote to reprimand him and Fisher came to regret 'the brutality' of his assault, but in the subsequent debate and in a letter to *The Times* he continued to oppose the government's policy strenuously.

19 *Wakey, wakey*

COME BACK TO CHURCH
CHRISTIAN BEARS.
HIBERNATION IS OVER.

Poster displayed outside Roydon Parish Church

20 *Revolution in a Leeds parish*

I first met Ernie Southcott when he came to speak at the King's College outpost at Warminster where I and about fifty others were in the final stage of our preparation for ordination. He had been imported to speak about the revolutionary aspects of church life at Halton, Leeds.

A very tall Canadian, with black hair, darkish skin and a hooked nose – there may have been North American Indian blood in him – he spoke with compelling fervour. His ideas and their expression at Halton seemed to be driven by a divine imperative. And he could not keep still – his long-fingered hands divided the air or banged the arms of his chair, his feet drummed the ground, and sometimes his body became contorted. This was obviously someone special.

I came to know him well, partly through our close collaboration in the Parish and People movement, and finally during his years as Provost of Southwark Cathedral. I gave the address at his Memorial Service in Blackburn Cathedral in 1976, he having ended his ministry in a small Lancashire parish, following a long-predicted emotional breakdown at Southwark.

His pioneering work at Halton – which became in the 1950s a much visited showplace for dynamic parish life – embraced the Parish Communion as the central focus of the local church's existence but emphasized that the congregation that gathered around the altar on Sunday must become a missionary movement during the rest of the week. A regular parish meeting, which all were expected to attend, planned the various aspects of the mission, and the baptism of infants was rescued from its semi-private, Sunday afternoon place to become an equal partner within the Parish Communion, parents and godparents having undergone a course of preparation. Next, the parish was divided into about a dozen sub-units, with members of the congregation gathering in a house in each neighbourhood to celebrate Holy Communion around the kitchen table, to study the Bible together, to organize pastoral work in the surrounding streets, and to invite non-churchgoing neighbours to join them. Thus began the house church (not to be con-fused with evangelical gatherings of the same name which developed during the 1980s) and these normally met weekly, either very early in the morning before their members had gone to work or late evening after their return home.

There is no evidence that these house churches, which were repro-duced in other parishes, had any direct influence on the missionary enter-prise, at least not in terms of conversions or churchgoing, but they helped to emphasize the organic character of the church as a 'body', rather than an institution or a building, and also to emphasize the relationship between Communion and community, worship and daily life. At Halton they and a multitude of other activities related to parish development had been pursued so relentlessly under Southcott's leadership that when in 1961 he moved to Southwark and I was invited to succeed him at Halton, the congregation was exhausted and in need of a long period of recuperation in which I did not feel called to share. I am not sure that Ernie ever really forgave me for declining, but we remained good friends.

21 Renewal in the suburbs

The Parish and People enthusiasts were by no means confined to the North. At Greenhill, near Harrow, Joost de Blank, a returned army chaplain, was exercising a dynamic ministry centred on the Parish Communion. He went there in 1948, found the church already well attended, but after a parish conference shifted the emphasis of the Sunday worship to a Parish Communion, with more lay involvement. Families were encouraged to attend with their children, rather than send them to Sunday school, and to bring them to the altar rail for a blessing at the time of Communion. A parish meeting was instituted for discus-sion of mission principles and planning of strategy. The parish was divided into four main areas, each with a lay leader, outside whose house was a noticeboard advertising church services and other events. Within the area were street representatives who established contact with every home and reported on pastoral or social need to the clergy or the area leader. They also delivered the parish magazine which contained community as well as church news, and attended the baptism of any children of families in the street.

Once every month invitations to attend the Parish Communion on the following Sunday went out, there was a Family Service every Sunday morning at 11 o'clock, and during the summer months a 30-minute epilogue at 9.30 p.m. At the Parish Communion queues often formed outside the church, so large was the congregation, and among those influenced by Joost de Blank's ministry was the young Monica Furlong, whose writing would before long be of considerable importance in the wider church. De Blank's own book *The Parish in Action* (1954) was widely read but after a mere four years he was enticed away from Greenhill to become Bishop of Stepney. There his dynamism and flair was felt in London's East End parishes for five years and when in 1957 the Archbishop of Cape Town, Geoffrey Clayton, collapsed and died, he was elected as his successor. Until his own health failed in 1963 he took a heroic stance of opposition to the evil of apartheid, and his final years were spent as a canon of Westminster.

22 Rural missions and a macabre ending

The Village Evangelists were formed by two remarkable men – Brother Edward and Bishop Walter Carey. The latter had resigned from the Bishopric of Bloomfontein, South Africa in 1935 and been found nothing better to do than a public school chaplaincy. In 1947, however, he was invited to a retreat-conference by Brother Edward and out of this came, by the 1950s, a 350-strong company of priests and laity, each devoting 10 days a year to village missions.

Divided into teams of ten or more, these went to a group of rural parishes where they carried out an intensive programme of visiting homes, meetings in pubs and private houses, open-air preaching and mission services in the main churches. The message was simple: 'Something is wrong with England and something is wrong with the souls of men – and the only remedy is to get God back into England and souls, and souls and England back with God.' Carey said, 'If we find the spiritual temperature of the parish 40 degrees, we try to leave it at 45; that's worth doing.'

A much loved bishop and, after service as a naval chaplain in the 1914–18 war (he was at the battle of Jutland), a lively church reformer, Carey worked full time with the Village Evangelists until retiring to Africa and missionary opportunities in Kenya. His final years were spent in Sussex where he sometimes declared his belief that the Church of England was better and stronger than ever before in her history. I never had the good fortune to meet him but in the late 1990s a 92-year-old priest told me how, in 1955, he had requested an interview with Carey and on arrival at the front door of the Sussex house informed the housekeeper that he had 'come to see the bishop'. He was immediately shown to a room where he found the bishop lying in the repose of death, having expired two days earlier. News of the sad demise had failed to reach the shocked visitor.

23 *A priest and a prince*

In 1922 a 36-year-old priest – Martin Andrews – was in the Duchy of Cornwall office in London, seeking an interview for a possible living in the Duchy's gift. His experience was wide: after a North London curacy he joined a Bush Brotherhood in Australia, spent the 1914–18 war in France, first as an army private, then as a chaplain, winning a Military Cross for bravery, followed by two years as chaplain of Khartoum Cathedral in Sudan. He was now in London to play in the Wimbledon tennis finals and had taken the opportunity to enquire about parishes in Cornwall. While in the waiting room, the Prince of Wales, the future King Edward VIII, entered the building, engaged him in conversation and appointed him Rector of Stoke Climsland, near Callington. He stayed for 46 years.

Six years after his institution Andrews asked his patron to let him have, at a low rent, a piece of land near the Rectory to enable him to provide work for some of Cornwall's many unemployed. With the help of his former army batman, a successful flower and vegetable farm was established and lasted 38 years, at its peak employing 45 men and women on 250 acres of land. The Prince took a particular interest in the scheme – 'Why can't this be done everywhere?' he asked – and on his accession as King in 1936 immediately appointed Andrews as one of his chaplains. Thus began a friendship with the Royal Family which continued throughout the reign of King George VI. He was appointed MBE in 1944 and CVO in 1946.

In the parish he proved to be a devoted pastor and was in great demand as a preacher, albeit of an emotional style – his sermons were sometimes accompanied by tears. He founded the Stoke Climsland Football Club, for which he played at centre-half until he was 46, and during the 1939–45 war was a company commander in the Home Guard. When he died in 1989 aged 102 he had been a priest for almost 80 years and an honorary canon of Truro Cathedral for more than 50 years. By this time he was one of Cornwall's best-known and best-loved characters. He never married and for many years enjoyed the close companionship of a male friend who was a flower-seller.

24 *MANsion House 9000*

No Church of England clergyman in modern times – or probably any other times – saved more lives or alleviated greater distress than Prebendary Chad Varah, who became Rector of St Stephen, Walbrook, in the City of London in 1953 and was still there at the end of the century.

He accepted appointment to this beautiful but little-frequented Wren church, sensitively rebuilt after wartime bombing, at the invitation of its patron, the Mercer's Company, and on the understanding that he could use its crypt as the base of a new kind of ministry to desperate people. He made it known that with effect from 2 November 1953 anyone contemplating suicide could telephone him at MANsion House 9000 – the dialling system at that time. Calls to 'The Samaritans' soon began to come in and doubled each year from 100 in 1954 to 1,600 in 1959. Eventually they would grow to 100 a day. Initially Varah used his church stipend to pay a secretary and, being a good journalist, lived off his Fleet Street earnings, but as the number of clients increased he trained volunteer helpers. A professional psychiatrist was also recruited.

During the early part of 1954, however, the original concept of a counselling service was abandoned in favour of a less demanding befriending service. This enabled a wider range of unqualified volunteers to be used, though these were carefully selected and their training taught them to recognize symptoms that required professional help. Religious tests and attempts to indoctrinate were strictly forbidden. Later the movement advertised its availability to the despairing as well as to the suicidal.

Once the London base was firmly established, Varah assisted in the founding of branches in other parts of Britain and within ten years few areas in the country were without a branch, and the number of active helpers had risen to 17,000. A national association was formed in 1963 and the expansion of the work to most other parts of the world led to the formation of an international body, with himself as chairman, then president.

A dynamic, combative priest of generous disposition and immense compassion, especially for those with serious problems, he was quite unshockable and, while the suggestion that he personally was responsible for inaugurating the 'permissive society' of the 1960s and beyond was quite untrue, it was not entirely incredible. On reaching the age of 75 in 1986, he retired from his various Samaritan offices, except that of Founder, but not from his position as Rector of St Stephen Walbrook, he having been appointed long before a compulsory retirement age for clergy was introduced.

He was a much loved figure in the City, had the distress of seeing his church closed for nine years when its walls and dome became unstable, but celebrated its reopening by installing a stone altar sculpted by Henry Moore. This led to a prolonged and expensive battle against the ecclesiastic lawyers, which he won after appealing to the Court of Ecclesiastical Causes Reserved – this being only the second time in its long history that the Court had been convened. In his autobiography *Before I Die Again* (1992), he announced his belief in reincarnation, and in his ninetieth year he was made a Companion of Honour.

25 Janet to the rescue

One of the most remarkable women to emerge in Britain's public life during the 1950s was Janet Lacey. In 1952, when she was at the end of a five-year contract as Youth Secretary of the British Council of Churches, she was asked to take charge temporarily of its Inter-Church Aid operation, then in a desperate crisis owing to the illness of its Secretary and to serious financial problems. She moved in, said she would do the job for six weeks, and immediately took the office and the churches by storm. Staying for 16 years, she brought the small, ailing organization, with a staff of only 3 and an annual income of £20,000, to the forefront of British charities with a staff of over 100 and an annual income of £1,500,000. Christian Aid, as it was renamed, made the contributions of the British churches to overseas aid the largest and most influential in the world.

A short, generously proportioned, bustling woman, generous to a fault, Janet Lacey had vision, imagination, energy and administrative skill in more or less equal proportions. She also had a marked fondness for the unorthodox and, having been born and brought up in Sunderland, never lost her North-country plain speaking. Originally she hoped to go on the stage and attended a drama school, but this did not work out and she had to be content with the role of impresario in the management of whatever she took in hand. She never lost her love of the theatre.

From 1926 to 1945 she had served on the staff of the YMCA and YWCA in Kendal and Dagenham where she displayed her great flair for dealing with young people. It was on the strength of this that she was sent to Germany as YMCA Education Secretary with the British Army and during this time unilaterally extended her brief to include work with young Germans. The experience of seeing at first hand the plight of the European refugees, linked to a deep religious faith, inspired all her future work for refugees and other suffering people. As Director of Christian Aid she travelled to all parts of the world investigating or pleading the cause of refugees and the hungry, and inspired a multitude of people to commit themselves to gifts of money or actual service either in Britain or overseas. She was the first woman ever to preach in St Paul's and Liverpool Cathedrals and St George's Collegiate Church in Jerusalem. She was also one of the founders of Voluntary Service Overseas (VSO).

26 A mite for the hungry

The collection at the Men's Service in the cathedral on June 15 was £33.5s.2d. Cathedral expenses were £8.8s.0d, other expenses were £22.0s.11d., leaving £2.16s.3d. to be forwarded to the Freedom from Hunger Campaign.

The Winchester Churchman

27 Forward from basics

It is rare, probably unprecedented, for a solid book on patristics – the study of the development of doctrine during the early centuries of Christian history – to have an almost immediate and far-reaching effect on the thought and practices of the contemporary church. But such was the impact made by the publication in 1951 of Geoffrey Lampe's *The Seal of the Spirit*. Lampe, a liberal churchman, a canon of Ely and a professor at Cambridge, was the editor of the massive *Patristic Greek Lexicon* and a leading authority on the patristic period. His studies led him to the obvious, but infrequently stated, conclusion that within the church there must be room for varieties of theological interpretation and that theology must always be expressed in the thought forms of the surrounding culture.

His concern in *The Seal of the Spirit* was with the relationship between baptism and confirmation in the New Testament and its development in the immediately following centuries. He concluded that baptism alone is the means of sacramental incorporation into the life of the church, and that confirmation is no more than a reaffirmation of the

Holy Spirit given in baptism. Once recognized – and it did not take long to win the argument in theological circles – Lampe's conclusion had considerable ramifications. Theologically liberal bishops and parish priests ceased speaking of confirmation as the 'completion' of baptism, and the liturgical revisers, working on the Baptism and Confirmation Services from the 1960s onwards, changed their content to reflect the recovered insight.

And that was not all: since baptism alone was now recognized as the only means of entering the life of the church, the case for resisting inter-communion involving the Church of England and the baptized membership of the Free Churches was seriously weakened, if not totally undermined. This was recognized by the General Synod and a major improvement in inter-church relations soon followed – much to Lampe's pleasure.

28 *Father Joe of Stepney*

Joe Williamson, a great priest and a remarkable character, was famed most for his ministry to prostitutes, though he had some other achievements. Born into poverty in London's East End during the closing year of Queen Victoria's reign, he felt drawn from an early age to the priesthood. When, however, he presented himself at the door of a Poplar vicarage to announce this fact he was thanked for the information and bade good afternoon. But he persevered and eventually was admitted to St Augustine's College, Canterbury – at that time a missionary training college.

After two short London curacies, he was at Grahamstown Cathedral in South Africa for four years before returning to England in 1932. Each of the four parishes in which he then ministered required the restoration, sometimes the rebuilding, of its church. At Fenny Drayton, Leicester, he spent all his own money on the work; at Shimpling, Suffolk, he had initially to stand in water while conducting services and continued to raise money for repairs while serving as an army chaplain during the 1939–45 war; at Little Dunham, Norfolk, he carried out urgent bricklaying and carpentry himself.

When Williamson moved to St Paul's, Dock Street, Stepney in 1952, the church, having been bombed during the war, required major restoration. The social life of the parish had also degenerated and its outspoken Vicar shocked the London Diocesan Conference with a colourful description:

We have developed into an area of low-level clubs for drugs, drink, gambling and women. We have a hot-bed of vice on gutter level. Humans are like rats, living in filth – two couples, four in a bed . . . Girls screaming and fighting for their money; girls taking man after man in the open streets; girls being smashed to the ground by men, thrown down bodily and kicked.

And much else that would, as is sometimes said, be 'unsuitable for publication in a family newspaper'. Besides constant campaigns for change in the social fabric of the neighbourhood, Father Joe – a frail figure but with a loud voice, and always to be seen in cassock and biretta – turned Church House, Stepney into a hostel for prostitutes, opened two more hostels in Essex and another in Birmingham. He travelled far to raise money for the Wellcome Square Fund he had founded to assist prostitutes in the building of a new way of life, and was also chaplain of both the Sailors' Home and the Red Ensign Club, catering for the welfare of seafarers.

Failing eyesight drove him into reluctant retirement in 1962, but he remained warden of the Stepney hostel for many more years and was appointed MBE in 1975. Explaining the driving force behind his concern in a graphic autobiography, he told how he had encountered a prostitute who appeared to him to be a beautiful young woman, but on further inspection turned out to be old and ugly with a razor-scarred face: 'My vision was of the lovely girl she had been before prostitution destroyed her. Her name had to be Mary. It was a message from God, I had to help women like her.'

29 The end of hanging

When on 6 February 1956 the House of Commons, on a free vote, rejected capital punishment by 283 to 262 votes the division of opinion thus reflected was probably close to that among the laity of the Church of England. A much larger majority of the bishops and the other clergy were known abolitionists, though Bishop Harland, who had ministered to condemned prisoners in Lincoln prison, was of the belief that the prospect of execution was good for a man's spiritual health. Christian Action, led vigorously by John and Diana Collins, played an important part in the long campaign for abolition. Meetings and seminars were held, the clergy were circularized, leaflets were published and petitions organized – the latter to the displeasure of Archbishop Garbett of York.

In the event, the House of Commons' decision was overthrown by the Lords, and the Conservative government introduced instead another Bill abolishing hanging for certain categories of murder and retaining it for others.

In my Stockton parish a husband murdered his wife with a sawn-off shotgun and was sentenced to death, his crime being premeditated and involving a gun. An anxious time for the community followed, with petitions to the Home Office and the powerful intervention of our MP. The murderer was eventually reprieved and soon afterwards, in 1964, capital punishment was finally abolished, a large number of bishops attending the House of Lords' debate and voting unanimously for abolition.

30 *Crime and sin*

In 1931 the number of homosexual offences known to the police was only 622, but by 1955 this had risen to 6,644, most of the increase having taken place since the end of the war. There is no evidence to suggest that this reflected an increase in homosexual activity in the British population or even that a change of morals had made homosexuals less discreet. There was at the time, however, a good deal of evidence that the police were much more active in pursuit and prosecution, and media reports of court cases and prison sentences, sometimes involving prominent people, began to cause concern. In 1955 there were 2,504 prosecutions and the question was raised, 'Is private behaviour of this sort necessarily a crime?'

Among the questioners was a young ordinand, Graham Dowell, later to become a university chaplain, then Vicar of Hampstead, who raised the matter in a letter to the magazine *Theology*. The Church of England's Moral Welfare Council took this up and after conducting its own investigation asked the Home Secretary to initiate an official enquiry. A commission under the chairmanship of J. F. Wolfenden, who had been headmaster of two public schools and was now Vice-Chancellor of Reading University, considered 'Sexual Offences and Social Punishment' and was greatly assisted by a major piece of research, *Homosexuality and the Western Christian Tradition*, carried out by a priest, Sherwin Bailey, on the staff of the Moral Welfare Council.

The commission recommended that homosexual acts between consenting adults in private should no longer be a criminal offence. It was also of the opinion that prostitution should not be illegal, provided no public offence was caused. The basis of these judgements was the belief that criminal law should not be regarded as synonymous with, or a substitute for, personal morality. In other words, that crime should not always be equated with sin. Archbishop Fisher agreed, and so did Bishop Barry of Southwell in a learned speech in the House of Lords in which he described homosexuality as a 'disability', which, by the grace of God, a man might overcome, whereas Fisher believed homosexual behaviour to be 'a sin against God', but both favoured a change in the law. When in 1967 the Wolfenden recommendations were finally accepted by Parliament, Archbishop Michael Ramsey offered his strong support. No one could foresee at the time what the implications of the changed attitude to homosexuality would be for the Church of England and for the whole Anglican Communion at the end of the century.

31 Suicide and sickness

While the homosexuality issue was still under discussion the church's Board of Social Responsibility issued in 1959 a report which affirmed that suicide should be regarded as a personal tragedy and not as a crime and that both it and attempted suicide should cease to be a breach of the law. In the following year a Suicide Act removed suicide from criminal law and the Home Secretary acknowledged the influence of the church's report. Prosecutions had already become comparatively rare and most of the clergy had already come to believe that suicide was a symptom of sickness and that the rules which forbade a church funeral or burial in consecrated ground could be ignored. Coroners also began to qualify their verdicts with 'while of unsound mind' and the overall effect of these changes in the parishes was to greatly reduce the sense of shame often felt by bereaved families.

32 The usefulness of a hearing aid

Before the inauguration of synodical government in 1970 the six-monthly Diocesan Conference could be a mixture of sharply contrasting stimulation and boredom. Consisting of all the diocesan clergy and an equal number of laity, it had no legislative power and the agenda consisted of a presidential address by the bishop and reports on various aspects of diocesan life, including the financial position. Where the bishop was a scholar – Ramsey at Durham, Barry at Southwell, for example – or a man of vision – Hunter at Sheffield, Bell at Chichester –

it was worth the journey and the Saturday afternoon to hear what was often a magisterial utterance. As to the reports, not all in the audience were able to adopt the tactics of the deaf Bishop Barry who, on observing that Canon Douglas Feaver, at that time Vicar of Nottingham, was about to address the Southwell conference ostentatiously turned off his hearing aid and asked to be informed when he had ceased speaking.

33 *Industrial mission starts at Sheffield*

The Sheffield Industrial Mission founded by Ted Wickham in 1944 was, under his leadership the most radical twentieth-century attempt by the Church of England to engage with the largely alienated industrial working class. The basic element in its work, carried out with the consent of trade unions as well as management, involved a large team of chaplains wandering around the shop floor, talking to the steel workers as opportunity arose, getting to know them and learning about the issues that concerned them. The chaplain was to remember always that he was a guest, with neither status nor rights. The result was a great deal of pastoral work which would never have found its way to the local vicarage. Next came the arranging of informal gatherings in snap breaks. The steel-making processes at that time allowed breaks during which the workers could have sandwiches or simply pause for a smoke. Wickham used these to initiate discussions on a variety of subjects – some suggested by himself, others by the men; some with a direct religious dimension, many raising ethical, social and political issues. Anything from 10 to 100 would gather and quick-witted Wickham was adept at stimulating discussion and encouraging involvement. And, since many subjects were too big to cope with in 15–20 minutes, further meetings were arranged out of working hours and away from the factory in a home, or a pub or a hall. The aims of all these activities was to build a modest bridge between the church and the industrial community – managers as well as workers – to stimulate the discussion of important human and social problems, and to encourage the small number of active Christians in the steel works to see their responsibilities not so much in the service of the parish churches but rather within their working environment where they might serve as shop stewards and trade union officials or simply demonstrate with sensitivity their love of their neighbours.

Wickham was born in London in 1911 and never lost his assertive Cockney style. Fairly small of stature, decidedly scruffy, with tousled hair and no-nonsense manner, people were often surprised to discover that he was a priest, and later that he was a bishop. He had worked in East London industry in the 1930s and claimed to be the only bishop ever to have stood in a dole queue. Having felt drawn to the priesthood, he taught himself Latin, Greek and Hebrew, obtained a London University BD and, after a few terms at St Stephen's House, Oxford, became a curate in 1938 in a poor Tyneside parish. This heightened his awareness of the gulf between the church and the working class and, after the parish had been more or less flattened by a single night's bombing in 1941, he spent the rest of the war as chaplain of a huge armaments factory in Staffordshire. The Bishop of Sheffield, Leslie Hunter, then invited him to experiment with something similar in the steel works of the diocese.

34 Priests among the workers

There was another approach to the industrial problem – that of the worker-priests who believed the Christian faith could only be effectively shared with industrial workers by those who shared fully in their life. A small group of these – five in all – emerged in the Church of England during the 1950s, inspired in part by the French worker-priest movement, but also by the example of St Paul who preached the gospel 'free of charge'. Sharing in the impersonal, soul-destroying nature of much manual work and the insecurity experienced by most workers was another motivation.

Long before he was aware of the French movement, Michael Gedge had started work as a machine operator with a South London firm of heating engineers, and in 1951 he moved to a Kent coal mine where he was joined by another priest, John Strong. The two men worked underground on alternate shifts and shared responsibility for the parish of Eyethorn. After five years, however, the partnership broke up (Gedge eventually became a Roman Catholic) and Strong moved to Harlington, a village near Luton, where he became priest-in-charge of the parish and travelled to Luton every day to check oil meters in a factory.

Martin Grubb started work as a layman in West London in 1951, then took a two-and-a-half-year break to train as a priest before returning to work as a semi-skilled engineer in the area's largest factory. John Rowe, born and trained in Canada, became a curate in East London in 1953 but after three years began to work as an electrician's mate in a local brewery where he remained for the next thirty years. Tony Williamson started work at the Pressed Steel Works in Cowley, near

Oxford, having completed his training for the priesthood in 1958, but it was not until 1960 that he was ordained. In the following year he was elected as a Labour member of Oxford City Council. A number of other priests joined their circle in the 1960s and their wives were usually involved in the experiment, as well as several laymen. Initially the priests picked up pastoral work on the shop floor and were sometimes asked about moral and religious issues, but they regarded their chief role as simply to be present in manual work situations.

Brave and important though this experiment undoubtedly was, it never entered into the lifeblood of the church and the witness of these priests is not to be confused with that of the non-stipendiary priests who emerged in the later decades and were mostly middle-class professionals leading worship and sometimes undertaking pastoral work in parishes. For several years Ted Wickham was strongly opposed to the expansion of the experiment, arguing that the situation in England was culturally and religiously different from that in France and that the Christian mission in this country could be carried out only by laity. But he came to recognize that the worker-priests had offered important witness in a church that was unwilling to face the consequences of its failure to meet the industrial challenge.

35 *Thomas the Tank Engine, the Fat Controller and all stations to heaven*

Other clergy had different preoccupations. In the early 1920s Wilbert Awdry, the young son of the Vicar of Ampfield in Hampshire, was taken by his father every Wednesday afternoon to an embankment to see the steam trains pass by on the Eastleigh to Romsey branch line. There was also conversation with the men working on the track, all of which created in the boy a fascination with railways.

Almost a quarter of a century later when, having followed his father into Holy Orders, this boy was now vicar of the large Birmingham parish of King's Norton, he found himself trying to entertain his own 3-year-old son, Christopher, who was ill with measles. He drew some engines with faces to illustrate the lines, 'Early in the morning down at the station/All the little engines standing in a row'. A few stories were written on the backs of circulars to go with them and, although Awdry regarded them as being of little value, his wife suggested that they be sent to a fine-art printer who paid £40 for the copyright and engaged a professional illustrator.

The first volume, small and easy to handle, was published as *The Three Railway Engines* and reprinted four times during the next twelve months; it was followed by *Thomas the Tank Engine*. Thus entered the world of several generations of children, Thomas, Gordon the Grumpy Express, the Fat Controller and many other human-faced rolling stock, giving endless delights. In the end some thirty books were published and these led to a television series and numerous commercial spin-offs.

Awdry remained a parish priest, serving mainly in Cambridgeshire and leaving Christopher to write more stories and manage their publication. Not long before he died in 1997 aged 85 he looked back philosophically on his two callings: 'Railways and the church have their critics, but both are the best ways of getting a man to his ultimate destination.'

36 *The church must meet – Sheffield again*

It was, I suppose, in the late 1940s while I was still a student that I first encountered Alan Ecclestone. The Communist Party had organized a meeting in Netherfield, a community largely made up of railwaymen not far from my Nottinghamshire home, and I went along to hear him speak. He spent 27 years (1942–69) as Vicar of Holy Trinity, Darnall, then one of the toughest of Sheffield's tough parishes, with an entirely working-class population of 15,000, which had suffered greatly during the wartime bombing. He was a widely cultivated man who tried to read the whole of Shakespeare's works every year and identified himself completely with his parishioners. He was assiduous in his concern for the sick, the poor and anyone in trouble, and he introduced gaiety into the community by means of colourful services in the parish church. A local branch of the Communist Party met at the vicarage and over the course of 20 years he stood as a Communist candidate in local elections, coming last on every occasion. He also attended Communist-organized peace conferences in Paris and Warsaw.

More influential in the Church of England was his initiation of the parish meeting – an expression of his belief, shared with those of the Congregationalist tradition, that the local church consists of all its members who ought to meet regularly, not only for worship but also for experience of Christian community life and the planning of the Christian mission in the neighbourhood. At Darnall, where the meeting was held weekly, this included the sending of delegates to meetings at the City Hall to ask questions about social policy. The number participating was never large, but the idea spread to other parishes, including those in the North of England where I served, and the Parish and People movement adopted it and public baptism as corollaries of the Parish Communion. But it never became widespread and was eventually overtaken by the process of synodical government, though this was not the same thing, it being elective rather than fully participatory and concerned almost exclusively with ecclesiastical matters.

In 1969 Ecclestone retired to a small, whitewashed cottage in Cumbria, where, surrounded by his 12,000 books, he began to share with a wider audience the deep spirituality which had informed and sustained his ministry in Sheffield. *Yes to God* (1975) was a bestseller, won a Religious Book Award and was said to have 'taken prayer on to the streets'. This was followed by *A Staircase for Silence* (1971), which drew heavily on the French poet, mystic and visionary Charles Péguy, *The Night Sky of the Lord* (1980) and *Scaffolding of the Spirit* (1987). In all these he related the life of the spirit to the challenges of the modern world.

37 *Inspiration*

The Bishop of Durham, Dr. Michael Ramsey, was the speaker at St. Ives Church, Leadgate Parish Meeting last Wednesday evening. His address was mainly on spiritual lines; it was nonetheless most inspiring.

Consett Guardian

38 *New housing and the church's response*

More than 3 million new houses were built in Britain between 1945 and 1960 and at the end of this period more than one-quarter of the entire population was living in houses and flats that did not exist when the war ended. Most local authorities still had long waiting lists of families who were without homes of their own and it was estimated that 300,000 new dwellings a year would be needed for as far ahead as could reasonably be foreseen. This represented the greatest social change in Britain since the Industrial Revolution and a particular challenge to the church which, in most places, responded speedily with the allocation of clergy and money for new churches.

Roseworth, the new housing area at Stockton-on-Tees to which I moved in 1954, was typical of its kind. Two thousand two hundred council houses had been erected on the northern outskirts of the small industrial town, and were occupied for the most part by young families enjoying their first homes. The high birth rate meant that the population was approximately 8,000 and still rising. At the end of 10 years, over 75 per cent were in either the 30–50 or under-15 age groups and only 2 per cent were over 65 years of age. More than one-third of the population was made up of schoolchildren. The church survey that produced these statistics also indicated that of the 2,500 men living on the estate, 2,266 were skilled tradesmen or clerks or unskilled workers employed mainly at the ICI chemical plant or two large engineering works. Only 154 were junior executives, foremen or teachers, and although 66 were listed as professional and self-employed these had small one-man businesses as furniture removers, agents and traders.

Since virtually all the men worked several miles away, Roseworth was a dormitory area, populated during the daytime for most of the week only by women and children. The council houses were well designed and comparatively spacious until the final phase of the development when a new housing minister, Harold Macmillan, paid a visit and ordered more houses to be built to the acre. No space was allowed for play and apart from a near-derelict Edwardian mansion, Kiora, there was no provision for community meetings or other social activities. The idea that schools might be used out of hours for these purposes was no more than a pipe dream. The building of a pub and a small parade of shops was long delayed.

Such an imbalanced community presented the church with some opportunities, particularly in its work among women and children, and especially among the lonely. But problems relating to leadership in both church and community were bound to arise and there could be no over-coming of the Church of England's longstanding alienation from the working class. The development of a second adjacent estate, Hardwick, to accommodate those displaced by central Stockton slum clearance would soon raise the parish population to almost 20,000 and provide ominous signs of the serious problems to come.

39 *Starting from scratch*

Appointment as priest-in-charge of this embryo new parish was very welcome to me, as it was to many other young new area clergy, since starting from scratch meant no lumber from the past to inherit and more or less complete freedom to implement the new ideas about worship and mission that were at the top of the Parish and People agenda. A small house was built for me just off the edge of the estate and I was told that a site for a church had been allocated at its centre and that the diocesan architect had been asked to design a building at a cost of about £15,000.

A leaflet to every house announced my arrival and the first act of worship in the Kiora house on the first Sunday in November 1954. About seventy came to the 9.30 a.m. Parish Communion, held in what had once been a large bedroom, with an improvised trestle-table altar, stacking chairs and an ancient harmonium to accompany the singing. There were about forty at Evensong, so this was an encouraging start to a ministry that would occupy me for the next eleven years and influence my outlook for the remainder of my life. Two churches, a vicarage and another clergy house were erected, and from 1958 onwards I had colleagues who eventually formed one of the early team ministries – five priests, all brimming with enthusiasm and ideas, and some with specialist gifts.

In many ways our approach was traditionally Anglican – daily Book of Common Prayer services, daily systematic house-to-house visiting, Sunday school, confirmation classes and eventually some work with young people. Marriages and funerals were conducted on accustomed lines, the sick were ministered to in their homes or in hospital. Where we broke new ground was in our refusal to have any of the usual church organizations and by our division of the parish into 12 areas each with its house church, the members of these responsible for pastoral and mission work in the locality. Baptism was administered only at large-scale services and after careful preparation of parents and godparents at the 'Baptism Clinic'. Preparation for confirmation extended over two years and involved regular involvement in the Sunday worship. House meetings, joint Bible study groups with Methodists, with whom we worked closely, and occasional teaching weeks provided laity education. Following the inauguration of the Teesside Industrial Mission in 1959 a special men's group for the consideration of workplace issues was led by the industrial chaplain Bill Wright, and sometimes attended by trade union officials and shop stewards. A monthly newspaper, *The Clarion*, dealing with community as well as church matters, went into virtually every house. Social concerns were often voiced by the churches and meetings with doctors and social workers facilitated the useful exchange of information and ideas. A monthly parish meeting, which anyone could attend (never more than about thirty ever did) discussed policy and plans.

This was demanding, but never specially difficult, work. The church was the only expression of corporate community life, television had yet to become addictive, a welcome still awaited clergy who visited houses, secularization was less advanced than it would become by the end of the century. The response was considerable – the first church, designed to accommodate 200, soon had to be enlarged to accommodate 300, and church life in Roseworth, and to a lesser extent in Hardwick, was vibrant and stimulating.

Much of what we were doing experimentally is now commonplace in parishes new and old, but at the time it was sufficiently novel to attract attention, with frequent requests from young priests and groups of theological students anxious to experience it for themselves. In many other new housing areas similar experimental work was being undertaken but, except in the new towns, without the clerical manpower resources available to us. And when eventually these resources were withdrawn the collapse was catastrophic.

40 A long way ahead of her time

Maude Royden, a popular broadcaster in her later years, died in 1956 aged 80. Earlier she had been one of the outstanding preachers of the century and the leading protagonist for the ordination of women. Having been forbidden to preach in Anglican pulpits, she accepted in 1917 an invitation to become a 'pulpit assistant' at London's City Temple – a leading Congregationalist preaching centre. There her sermons attracted huge crowds and police were needed to control the long queues of people seeking admission. After her first appearance the *Daily Express* reported 'Girl Preacher in Parker's Pulpit'. A fortnight later she was in the Albert Hall speaking to thousands celebrating the Russian Revolution.

Earlier she had been deeply involved in the women's suffrage movement, serving on the Executive Council of its National Union and editing its journal. When this battle was won she directed her considerable energy to the cause of securing for women an equal place with men in the life of the church. She declared women's ordination to be 'the most profoundly moral movement since the foundation of the church'. Another special concern was the peace movement and she was at different times involved in the leadership of the Fellowship of Reconciliation and the Peace Pledge Union, but, to widespread astonishment, she renounced pacifism in 1940 and supported Britain's involvement in the war. Following her death, the voice of advocacy of women's ordination was reduced to a whisper.

41 *Bottles and bottles – and more bottles*

Ever in quest of money for the building of the new church at Roseworth, I was driven to organize a 'bottle party' – a not very original idea which involved parishioners bringing bottles of various products to a coffee morning, these to be put on sale at the following Christmas Fair. In my notice of the event in *The Clarion* I suggested bottles of sauce, scent, vinegar, ink and so on, and added, tongue in cheek, perhaps wine, beer or whisky. The local evening newspaper picked this up, gave it a heading 'Vicar's Bottle Party', and evoked an immediate response from a Baptist minister who declared it to be sinful that a clergyman was encouraging people to 'take to the bottle'. The ensuing controversy spread to the national press and before long I was receiving letters of support from many different parts of the country, some enclosing money, others attached to cases of wine or beer. A Customs and Excise official wrote to point out that I would be breaking the law if I sold alcohol without first obtaining a liquor licence. Success was assured, and neither bottles nor law were broken.

42 *Giving is good for you*

By the end of this decade the Christian Stewardship movement, spearheaded by the American Wells Organization, was beginning to make its presence felt in the livelier parishes. Working under the slogan 'Giving is Good for You', its theology and methodology were simple. The New Testament affirms that 'God loves a cheerful giver' and tells how the earliest Christians were instructed to set aside a certain sum of money, according to means, for the furtherance of the Christian mission.

Away then with church bazaars, fêtes, jumble sales and such like; bring on a campaign manager, organize a free dinner, invite to this all church members and anyone else who may be seriously interested, produce an illustrated brochure about the church's needs and the doctrine of stewardship, make speeches at the dinner on these subjects, recruit an appropriate number of canvassers, who having made their own 'pledge', visit the homes of the diners to secure their 'pledges' of specific weekly support. Result: church income tripled or even quadrupled within a matter of weeks. 'Pledges' of 'time and talents' also reduced church running costs or led to an expansion of activity. The fact that the fundraising firms exacted a hefty fee was a deterrent to many parishes (at Roseworth we did it ourselves, using the professional method and with comparable results), so in due course most dioceses employed a Stewardship Adviser to help avoid this cost. But the bazaars and fêtes had a tendency to return – to augment direct giving and to meet a social need.

43 Music and the Mass

In 1956 the Rector of St Dunstan's, Stepney commissioned Geoffrey Beaumont, a Mirfield monk and also Vicar of the Trinity College, Cambridge mission in Camberwell, to compose a setting of the Mass in a modern idiom. When broadcast later in the year from St Augustine's, Highgate, it made a considerable impact. No one could even pretend that it was fine music, or even that it was truly contemporary. It reflected the rhythms of 1930s' musicals, but it was something new and lively, and when accompanied by guitar, saxophone and drums had a dramatic effect on the worship. When tried out at Roseworth in the recently dedicated new church it was welcomed enthusiastically, and the addition of Beaumont hymn tunes – a swinging version of 'Now thank we all our God' became specially popular – heightened the celebratory atmosphere. It was not hard to believe that the composer was an accomplished pub pianist.

44 Man of Christian action

The most notable cathedral canon of the second half of the twentieth century and the most prominent social reformer of his time was John Collins, who went to St Paul's in 1948 and remained there until shortly before his death on the last day of 1982. He was appointed by the then Prime Minster, Clement Attlee, not primarily to serve the cathedral, though he was in fact a very diligent member of the chapter, but to run a small organization named Christian Action. This became his life's work, to which was added later the Campaign for Nuclear Disarmament (CND) and the Defence and Aid Fund for the victims of apartheid in South Africa.

Returning, after wartime service as an RAF chaplain, to his pre-war post as Dean of Oriel College, Oxford, Collins formed in the college a Christian fellowship which, after reading together *Our Threatened*

Values (1946) by the left-wing reformer Victor Gollancz, decided to hold a public meeting about it in Oxford Town Hall. The Bishop of Chichester, George Bell, was in the chair, Gollancz, Richard Acland, Barbara Ward and Roger Wilson, the former secretary of the Friends' Relief Organization in Europe, were the speakers. The Town Hall was filled to capacity, the university church was used for an overflow meeting and it was estimated that some three thousand people had turned out for the event.

It was from this meeting that Christian Action came into being and was based at Oriel College until Sir Stafford Cripps, the Labour Chancellor of the Exchequer, who had a great admiration for Collins, persuaded the Prime Minister to offer him a canonry of St Paul's in order to provide the fledgling organization with an office and a sphere of influence in London. Although a small but influential committee was formed and several hundred members were recruited, and there was at one time talk of establishing a national network of branches, Christian Action became and remained basically a support organization for Collins's own dynamic and courageous personal prophetic ministry.

Initially, the concern was chiefly with reconciliation and the care of some of the war's casualties, with particular emphasis on the future of the many millions who had been displaced from their own countries. Then, during the 1950s, an 'Anti-Capital Punishment' campaign was launched by Victor Gollancz and run by Collins from the Christian Action office. A 'Homeless in Britain' campaign drew attention to a national problem and 19 housing associations were opened, together with homes for unmarried and deserted mothers, a shelter for vagrant women at Lambeth and several houses for the rehabilitation of alcoholics and other addicts. Financial and administrative support, including office accommodation, was provided for other small projects, such as 'Radical Alternative to Prison' and 'Campaign for the Homeless and Rootless'. No less committed to the work of the new movement was Collins's wife Diana, whose contribution to the work of Christian Action was later recognized by appointment as a Dame.

In 1950 there was little concern in Britain about the rapid development of racist rule in South Africa. But Collins was deeply concerned, having read Alan Paton's *Cry the Beloved Country*. Trevor Huddleston asked him to raise money for the families of men who were being imprisoned for their non-violent resistance to apartheid, and in 1956 Christian Action launched a Treason Trial Defence Fund and raised £170,000 for the defence of 156 black and white South Africans whose opposition to government policy had led to their trial on charges of high treason. This led eventually to the founding of the International Defence and Aid Fund, through which the Swedish and several other governments channelled their assistance of apartheid's victims, and when the fund became too large to shelter under Christian Action's umbrella a separate organization was started, but with Collins still at the helm. The United Nations, which also channelled money through the Fund, honoured him with its gold medal for his work against apartheid.

Deeply shocked by the use of nuclear weapons to end the war in 1945, he convened a meeting at his office at St Paul's in January 1958 to consider the possibility of organizing a campaign against their stockpiling as well as their possible use. This was attended by a number of notable left-wing figures, none of them Christian, and led to the launching of the Campaign for Nuclear Disarmament, with Collins as chairman. This soon became a mass movement and its annual march at Easter from the nuclear research station at Aldermaston in Berkshire to Trafalgar Square, in which anything from 7,000 to 20,000 people took part, with Collins leading the way in his cassock, always attracted massive media attention.

Collins's involvement in these and other radical reformist causes did not please everyone and during the 1950s slogans of a threatening sort, including 'Hang Canon Collins', were painted on the walls of his house in Amen Court. When he retired from St Paul's in 1981 he gave up the leadership of Christian Action and this was, after a short break, taken over by Canon Eric James, with myself as chairman. A new policy was adopted which involved the financial, and sometimes administrative, support of the many social reform organizations that had come into being since John Collins began his great work. Eric James was deeply involved in the production of the seminal report *Faith in the City* (1985) on urban priority areas.

45 *The Bible, history and faith*

The theology in vogue in the 1950s was still that of biblical theology – an approach with a history going back to the seventeenth century, revived by the Swiss theologian Karl Barth after the First World War and taught influentially in England in the 1930s by the Cambridge scholar Edwyn Hoskyns. In this latter manifestation it was a reaction against liberal, historical and scientific approaches to the Bible, and argued that the scriptures were self-authenticating and could only be properly understood in the context of the faith they expressed.

Lionel Thornton, Gabriel Hebert and Michael Ramsey belonged to this school of theology, though they were not actually biblical scholars, and its chief exponent in the 1950s was Alan Richardson of Durham. In *The Miracle Stories of the Gospels*, he stated his position clearly:

> History cannot be detached from theology in such a way that the miracle stories (or indeed any other part of the Gospel tradition, such as the teaching of Jesus) can be treated as the subject of a strictly scientific investigation. The question of whether the miracles really happened is not within the competence of the historian to decide, if we mean by the historian someone who approaches the subject with an open mind and without preconceived ideas – for the sufficient reason that it is impossible to approach the Gospel records this way. There is no such thing as an impartial historian in the sense that everyone who comes to the Gospels is already either a believer or an unbeliever. The multitudes, according to the Gospel accounts, witnessed the miracles of Jesus as 'signs and wonders'; they came and went away with an 'open mind' but they were not edified; seeing, they had seen and not perceived. Only those who came in faith understood the meaning of the acts of power. That is why any discussion of the Gospel miracles must begin with a consideration of the biblical theology, with the faith which illuminates their character and purpose.

This approach could not survive beyond the 1950s, since the development of biblical scholarship and the urgent need to relate the Christian faith to other fields of study undermined its somewhat narrow presuppositions.

46 Modern miracle – answered prayers

The young boys in the cathedral choir stopped daydreaming when they heard the clergyman in the pulpit say, 'Now let us pray for professional footballers.' The prayers were offered in Carlisle Cathedral, so the choristers naturally thought of Carlisle United struggling at the bottom of Division II and without a win. Since then Carlisle have played eight matches without losing. And in seven they have not conceded a goal. Canon Batty said, 'There is no doubt Carlisle have made a miraculous recovery. We would like to think we have been able to help.'

Daily Sketch

47 *Save our schools*

When the Butler Education Act came into force in 1944 there were about 9,000 Church of England schools. By the end of the 1950s this had been reduced to 2,000, though the church retained some degree of influence in the rest. In order to keep direct control over the management, the appointment of teaching staff and the religious education syllabus of its schools, the church was required by Butler to find 50 per cent of the cost of repairing and developing the buildings. This was not an unreasonable demand but, given the number of schools involved and the backlog of renovation needed, it was quite beyond the capacity of the Church of England. In any event, there was a division of opinion among its bishops as to whether or not it was desirable for the church to retain such a direct control over the schools. Some believed it would be best for them to be handed over to Local Education Authorities with the church providing, as allowed by the Act, one-third of the members of school management boards and seeking to ensure that religious education, in accordance with an agreed syllabus, was recognized as important by all schools.

In the end, lack of money dictated a compromise and government action was needed to ensure that the Church of England remained a significant partner in the national education system. As the 1950s advanced it seemed likely that the church would be able to finance no more than about 500 of its own schools, but a new Education Act in 1959 reduced the buildings levy from 50 per cent to 25 per cent, and by this time it was only too evident that the church's influence on religious education in all the other schools had been, and was likely to remain, insignificant.

The Church of England made, therefore, a renewed effort to retain as many as possible of its schools. In some dioceses it was too late – Durham, for example, now had only a handful of schools – but in Blackburn, where there was a long-standing commitment to church schools, a large number were retained. Everywhere they became a diocesan, rather than a parish, financial responsibility, central church funds were allocated to their support and, besides pouring huge sums of money into its teacher-training colleges, it would eventually become possible for some new church schools to be built.

It could hardly have been foreseen that by the end of the century church schools would be regarded, on educational grounds alone, as the most successful in the maintained sector and that a Labour government would be holding them up as examples of healthy local partnership.

48 *The last days of the Sunday school*

Sunday schools were, in the 1950s, still going strong. At Stockton we started with 80 children, and within 6 months this had grown to 800 – filling on Sunday afternoons every nook and cranny of the old house which was the only community building. There were special reasons for this phenomenal growth, one of which was that in the early stages of the community's development there was little else for children to do, and there was the further point that even though most parents were not churchgoers they still had a genuine desire that their children should be exposed to some Christian influence.

A Sunday school of 800 required time for organization and the training of 40 volunteer teachers in weekly preparation classes. The annual outing to the seaside required a fleet of eight double-decker buses to accomplish the invasion of nearby Redcar or Seaton Carew. By a miracle no child was ever lost. Many confirmation candidates were produced by the school and an intensive course of training, extending over two years and conducted by the clergy, was introduced, together with a requirement of weekly church attendance as a safeguard against casual commitment. Even so, as many as 100 young people, together with 50 adults, were presented to the bishop among a 1,000-strong congregation in Stockton Parish Church in 1963.

Yet we were aware, as clergy in every parish were aware, that unless the Sunday school children and young confirmation candidates came from homes in which at least one parent was a regular churchgoer the chances of any of them becoming integrated into the life of the congregation was remote. Was it worth the considerable effort involved? This was the question we frequently discussed. On the positive side there were some successes, and all received a grounding in the basics of the Christian faith that they might value later. On the other hand, and this was particularly true of those who did not progress beyond Sunday school, there was the serious risk that they would be left with an infantile understanding of the Christian faith that might well prove to be an 'inoculation' against further growth to something more mature.

In the end we decided to give this educational work lower priority in an overfull parish programme and before long, and for a variety of reasons, the traditional Sunday school would in most places be no more. Its replacement was a very much smaller educational programme, confined largely to the children of regular churchgoers and integrated into Sunday morning worship. A consequence of this was loss of all contact with a very large number of children and their parents, the

49

cost of which, in terms of Christian influence, is still impossible to calculate.

49 *Reformers take up their pens*

The first stirrings of reform came in 1957 with the publication of a new magazine, *Prism*. This was the bright idea of two recent Oxford undergraduates, Christopher Martin, who was now working as an Inspector of Taxes, and Robert Minney, teaching in a church school in Hackney. They said they were writing for their own generation, primarily graduates and professional people, and wanted to provide interest in the Church of England that would stimulate more than nominal membership and to encourage the drawing together of the different traditions of the Anglican Communion. This was an ambitious policy for a 16-page octavo magazine, appearing monthly at the price of 1 shilling, but it soon took off and at the end of its first year had expanded to 40 pages with a different glossy cover every month. Robert Minney became business manager and his place as journalist was taken by Nicholas Mosley, who was on the way to becoming a leading novelist.

The contents were nothing like as mild as the original policy statement had seemed to suggest. Support was offered to Mervyn Stockwood of the University Church at Cambridge for an attack on the Church of England's complacency. Eric James had been roped in as a regular columnist; the editors were unhappy with the church's established status and it was announced that a weekend conference for 'Cross Young Men' would be held that summer. So it continued, increasing its circulation rapidly among a new breed of church reformers, until by the early 1960s it had become the unofficial organ of the radical movement in the church. At which point Timothy Beaumont appeared on the scene, took over the ownership, injected necessary capital, became editor and helped to raise the circulation to about 5,000. Its writers and readers were enthusiasts and, although *Prism* began as a lay enterprise, they included the most able of the younger clergy of that era. To the conservative elements in the church its existence became a source of intense irritation and its influence extended into a new parish magazine inset *Outlook*, with a circulation in excess of 100,000 monthly.

50 *An overlarge Lambeth agenda*

At the 1958 Lambeth Conference good things were said about the need to reconcile conflicts between and within nations and there was a strong denunciation of racism in all its forms, with the Archbishop of Cape Town, Joost de Blank, urging his colleagues on. It was impossible, however, to achieve agreement over the possible use of nuclear weapons. Entry into full communion with the recently constituted United Churches of North India and Pakistan and of Sri Lanka, was agreed without any of the bitterness and division that attended the formation of the United Church of South India ten years earlier. Particularly notable was a pre-conference report on *The Family in Contemporary Society*, which encouraged the bishops to reaffirm the statement of the 1930 conference that the use of contraceptives within marriage was permissible for Christians.

Bishop George Bell, who was attending his fourth and last conference (he had been present in 1920 as Archbishop Davidson's chaplain and assistant secretary of the conference), complained however that the agenda this time had been far too large and that sufficient time was not given to important subjects. He was worried also about the lack of 'weighty bishops' and the failure of the English bishops to give leadership, the newer ones being very disappointing. Nonetheless 'the spirit of genuine brotherhood and friendship: and the sense of Anglican Communion was much deeper and stronger than at any previous conference'.

51 *Lambeth-speak examined*

Valerie Pitt, a lecturer in English, was not happy with the language of the official conference report. Writing in *Prism* she complained:

This is the voice of our Lords and Masters talking down to us. The Lambeth Fathers came to London sane and healthy and have gone back to their dioceses afflicted with the worst disease of the Establishment – Fisher's disease or Headmaster's Infallibility – the conviction that they know what is good for the boys. They take (it is one of the symptoms) themselves seriously and stand in awe before their own deliberations. They swell with wisdom, travail (and in public too) with inspiration and are delivered of a platitudinous mouse . . . Now there is a great deal of good sense in the Lambeth Report and the bishops sensibly claim no authority for it. But their speech betrays them. Their language is the language of those who expect no contradiction, and would indeed consider it blasphemous. The Encyclical Letter is couched in the language of proclamation:

> We, the Archbishops and Bishops of the Holy Catholic and Apostolic Church in communion with the See of Canterbury, three hundred and ten in number, assembled from forty-six countries, etc. etc. etc.

From time to time the authors of the Letter and of the Resolutions try to live up to this grandiose beginning. The only trouble is they haven't the skill to manage the rhythms of formal speech.

52 Miss Pitt

It will be readily understood that Valerie Pitt was not a person to be trifled with. She was for several years in the 1950s a Fellow of Newnham College, Cambridge, but gave this up in order to care for her aged mother, combining this with the post of Senior Lecturer in English at Woolwich Polytechnic. She was a highly regarded literary critic and, a disciple of Austin Farrer, had an acute theological mind which led her to embrace the doctrines and spirituality, of the unfrilly variety, of Anglo-Catholicism. That she was a conservative was not open to doubt, but not of the dyed-in-the-wool sort and politically she was left wing. Moreover her objections to the theological explorations of the 1960s were based on what she believed to be their intellectual inadequacies. Most of the proposals for reform struck her as being trivial; bishops were objects of pity.

For more than a decade she edified, entertained and often enough infuriated the readers of *Prism*, then of *New Christian*; a sad consequence of the demise of these journals was that she was deprived of a regular platform for her stimulating views. She ought really to have been a columnist; authors prayed that their books would not be sent to her for review, though she was never other than perceptive and fair.

53 The Red dean

Only the Church of England could have tolerated a dean of its historic, central cathedral who spent much of his time defending the monstrous

Stalinist regime in the Soviet Union during the 1930s and 1940s – but it had no choice since he had committed no ecclesiastic offence that merited deposition.

Hewlett Johnson was at Canterbury from 1931 until his retirement in 1963 at the age of 88. By the standards of his time he was an effective Dean and during the severe wartime bombing of Canterbury a courageous Dean. Certainly he looked the part – tall, big boned, endowed with a fine face and a splendid domed head, framed by plentiful white hair, he was an imposing figure and at the enthronement of Michael Ramsey in 1961 the sight of the Dean and the Archbishop, who had a not dissimilar appearance, suggested a flashback to the Middle Ages.

The problem lay in the fact that, in common with some others who should have known better, he was completely taken in by the propaganda emanating from Moscow during the darkest days of Stalin's reign of terror. Even during his frequent visits to Russia he allowed himself to be bamboozled by what he heard and was permitted to see. That the Russian Orthodox Church had been decimated and millions consigned to prison camps or firing squads did not seem to trouble him, and he was an ardent propagandist for the Communist cause. His book *The Socialist Sixth of the World*, published in 1939 soon after the outbreak of the Second World War, brought him instant world fame. It was an account of a three-month-long stay in the Soviet Union as a guest of the government, sold several million copies in 22 editions and 24 languages. In 1951 he was one of the first recipients of a newly created Stalin Peace Prize and he received other awards from the Chinese government.

It was unfortunate that in many countries the distinction between the Dean of Canterbury and the Archbishop of Canterbury was not always discerned and Johnson's activities and utterances were a constant source of embarrassment and irritation to Geoffrey Fisher. By the time Michael Ramsey succeeded to the Primacy he was much less active and more easily accepted.

54 *The connoisseur*

No one did more to re-establish contact between the church and the artist in the twentieth century than Walter Hussey. At St Matthew's, Northampton, where he was Vicar from 1937 to 1955, he commissioned one of Henry Moore's greatest works, a seated figure of the Madonna and Child, and a painting of the crucifixion by Graham Sutherland. Benjamin Britten composed *Rejoice in the Lamb* and

Gerald Finzi *Lo, the Full Final Sacrifice* for an annual festival, to which contributions were also made by Lennox Berkeley, Kirsten Flagstad, W. H. Auden, Norman Nicholson and Peter Pears. He knew everyone in the arts world and was strongly supported by Sir Kenneth (later Lord) Clarke, the Director of the National Gallery. When he moved to Chichester as Dean in 1955 he transformed the cathedral by restoring a fifteenth-century stone screen to its proper place (as a memorial to Bishop George Bell), introduced a splendidly colourful tapestry by John Piper, a dramatic painting, *Noli me Tangere*, by Graham Sutherland, an altar frontal *The Lens of Divine Light* by Cecil Collins and a blazing red window on the creation by Marc Chagall. Among the musicians recruited were William Walton, Leonard Bernstein and the American Wilhelm Albright, and the Chichester Festival became, and remains, an important event in the cultural life of southern England. Hussey had some of the traditional assets of a dean – an impressive appearance, a cultured and sonorous voice – and he was a remarkable raiser of funds for his artistic projects. In other important ways, however, he was a disappointment.

55 The last hunting parson?

Bill Llewellyn, who lived to be 93, was Vicar of Badminton with Acton Turville, then Rector of Tetbury with Beverston, in Gloucestershire, and subsequently became Bishop of Lynn in Norfolk. While at Badminton he rode with the Beaufort hounds and, having said Mattins in the parish church, wearing breeches and boots under his cassock, he donned his black coat and top hat in the vestry before mounting the horse which one of the Duke of Beaufort's grooms had been walking up and down outside the church. He continued to ride until he was 83. Besides this he was a considerable ornithologist and a skilled angler, as well as a fine oarsman. He won an Oxford Blue at stroke in the 1928 Boat Race and during his years as a bishop frequently rowed off the north coast of Norfolk. He belonged to an older school of aristocratic clergymen and, himself an old Etonian, described as 'among the most beautiful of his generation', he once wryly remarked, 'A man does not know what poverty is until he has two sons at Eton.' Llewellyn had a distinguished war record as a chaplain with the Eighth Army in the Western Desert, and his rural interests and pastoral gifts made him a much loved first Bishop of Lynn.

56 *Evangelical revival – beginnings*

During the late 1950s and early 1960s there was widespread belief that the Anglo-Catholic and Evangelical wings of the Church of England were in terminal decline. The Evangelicals were small in number, introverted, backward-looking and divided. Yet within 50 years there was an evangelical Archbishop of Canterbury, several diocesan bishops of similar convictions and in all parts of England a network of dynamic churches inspired by the evangelical spirit. Moreover these churchmen and churches had social consciences and marked affinity with their forebears of the early nineteenth century who provided the driving force behind the anti-slave-trade movement.

The reasons for this dramatic revival were several but chief was the leadership of John Stott who was Rector of All Souls', Langham Place in London's West End from 1950 to 1975. He received no ecclesiastical preferment – at least he accepted none – but, apart from Archbishop William Temple, was the most influential Church of England clergyman in the twentieth century. What was the secret of his success?

First, he turned All Souls' into a showplace evangelical parish in which every church member was involved in mission. He had already been a curate there for five years and was on the verge of leaving, when, aged 29, he took over the leadership of a church that still needed rebuilding after wartime bombing and was no less in need of spiritual renewal. Both were achieved by dint of hard, dedicated and imaginative effort and, besides the worship and inspired preaching, a clubhouse for the underprivileged young people of the area had over 300 members and was run by 60 volunteers. All of which became much talked about, and others came to see what they could learn.

Next in importance was the founding of the Eclectics Society – a group of young and able clergymen who were deeply influenced by Stott's personality, teaching and methods. They met with him regularly and by the mid-1960s had 17 linked groups in different parts of the country, with a combined membership of over 1,000. They joined him in the organization of a National Evangelical Anglican Conference at Keele University in 1967. This was addressed by the Archbishop of Canterbury, Michael Ramsey, and repeated 10 years later at Nottingham University when nearly 2,000 delegates attended.

During this period of growth Stott was unequivocal in declaring his intention never to become the leader of a sect but to take Evangelicalism into the mainstream of the Church of England. Which is precisely what he did. His writing was also hugely influential. He was the author of about 50 books – some of them Bible commentaries, the others dealing with the basic elements of Christianity and achieving wide paperback sales on church bookstalls. A bibliography of his writings runs to 156 pages and by 2000 the royalties, virtually all of which went to a charitable trust, totalled almost £750,000.

It might be supposed from all this that Stott was a larger-than-life figure, given constantly to banging the big drum. Not at all. Although he was a close friend of Billy Graham and conducted many missions he had none of the American evangelist's histrionics. He was a compelling preacher and spoke in a distinctive style, but the emotional content of his message was balanced by the intellectual demands he made on his mainly middle-class professional audiences. He seems to have resembled Charles Simeon, the great leader of the eighteenth-century Evangelical Revival, not least in his evident godliness.

57 Strong moves on the leadership chessboard

Although by the 1950s the supply of outstanding men for the bench of bishops was beginning to be depleted, it was nonetheless still possible during that decade to make strong appointments to some of the 32 dioceses that became vacant. The elevation of Michael Ramsey, who was in a class of his own, to Durham in 1952 and his translation to York a mere four years later, more or less guaranteed his succession to Canterbury when Geoffrey Fisher died in 1961. Donald Coggan, who succeeded Ramsey both at York and Canterbury, went to Bradford in 1955 and probably did his best work there. Edmund Morgan, one of the godliest of bishops, had gone to Truro in 1951 and Leonard Wilson, the heroic survivor of a Japanese war camp, began a distinguished episcopate at Birmingham two years later.

Gerald Ellison's appointment to Chester in 1954 was a recognition of the gifts and experience of another of Archbishop Garbett's former chaplains and strengthened the ranks of the enlightened traditionalists. In the same year Launcelot Fleming, a former polar explorer and wartime naval chaplain, was translated from Portsmouth to Norwich to begin a notable ministry in fast-changing rural Norfolk. The translation of the elderly, sardonic Henry Montgomery-Campbell from Guildford to London in 1955 was baffling and turned out to be no more than a stopgap appointment.

Not so that of Cuthbert Bardsley to Coventry in 1956. He proved to be just right for a diocese planning the resurrection of its cathedral after wartime bombing and was an inspiring leader as well as the maker of brilliant appointments to the cathedral chapter. The translation of the admirable Noel Hudson from Newcastle to Ely in 1957 was a mistake but Harold Macmillan, who became Prime Minister that year and had a special interest in episcopal appointments, served the church better when he sent the scholar-pastor John Moorman to Ripon and the ecumenist-pastor Oliver Tomkins to Bristol. Most bold of all was the appointment of Mervyn Stockwood to Southwark.

58 *Yes, but . . .*

The Archbishop of York, Michael Ramsey, on learning that the Bishop of Lincoln, Maurice Harland, was to be his successor at Durham:

> 'Very good, very good, very good,
> but it mustn't happen again.'

59 *Fizz at Southwark*

The appointment of Mervyn Stockwood to be Bishop of Southwark in 1959 brought to the bench of bishops its most colourful and enigmatic member in the second half of the twentieth century. Arriving at Southwark to a fanfare of trumpets, after hugely successful ministries as a parish priest in the East End of Bristol and as vicar of the University Church at Cambridge, he was seen by many as a beacon of hope in the renewal of the Church of England. Under his leadership some of the most able clergy of the post-war era tackled the long-standing problem of the church's alienation from all but a tiny percentage of London's population. A lot of noise was made and some development of permanent work activated, but when, after 21 years, Stockwood retired, the number of people in his diocese attending church was fewer than ever before and he had spent the final year of his episcopate in debilitating depression.

The failure to arrest decline was certainly not his fault and it served to demonstrate beyond dispute that the church's inner-city problems could not be solved simply by recruiting gifted and dedicated clerics. Stockwood was both, and for the greater part of his time at Southwark his leadership was inspiring. Yet those who observed him closely were aware of strange inconsistencies. Unmarried, he craved for affection, but was a demanding and sometimes ruthless friend whom it was not always easy to love. Michael De-la-Noy subtitled his biography of Stockwood 'A Lonely Life' and there was broad agreement among those nearest to him that his disciplined homosexuality precluded the establishing of a permanent, sustaining relationship which might have brought him happiness and fulfilment at the deepest level. He made no secret of his socialism, though it was of the champagne sort and he employed both a liveried servant and a cordon bleu cook. Lunch at Bishop's House, Tooting Bec Gardens was memorable – and dangerous for any guest who had travelled by car.

Stockwood was genuinely concerned for the poor, and spoke up for them in the House of Lords, but he was more often in the company of the titled rich, among whom he was at various times pleased to number the Duke and Duchess of Windsor, Princess Margaret and the Prince of Wales. He hated fascism, but was a close friend of Sir Oswald Mosely who had been the leader of the British fascists in the 1930s. In church matters he was the *enfant terrible* of the Establishment. The Church Assembly and its successor the General Synod bored him greatly and he made no secret of his frustration with its lack of vision and courage. The pastoral care of his clergy was a high priority for him, though he quarrelled badly with some and at one time had the inconvenient habit of summoning priests for interview at midnight.

He was left at Southwark far too long, for he was essentially an innovator rather than a sustainer and needed the stimulus of excitement and success. On the whole the diocese appreciated the leadership of a colourful bishop and when at his final service in Southwark Cathedral he was presented, among other things, with a Jeroboam of champagne he acknowledged this to be an appropriate gift since, 'I have attempted to bring a little fizz into the diocese.'

60 *A false dawn over Scotland*

The proposals for uniting the Church of England, the Church of Scotland and the smaller Episcopal Church of Scotland and the Presbyterian Church of England promised much when they were published in 1958, but they came to nothing. The Church of Scotland and its English counterpart were to have bishops who would exercise their leadership in the context of the existing Presbyterian policy, while the Church of England and its Scottish counterpart would adopt a corporate and conciliar style of episcopacy. They would also introduce a form of lay eldership similar to that of Presbyterian churches.

It seemed a positive step forward for all concerned – but not to the Scots. The Church of Scotland's representatives in the conversations were nearly all academics who lacked close contact with the grass roots of their church. Sensing this, the *Scottish Daily Express* and other Beaverbrook newspapers mounted a sustained and often vitriolic campaign designed to torpedo the scheme, which it succeeded in doing. Day after day front-page headlines screamed 'Outrage' and the supporting text denounced a secret ecclesiastical plot to enslave the Scots. The General Assembly of the Church of Scotland, more seriously, decided that the proposals implied a denial of the validity of its present arrangements. So that was that, and half a century later these churches remained divided.

61 *The statistics of clergy decline*

The size of the Church of England's ordained manpower peaked in 1901 with 23,670 clergymen serving a population of 30.6 million. By 1950 this had been reduced to 14,972 parish clergy serving 41.3 million and retirement was exceeding recruitment by about 600 every year. The reduction was most keenly felt in the supply of curates, especially in the North of England. Whereas Manchester diocese had 141 curates in 1938, it now had 54; Liverpool went down from 158 to 58, Sheffield from 106 to 43. But the overall number was still high enough to enable the traditional parochial system to be maintained in most places, although single-handed incumbents in large urban parishes were often under considerable strain. On the other hand, young priests in rural areas complained that they did not have enough to do. In Hereford, Norwich and Exeter dioceses there was one clergyman for between 1,000 and 2,000 population and even at the end of the decade 4,630 clergy (41.7 per cent of the total number) were in charge of parishes each of 1,500 population or less. Sixty-four per cent of those accepted for ordination were under 24, and of these 35 per cent had been educated at public schools. This would change dramatically.

62   *Getting together in Lincolnshire*

South Ormsby, a village some seven miles from Louth, was known to few people outside that remote part of Lincolnshire when Arthur Smith became its Rector in 1946. The total population of the parish, which was associated with three other villages, was 215. Smith had been a wartime naval chaplain and he accepted the living under the patronage of a friend. The Rectory was lit by oil lamps and on his first Sunday there were no communicants and about a dozen people present. He soon came to believe he had made a serious mistake, for although he had a number of outside interests, including the RNVR Humberside chaplaincy, he could not find enough to do. With the rural population of Lincolnshire declining, he declared the traditional pattern of one parish with its own parson to be not only outmoded but actually undesirable, as it encouraged idleness and caused loneliness and low morale.

He was seeking a new urban appointment when the Bishop of Lincoln, Maurice Harland, pressed him to stay in order to take on a further 11 parishes and to form a team to experiment with a new approach to rural ministry. At first he declined but then agreed to devote several years to the project. The 15 parishes covered 75 square miles and had a population of about 1,100. Twelve churches, some of outstanding architectural importance, were open for worship and the rector, two curates, a deaconess and a lay reader were located strategically in different parishes in order to be able to travel easily to conduct services and to undertake pastoral work.

A group bus, driven by the clergy, conveyed parishioners to churches other than their own for shared worship and also brought young people together for joint Sunday schools and youth clubs. Four hundred acres of glebe were jointly administered. The effect of all this was dramatic. Prior to the setting up of the group in 1949, several of the churches had tiny and in some instances non-existent congregations. By Easter 1959, however, 500 people were attending one or other of the churches. There was lively youth work, a monthly magazine going into every home, much new lay involvement in parish life and a buildings restoration programme under way.

Smith, who left after 14 years to become Archdeacon of Lincoln, wrote a book, *The South Ormsby Experiment: An Adventure in Fellowship* (1960), which aroused widespread interest. The group ministry came to be seen as the answer to most of the church's rural problems and a large number of them were formed in every part of the country. It was believed that these would lead to revival of rural church life, but it was not foreseen that a serious reduction in the size of the ordained ministry would not allow them to be provided with South Ormesby-scale resources. By the end of the century the South Ormesby Group had one priest – a woman.

63 *Rehousing the clergy*

At the beginning of this decade virtually all the Church of England's clergy, apart from the curates and those ministering in new housing developments, lived in large houses, usually with an extensive garden. Most were Victorian, solid rather than elegant and sometimes with elements of Gothic reflecting the nineteenth-century churches alongside which they had been built. Some of them, however, had been replacements for earlier, eighteenth-century rectories and vicarages, and of those that remained – a significant number – some were buildings of considerable grandeur and elegance with a sweeping drive for carriages. They had been erected by very wealthy clergymen with the aid of either family money or the profits from glebes and tithes – the value of which increased considerably with the late eighteenth-century revival of agriculture.

The size of the rectory or the vicarage indicated the status of the parson in society. He was a gentleman in Holy Orders, positioned with the squire, the magistrates and only a step below the aristocratic inhabitants of the 'great' house. He was also likely to have a large family and a sizeable domestic staff. As late as the 1930s the rector of the Nottinghamshire parish in which my boyhood was spent employed a butler, a cook, several maids, a nanny and three gardeners, one of whom served as his driver. The vicarage of a County Durham parish to which I went for a Harvest Festival one year was of curious shape and, on enquiry, I was told that successive vicars had enlarged it to accommodate their growing families, with the result that it now had 25 bedrooms.

During the Victorian era the houses were scaled down somewhat but remained large and became centres of hospitality and social life in the parish. They were deemed to be over-large by 1950 since there was insufficient money available to meet the cost of maintenance, and the clergy lacked the means, and often the will, to keep them warm and clean. A garden of an acre or more could be a burden to a priest who could no longer afford help, and there was no tradition of financial assistance from parishes for either house or garden.

The centralization of endowment income and the move towards the equalization of stipends from 1960 onwards enabled the dioceses to start selling the large parsonages and replace them with very much smaller four- to five-bedroom houses, built usually in the garden of the grander place. In retrospect it appears unfortunate that this policy was carried out during a period of relative stagnation in the housing market and most of the houses went for bargain prices, though a large proportion of these required considerable renovation and redecoration. Before long, houses purchased for £15–20,000 would be worth £1 million or more and The Old Rectory or The Old Vicarage became a property with a certain caché and the home of a business tycoon or a media personality. The splendid eighteenth-century former Rectory at Michelmersh in Hampshire, where I preach regularly, is the home of the broadcaster Sir David Frost. When the Dowager Duchess of Devonshire left Chatsworth House she moved into a conveniently placed former rectory. The down-sizing of clergy housing was inevitable as the twentieth century advanced, but it was not without some loss to the parishes and it was clear evidence of the changed position in society of the Church of England and its rectors and vicars.

64 The advent of the managerial bishop

The 1950s saw the development of what was to become a marked change in the relationship between bishops and the parish clergy. When I was ordained at the beginning of the decade the rectors and vicars had no desire to see their bishop unless he was needed to conduct a confirmation or to grace some other important event. They had nothing against them (at least generally not) but they resented any suggestion of interference in their parish territory. They were, in other words, clear about their responsibilities and secure in their belief that they could carry these out. The bishops, too, who had often been professors of theology or public school headmasters, were not always anxious to be driven to the far-flung corners of their dioceses for an inconsequential event. They had books to write and in some cases the House of Lords to attend.

Things began to change when the Liturgical Movement identified, correctly, the bishop as the chief minister of the Eucharist and recommended that the rites of baptism and confirmation were best administered in the context of the Eucharist. Confirmations involving several parishes gave way to single parish events requiring more frequent episcopal appearances. These were increased further as church attendance began to take a dramatic dip and the clergy, feeling increasingly marginalized, were less secure. Bishops were needed to hold hands and provide encouragement.

Soon more suffragan bishops were needed to share this responsibility (their number increased from 40 to 63 by the end of the century) and when eventually even they could not cope with the pastoral demands archdeacons spread their wings and added to their traditional concern for drains and legal matters some of the functions of a bishop. Thus the leadership of the church was diverted from a strategic to a managerial role.

65 No need to overdo it

The Watch of Prayer is in response to Our Lord's words to his disciples in the Garden of Gethsemane. 'So you hadn't the strength to keep awake with me for one hour?' The time will be divided into half-hour periods.

Woodville Parish Church Magazine

66 The media and the message

It was hardly surprising that Archbishop Fisher, who loathed the media and had no idea how to handle it, was not at his best when awakened in the middle of the night by a telephone call from a journalist seeking his opinion on some aspect of church or national life. He had no press officer, the church had no Information Office, which was not only inconvenient for an archbishop, but meant that the church lacked expertise in the dissemination of its own news and opinion.

This was remedied – up to a point – in 1959 by the establishing of an Information Office in Church House, Westminster. Colonel Bob Hornby, a lively character with much experience of army public relations work, became the first Information Officer and stayed long enough to see the enterprise firmly established. He was succeeded by another army man, the perhaps unfortunately named General Adam Block, and he acquired an assistant, Michael De-la-Noy, a young journalist who was also made Archbishop Ramsey's personal Press Officer.

At this point things began to wake up. De-la-Noy prepared for the bishops attending the 1968 Lambeth Conference a guide to London, which included some of the most expensive restaurants in Soho – possible maybe for journalists on expenses, but emphatically not for impecunious bishops from the developing world. There was a row. This was soon followed by the publication in *Forum* and *New Society* of articles by De-la-Noy about a transvestite army colonel and, in frank terms, the life of a bisexual man. Ramsey's advisers convinced him that these were inappropriate from the pen of a member of an archbishop's personal staff, so he was obliged to leave.

These incidents apart, the operation ran smoothly and reasonably competently. A radio and television section was established and an Enquiry Office dealt with requests for non-topical information – many thousands of these every year. General Block was succeeded as Chief Information Officer by John Miles, an experienced BBC man, and Archbishop Runcie was provided with his own press secretary at Lambeth, Eve Keatley, also from the BBC.

The serious newspapers and the BBC still employed experienced correspondents who were largely sympathetic to what the churches were about. But during the 1980s this changed. The media generally adopted a more aggressive approach to all established institutions and the Church of England found itself without the skilled resources necessary for dealing with the changed situation. Many years of bad publicity followed and it was not until the end of the century that the Archbishop's Council took steps to recruit a different breed of communicator.

67 A Son of Thunder at York

Cyril Garbett was 67 when he was translated from Winchester to York in 1942 – a move that he took a lot of persuading to accept – but few archbishops have enjoyed such widespread admiration as a church leader, particularly by the laity, and he was the perfect partner for William Temple and Geoffrey Fisher during their years at Canterbury. He had been a curate, then the Vicar of Portsea during its greatest days, and throughout his long episcopate retained the outlook of a parish priest.

As a bishop, he gave priority to visiting the parishes and after two years at York, where he had immense extra-diocesan responsibility, he reproached himself for having preached at only 260 out of 460 parishes. Yet one of his many Portsea curates, who admired him greatly, felt moved to write:

He was not a loveable person. He inspired tremendous devotion and enormous admiration . . . but there was something about him which did not permit straight forward affection. He could not unbend and he was never utterly and completely relaxed.

Charles Smyth, his brilliant biographer, portrayed him as a tyrant, more of an inspector than a pastor and one who could be devastatingly cruel when dealing with an erring clergyman. On the other hand he was sometimes generous and supportive of the delinquent, especially if they had a tough parish, and if he was demanding of others he was even more demanding of himself.

He had been Bishop of Southwark before moving to Winchester and his arrival at York coincided with the darkest days of the war. Although he did not court publicity, he knew how to use the media and, having made himself available for sermons and speeches throughout the North of England, his utterances were widely reported. In the House of Lords he was always heard with great respect, particularly on the subject of housing, in which he had made himself something of an authority. He denounced the Nazi massacre of the Polish Jews in 1942, later supported the retention of nuclear weapons in order to maintain peace, took a pro-Arab stance in the conflict over the Jewish settlement of Palestine and welcomed the Welfare State.

An official visit to Russia in 1943, not long after the Soviet Union's entry into the war, captured the popular imagination, and wartime visits to America and Canada, then to the Home Fleet at Scapa Flow, the troops invading the Low Countries and Germany and the Mediterranean forces, were all deemed to be highly successful. They continued to be an important aspect of his work in the post-war era, though questions have recently been asked about the extent to which he was made, unwittingly, an agent of British foreign policy.

Garbett professed to be a reformer, but whenever specific reforms of the Church of England were proposed he usually counselled caution. The three books of his years at York – *The Claims of the Church of England* (1947), *Church and State in England* (1950) and *In an Age of Revolution* (1952) – were widely noticed, but they were the expression of an essentially conservative mind. I first encountered him in 1943 when he shared a platform with William Temple at a public meeting in Leicester, but not again until 1955 when I met him in a Middlesbrough vicarage. By this time he was 80 and seemed as gentle as an old grandfather. Smyth explained: 'The Son of Thunder was transformed into an Apostle of Love.'

2

The Rebellious Sixties

In retrospect it appears that a decade of reconstruction and restored confidence may have been needed before the idealism and the demand for change engendered by an appalling war could gather strength to embark upon a social revolution. When it came in the 1960s it affected in one way or another virtually every aspect of life – music, politics, morality, education, sexuality and the religious faith expressed by all the churches. Power was now passing from those who had held the reins before the war to a new generation which, having experienced the consequences of political and social failure, was determined that the future must be different.

Within the Church of England those who had been ordained since 1945, often as a consequence of their wartime experience, were not motivated by a calling to serve the church as it had been in the first half of the century. The jet age needed something very different and study of theology pointed to the urgency of renewal – of reformation, even.

By the end of the 1950s it had become apparent that, although interesting and encouraging experiments were taking place in a handful of parishes, the long-established parochial system was now a hindrance to significant missionary enterprise in towns and cities. Experience in Sheffield demonstrated the need for more specialized work. Equally, new biblical insights into the nature of the church demanded much greater involvement of the laity in its life and wider consultation at every level. Why were women still excluded from positions of leadership? Again the movement towards unity needed reinforcing if the church was to be credible and efficient.

Hence the torrent of proposals for change on these and other matters that engulfed the church (and not only the Church of England) in the 1960s. So considerable was the momentum of this and so radical the potential of its consequences that there was talk of a New Reformation.

On the south bank of the Thames some spoke of the need for revolution in the church's life.

Before all this got under way, however, there was a theological explosion created, mainly in Cambridge, by a new generation of scholars who discerned that the current belief system of the church could no longer be shared convincingly with a better educated and more sceptical population. The consequences of this, demonstrated by the response to Bishop John Robinson's Honest to God *(1963), were exciting for some, but deeply threatening to others. As were new responses to changing ethical norms in a so-called permissive society.*

This was a stimulating and encouraging decade for reformers, young and old. Never again in the twentieth century would the church experience the bubbling of so many new ideas or such zeal for a more dynamic approach to its mission. But by the end of the 1960s many of the would-be reformers had reached the conclusion that optimism about the church's willingness to change, or even its ability to change, had been misplaced. A long haul was going to be needed and the challenge posited by this met with a mixed reception.

1 *Lady Chatterley on trial*

The prosecution of Penguin Books in 1960 under an Obscene Publications Act for their publication of the first unexpurgated edition in Britain of D. H. Lawrence's novel *Lady Chatterley's Lover* became a cause célèbre, and the appearance in court of Bishop John Robinson for the defence shocked some in the Church of England, including the Archbishop of Canterbury.

Robinson had been Bishop of Woolwich for only just over twelve months and was little known outside academic circles. This would soon change. His offence in the eyes of the book's churchgoing opponents was partly that of supporting its publication but also, and for some chiefly, the content of his support. While in no way condoning the kind of adulterous relationship portrayed by Lawrence, Robinson spoke of the author trying 'to portray the sex relationship as something essentially sacred, akin to holy communion'.

Following the jury's 'Not guilty' verdict, which had a profound effect on the future of publishing, Lambeth Palace was flooded with telephone calls protesting against Robinson's action and Archbishop Fisher felt constrained by what he called his pastoral responsibility to rebuke him in public for causing confusion among ordinary people. The bishop was, he said, much mistaken in believing that he could take part in this trial without becoming 'a stumbling block and a cause of offence to many'. Robinson was now marked as a controversial bishop, which ensured maximum media attention to his *Honest to God* when it appeared.

2 *A far-reaching 'courtesy call'*

The visit of Archbishop Fisher to the recently elected Pope John XXIII in 1960 was quite unofficial and described as no more than a 'courtesy call' made in the course of an ecumenical journey that would also take in Jerusalem and Istanbul. Vatican officials viewed it with considerable suspicion and, having failed to prevent it from taking place, did everything possible to reduce media coverage. Doubtless they were aware that five years earlier Fisher, in a speech to the Convocation of

Canterbury, had declared the Roman Catholic Church to be 'the greatest hindrance to the establishing of the Kingdom of God among men'. Much more seriously, from the Vatican's viewpoint, the meeting of Pope and Archbishop might conceivably hint at a degree of recognition of Anglican claims.

It was in fact the first time since 1397 that an Archbishop of Canterbury had visited the Pope, and Fisher, wearing a cassock and square Canterbury cap, appeared to be a throwback to the Reformation as he passed the Swiss guard at the entrance to the Vatican. The conversation between them was off to a sticky start when the Pope read from a recent address in which he looked forward to 'the time when our separated brethren return to the Mother Church'. But when Fisher responded by suggesting that this was not the time to be going backwards but only for looking forward to the time – 'God's good time' – when their two Christian communities would converge, the Pope warmed to their encounter, and Fisher wrote of his visit later, 'We talked as two happy people.'

An immediate outcome was the setting up of an Anglican Centre – a kind of embassy – in Rome, with a resident archiepiscopal representative who would study the preparations for the forthcoming Vatican Council and keep the Archbishop informed of its progress. It was also understood that he would on request supply the newly established Secretariat for Christian Unity with information about the Anglican Church. Bernard Pawley, a scholarly canon of Ely who had learned Italian during his years as a prisoner of war, proved to be an ideal choice for this post and, although Fisher's visit had not been official, it opened the way to a speedy thaw in relations between the two churches. It was no mean achievement.

3 *The birth of a ginger group*

The Keble Conference Group had a short, independent life but one of considerable influence. A conference at Keble College, Oxford, in 1960 convened on the initiative of the Rector of Woolwich, Nicolas Stacey, was concerned solely with group and team ministries, which were then being formed in urban as well as rural areas. The highlight of the conference was a paper by Bishop John Robinson in which he called for the adoption of many new forms of ministry, lay as well as ordained, and in the subsequent discussion much dissatisfaction with the traditional parochial system was expressed. It was said to have broken down in many places, and those present decided to maintain contact with each other by means of a quarterly newsletter and a simple organization, with Robinson as chairman and Timothy Beaumont as secretary.

The membership grew to just over 500, of which a high proportion came from the liveliest and best of those who had been ordained since the war and, in their first incumbencies, were experiencing the frustrations of trying to turn an antiquated organization into something like a dynamic instrument of mission. A couple of suffragan bishops and a handful of archdeacons also joined. In the newsletter and local conferences their concerns soon extended beyond group and team ministries to other areas where reform was needed – church government (a few laypeople had joined the group), church unity, clergy training, finance, clergy appointments. By the end of 1962 the group felt strong enough to consider the question of whether it should continue as a small, behind-the-scenes movement, exercising some influence, or embark on something far more ambitious – a wide-ranging reform movement.

Most members, of whom I was one, favoured the second but it was apparent that it would take some time to gather further strength and create the necessary momentum. It was then noticed by the leadership that the Parish and People movement needed a fresh infusion of life and some new objectives. So negotiations for the possible merger of the two organizations were opened. These, in which I was heavily involved as General Secretary of Parish and People, turned out to be far from easy. There was only a small overlap in membership – Parish and People had about 1,500 on its active list – and members of the Keble Conference Group tended to believe that the concerns of most of these did not extend much beyond the ordering of worship, and that in other matters they were conservative. This was only partly true, but many of them were certainly convinced that the Keble people were impatient hotheads whose activities would be more likely to impede than to advance reform. After much discussion between the leadership and the canvassing of members' opinions, however, proposals for a merger were put to a further conference at Keble College and accepted with enthusiasm.

4 A towering figure at Lambeth

It seemed, and still seems, appropriate that Michael Ramsey should have been the one-hundredth Archbishop of Canterbury. He combined in a remarkable way a formidable intellect and a deep spirituality. His early Anglo-Catholic loyalty had been greatly tempered by his studies, particularly in the realm of biblical theology, and this was influenced by a liberal mind often in conflict with a conservative heart. It is hardly surprising that such a mixture was accompanied by a degree of engaging eccentricity. His appearance was singular: a massive, somewhat lopsided frame, a large head, a bald dome ringed by fluffy white hair, ample, ever-moving eyebrows. This was a venerable figure and when at his consecration in York Minister on St Michael and All Angels' day, 1952, I had commented on this to my neighbour I was assured that he had looked exactly the same when he was in the sixth form at Repton (he was now 48).

It was Ramsey's lot to preside over the Church of England during the rebellious 1960s and he proved equal to the task – a towering figure who could not help but be involved in much of what was taking place, yet stood detached from it and provided a stable centre around which the tempest could rage. This is a retrospective judgement. At the time those of us who were pressing for reform found him a problem. He did not welcome change and often opposed change, particularly in those areas most precious to him – worship and the understanding of the Christian faith itself. It took time for him to recognize that what was being proposed was intended to further, not hinder, these key areas in the church's life. Again, we often wished that he might use a little more energy in the promotion of changes he believed to be necessary, not least the Anglican–Methodist reunion scheme, the rejection of which left him distressed. Only late in the day did he put his full weight behind it.

Church government bored him stiff – a healthy failing, perhaps – but he strongly backed a Worship and Doctrine Measure in 1973 that liberated the church to make its own decisions on these matters without having to secure the consent of the state. On social and political issues he stood firmly in the reforming tradition exemplified by F. D. Maurice and William Temple, both of whom he greatly admired, and his speeches in these areas were often truly courageous. The first of his many books, *The Gospel and the Catholic Church* (1936), proved to be a seminal work; most of the rest were on spirituality and widely read.

He was shy and had no small talk, sometimes with embarrassing consequences for others in his company, but beneath his complex personality there was great warmth and affection for those he had known for a long time. Following the announcement of my appointment as a canon of Westminster in 1976 a postcard from him (then living in retirement in Durham) said, 'Well! Well! Well! Love and prayers, Michael.'

5 *In the true wilderness*

Father Harry Williams spent 18 years as a Fellow of Trinity College, Cambridge (1951–69) and served as Dean of Chapel from 1958. It was during these Cambridge years that he exercised his greatest influence – as a teacher, preacher and spiritual counsellor in the university, and also through his books which were widely read in Britain and North America. He began his academic career as a fairly orthodox New Testament scholar and was a priest in the Anglo-Catholic tradition.

But following a breakdown, not long after his appointment to Trinity, he underwent long-term psychoanalysis. The combination of anguish and insights received through analysis, and an acute theological mind, produced a deeply personal interpretation of Christianity which many found illuminating and helpful, though many others regarded him as a menace. His views often caused controversy. 'Religious establishments invariably give me the creeps,' he once confided to his readers, before informing them that 'Religion is to a large extent what people do with their phobias, their will to power and their sexual frustrations.' His ethical views were no less startling and in his autobiography *Some Day I'll Find You* (1982), which seemed disappointingly self-indulgent, he spoke of his homosexual relations with several men and said, 'I have seldom felt more like thanking God than when having sex. I used in bed to praise Him more and more for the joy I was receiving and giving.'

His decision to become a monk in the Community of the Resurrections at Mirfield in 1969 came as a surprise to many and, in spite of his Friar Tuck-like appearance, proved to be some way below satisfactory, but the Community was now a more relaxed society and readily provided him with a second home until his death in 2006. He always regarded Trinity as his real home and, to the great pleasure of his friends, often returned to Cambridge and the flesh pots of London until ill-health intervened. His collection of sermons *The True Wilderness* (1965) became a bestseller and one of the twentieth-century's spiritual classics. He could be wonderful company.

6 *Cambridge religion*

During the late 1950s there was much talk of a religious revival in the universities, and bishops were greatly encouraged by favourable reports, especially from Oxford and Cambridge. Early in 1960 a survey carried out by *Cambridge Opinion* indicated that 33 per cent of the student body belonged to some religious society or group, while 66 per cent were definitely prepared to call themselves Christian; 49 per cent were professedly Church of England, and of these 61 per cent went regularly to church, 21 per cent occasionally.

Compared with the rest of the country these figures were astonishing. But Hugh Dickinson, at that time Chaplain of Trinity College and later to become Dean of Salisbury, raised a number of questions about their significance. His experience had led him to believe that a good deal of religious observance among students was motivated by personal need – loneliness, insecurity and so forth – rather than by response to a challenge. He complained that no one in Cambridge ever preached about sacrifice or heroic generosity, and that church leaders were lacking the passion or the vision to present a vocation for the church that was powerful enough to capture the imagination of undergraduates. Complacency ruled. The chaplain would not have long to wait before Cambridge stirred itself, but the result of the 'new theology' and the consequent excitement was to reduce chapel attendance and also to decrease vocations to the ordained ministry of a church that was unwilling to embrace reform.

7 *Oxford religion*

It remains true that no undergraduate need go without expert help in the all-important task of discovering for himself what Christianity is and deciding his attitude towards it. To take first the University Church. On the first Thursday before Full Term at 8.00 a.m. the Vice-Chancellor and Proctor attend a celebration of Holy Communion in Latin.

Handbook to the University of Oxford

8 *Making theology interesting*

Still influential during the 1960s was the monthly magazine *Theology*, which, under the editorship of Alec Vidler, succeeded in making its subject interesting and the handling of it stimulating. Vidler had taken over the editorship in 1938 when he became Warden of St Deiniol's Library, Hawarden, and, although wartime restrictions precluded much expansion of the 1,700 circulation, the return of the forces' chaplains and the recruitment of an eager breed of young clergy soon enabled him to more than double this figure.

The secret of this, as with all publications, lay in the editor. Vidler, a church historian with a specialist knowledge of the early twentieth-century Modernist movement in the Roman Catholic Church, often described himself as 'an agnostic believer' and sometimes as a 'theological midwife'. He had an acute mind and an unusual ability to gather around him other gifted scholars to share the results of their research and to spark off ideas. Add to this a pungent pen and a series of posts that gave him freedom to pursue his own interests, and the conditions for editorial success were ideal.

The magazine itself was modest in appearance – 40 or so octavo pages with no concessions to the eye – but Vidler's own editorials, selection of articles and choice of books for review ensured that it was eagerly awaited by thoughtful clergy in the parishes as well as in academic circles. It was the place to float new ideas and occasionally an issue would be devoted to a single subject. Astonishingly Vidler sustained the interest and stimulation for a quarter of a century and, although the circulation never exceeded many more than 5,000, this was probably the to be expected ceiling for a publication of its kind. The actual readership was very much larger since copies were shared.

9 *A candid book review*

It is an unusual type of book for one of the Bishop of London's Lent series; as a mind-stretcher it confronts us with tough and sometimes important questions.

Theology

10 *Into the theological depths*

It is not commonly recognized that the new direction in theological reflection that characterized the 1960s in Britain was not initiated by Bishop John Robinson in his paperback *Honest to God* (1963) but twelve months earlier in a more substantial hardback volume of essays, *Soundings*, edited by Alec Vidler. A group of able, and mainly young, Cambridge scholars had become concerned that some important questions, which had for some time been widely discussed in Germany and America, were being disregarded by the theological and church establishments in Britain. One of their number, Howard Root, Dean of Emmanuel College, chanced to meet Vidler, then Dean of King's, in the street and suggested to him that he might convene an informal meeting of the concerned theologians to consider what might be done.

Besides Root and Vidler, they were John Habgood, George Woods, Harry Williams, Ninian Smart, J. N. Sanders, Hugh Montefiore, Geoffrey Lampe and John Burnaby, and constituted a company of such distinction that their very existence at one time and in one place is now a matter for wonderment. They met occasionally in Vidler's rooms over the course of about a year, exchanged papers, spent a long weekend away together, then produced essays which covered the main theological issues of their day – issues that now require even more urgent consideration.

In his introduction, Vidler, who had suggested the title *Soundings*, explained:

> The authors of this volume of essays cannot persuade themselves that the time is ripe for major works of theological reconstruction. It is a time for ploughing, not reaping; or to use the metaphor chosen for our title, it is a time for making soundings, not charts or maps. If this be so, we do not have to apologise for our inability to do what we hope will be possible in a future generation. We can best serve the cause of truth and of the church by candidly confessing where our perplexities lie, and not by making claims which, so far as we can see, theologians are not at present in a position to justify.

Curiously as it would later seem, the Dean of Clare College, John Robinson, was not invited to join the group, as he was believed to be still in thrall to the neo-conservative biblical theology. It heralded what proved to be an exciting decade for the theologically reflective.

11 *Honest bishop creates sensation*

The publication of Bishop John Robinson's *Honest to God* in 1963 created a sensation and, still in print in its twenty-fifth impression, is remembered as a turning point in the study of theology outside the professional field. Just 141 pages long, it had been written while its author was off duty with a severe back problem and was intended as a statement of personal belief, drawing heavily on and attempting to conflate the thought of three important German theologians – Rudolf Bultmann,

Paul Tillich and Dietrich Bonhoeffer. This did not make for easy reading and at some points it seemed confused, but the broad message was
that in the modern age God could no longer be conceived as being 'up
there' or 'out there' (even if not taken literally), but rather as 'in the
ground of our being' – using here the language of depth psychology.

Likewise, Jesus was no longer to be regarded as one who had, as it
were, come down to earth from heaven as the embodiment of God.
Rather was he 'the man for others' united with 'the ground of his being',
and thus opening for humanity a window to God. Worship was not
therefore to be treated as if it were a temporary withdrawal from the life
of the ordinary world in order to be with God: on the contrary, it should
make the worshipper more sensitive to 'the beyond in the midst' and
also to the presence of Christ in the hungry, the needy, the homeless and
the prisoners.

The original print order for this 5-shillings paperback was 6,000
copies for the United Kingdom and another 2,000 for the USA, but
those all went on the day of publication, and in the end over 1 million
copies were sold in 17 different languages. The profits enabled the SCM
Press to publish many other good books in the 1960s. Besides the book
there were numerous television and radio programmes, articles and
lectures; volumes of rejoinder followed. Robinson received 4,000
letters, most of them expressing gratitude, but there was severe criticism
by Archbishop Ramsey who said in a television interview,

> It is utterly wrong and misleading to denounce the imagery of God
> held by Christian men, women and children; imagery that they have
> got from Jesus himself, the image of God the Father in Heaven, and to
> say that we can't have any new thoughts until it is all swept away.

Some other bishops joined in the condemnation before they had read the
book. The *Church Times* commented, 'It is not every day that a bishop
goes on public record as apparently denying almost every Christian
doctrine of the church in which he holds office.' Among many of the
younger clergy and better educated laity, in all the churches, however,
Robinson became a beacon of hope, and later Ramsey admitted that his
criticism had been misplaced.

There were several reasons for the book's extraordinary impact. The
fact that its author was a bishop made a great difference. Some academic
theologians had for several years been writing something similar, albeit
in a less accessible form, and no one outside their own circle had taken
much notice. An *Observer* headline, 'Our image of God must go', which

Robinson had unsuccessfully resisted, but which announced an introductory article on the Sunday before publication, ensured massive publicity. The author's recent court appearance in defence of *Lady Chatterley's Lover* added spice. But the chief reason was the existence of a large number of people who held some degree of religious belief but could not accept the tenets of orthodox doctrine. The appearance of *Honest to God* was as if a cork had been removed from a bottle that was about to explode, so the consequences were bound to be somewhat noisy, messy even, but refreshing in the end.

12 *The debate about God*

As with all books that receive massive publicity, it was impossible to discern just how many of those who bought *Honest to God* actually read it or even got beyond the first few pages. It was, however, widely discussed in university circles, as a professor of theology reported two months after publication:

> It has had a wonderful effect in opening up serious conversations with non-Christian academic colleagues. I think in particular of a young research fellow in physics in my college with whom I have had a good many rather futile exchanges in the past, but who now tells me that he begins to see what it is all about and wants to discuss it at a different level than before.

Two professors at King's College, London disagreed about it. Eric Mascall, a distinguished Thomist theologian was sharply dismissive:

> Much of what he [Robinson] says a theologian will recognise as platitude in the form of paradox; some of what he says, if taken literally, would make Christianity, in any sense that the world has ever held, altogether superfluous. Some readers will no doubt think he has abandoned the Christian religion, but I do not think he is guilty of anything more than confusion of thought. But when I see at the head of his article the words 'Our image of God must go' I am comforted to reflect that 'our image' must presumably refer to the author's.

Christopher Evans, a no less distinguished New Testament scholar, took a different line in a broadcast talk:

I ask myself what kind of a book it is, that is, where would I place it on my book shelves. I think I would say that I would put it among the books of devotion. For all the radical and disturbing things it says, this is where it belongs. For it is passionately concerned with God, and that is the mark of a book of devotion . . . The book is a *cri de coeur* against any tying up of our talk about God with outmoded views of the universe which modern man cannot, with the best will in the word accept. And surely there is ample evidence that this cry finds an echo in the hearts and minds of many not only inside the church but outside it.

T. E. Utley, a *Sunday Telegraph* journalist, was outraged:

It is not always clear whether the bishop's aim is to convince agnostics that they can conscientiously go to church or to persuade Christians that there is no real need to do so. At the lowest, he seems to me to be violating the principles of honest commerce by trying to sell a Christian a commodity that bears no relation to the historical accepted meaning of that word.

So it thundered on for many more months.

13 *Dignified fancy dress*

It was hardly a revolution, but the enthronement of Michael Ramsey in the chair of St Augustine quickly led to abandonment of the breeches, gaiters, apron and frock coat which had, for the previous two centuries, been the official outdoor dress of bishops, archdeacons and deans. Like most church vesture, this distinctive dress had begun for a practical, secular purpose: it was riding kit, required by bishops and archdeacons for getting about their dioceses and by deans for visiting cathedral estates. Something close to it was worn by the more prosperous parish clergy who owned a horse. As the nineteenth century advanced, other means of locomotion led to the adoption of jacket and trousers, but not by the conservative dignitary, who retained his riding suit as a badge of rank.

By the mid-twentieth century the usefulness of the distinction was beginning to be questioned. In an increasingly secular culture, more and more courage was required of those who walked the streets in so quaint a garb. There was an economic factor, too, inasmuch as by the 1950s the cost of the outfit in good cloth, well tailored, had risen to upwards of £700. But Archbishop Fisher insisted that dignitaries should continue to wear the now traditional uniform, and sternly rebuked any who turned up to meetings in London clad in trousers – 'If I can wear the correct attire, so can you.' The Queen also let it be known that bishops summoned to Buckingham Palace were expected to wear 'gaiter suits'.

Anthony Otter, who was Bishop of Grantham, went about Lincolnshire on a motorbike and found the uniform useful, while impoverished bishops solved the financial problem by inheriting or purchasing the attire of their predecessor – and presumably arranging for the necessary alterations to be made. Michael Ramsey issued no edict of liberation but, except on very formal occasions, appeared in either a cassock or an ordinary suit, so dignitaries leapt from the eighteenth to the twentieth century virtually overnight. A handful who wished to demonstrate their attachment to tradition or simply enjoyed dressing up, continued to amuse, or bemuse, the public.

But what happened to all the surplus attire? The *Yorkshire Diocesan Leaflet* provided the answer in the early part of 1967:

> If you have any gaiters or breeches you want to get rid of please do not send them to the local Jumble Sale, but please send them instead to the Bishopthorpe Pageant Wardrobe, c/o Mrs. Cobb, The White House, Bishopthorpe, York. These garments are getting scarcer, and we have three eighteenth century archbishops to dress, of differing sizes, for every production. Worn Episcopal Robes are very acceptable too.

14 A Protestant think tank

Latimer House, Oxford was the brainchild of the Calvinist theologian James Packer, who became its first Warden in 1961. As the evangelical revival in the Church of England gathered pace, he and two of his colleagues on the teaching staff of Tyndale Hall, Bristol perceived the need for a research centre to provide the movement with strong theological underpinning, and at the same time deal with what they regarded as the subversive influence of liberalism.

The publication of Bishop John Robinson's *Honest to God* in 1963 confirmed their worst fears and brought an immediate response in the form of a 20-page pamphlet *Keep Yourself from Idols*. Packer's language was robust; he accused Robinson of 'changing the truth about God into a lie'. 'Every page', he said, 'bears the unmistakable marks of unfinished thinking. The Bishop presents a new religion.' In the same year the Anglican–Methodist Unity Scheme was also given a hostile reception on the grounds that it would, if implemented, stifle evangelical witness.

Later Latimer House produced solid books and monographs on various aspects of Evangelical conviction and Packer became a leading figure in the evangelical movement – he played an important part in its national conference at Keele in 1967 – but, as numbers increased, he became increasingly isolated from those who could not share his Calvinist beliefs, and he left England in 1979 to become Professor of Theology at Regent College, Vancouver.

15 On the eve of a royal wedding

Dr. Ramsey, beaming and waving to the crowd, sang to himself a little song with words which went 'Bom-tiddy-bom-tiddy-bom.'

Guardian

The Princess [Alexandra] is a religious girl. Therefore the neckline of her wedding dress will be high, the bodice shaped, sleeves narrowing to the waist.

Daily Express

16 A breakthrough in ordination training

The Southwark Ordination Course, founded in 1960, and the first of its kind, was the brainchild of Bishop Mervyn Stockwood and designed to provide a new kind of training for the priesthood and also for a new kind of ministry. It was for men with established jobs who, for family or financial reasons, found it impracticable to go away for a full residential course at a theological college. It was also for men with established jobs who felt called to the priesthood but to exercise their ministry within the sphere in which they were already working. In other words to become worker-priests, after the French model. There would be space, too, for young graduate ordinands who felt the need to do at least part of their training in the context of the industrial world in which they expected later to work.

Responsibility for launching the course was given to the Bishop of Woolwich, John Robinson, and within 2 months more than 90 enquiries had been made, of which 60 became firm applicants for admission. It was, in the event, possible to accept only 30 for the first year of the designed 3-year course, and in September 1960 this started and was based on the Cathedral, with some of the canons becoming the lecturers. A brilliant appointment from outside was that of Stanley Evans, one of the Church of England's most gifted priests whose somewhat extreme socialist views had stood in the way of his preferment. For some years he had been Vicar of Holy Trinity, Dalston, in London's East End, and was now brought to Southwark as Chancellor of the Cathedral and Director of Training. He led the course during its early years with a rare combination of skill and integrity, but he was tragically killed in a road accident in 1965.

Meanwhile the course had been given its own base at Wychcroft, a large house near Bletchingley in Surrey. Students were not exempted from tough theological education, but this was related always to secular issues and the quality of the staff (specialists were recruited for a wide variety of subjects) ensured that it was without rival among the theological colleges. It continued to thrive for the rest of the century, but it was a disappointment to Stockwood, Robinson and many others that relatively few of the students became worker-priests, and that of those that did many eventually moved to full-time parish ministry.

17 A rural archdeacon looks ahead

Frank West, who served as an army chaplain throughout the 1939–45 war, then became Archdeacon of Newark, combining this post for several years with that of Vicar of a small rural Nottinghamshire parish. In 1960 he published a small book, *The Country Parish Today and Tomorrow*, which was widely read, and he went on to become Bishop of Taunton and the church's leading authority on rural ministry. His book offered no blueprint for the future and he, no more than anyone else at the time, did not foresee the dramatic effect that changes in farming methods and shortages of clerical manpower and money for stipends would make to the traditional pattern of the church's work in the countryside. He was only too well aware, however, that all was not well in that large sphere of ministry but doubted whether the bringing together of parishes into groups and the clergy into teams would solve the problems. Better to encourage young priests of ability to become country parsons and to make greater use of the laity:

Every diocesan bishop should initiate a drive for more lay readers and more teachers and there would only have to be a very moderate response in numbers for every parish to have regular instruction for the young and at least as many services as the people require. There must be a great number of cultured laymen who are capable of reading a service reverently and well, but who do not feel they have either the vocation or training for preaching. These, with the bishop's licence could supplement the work of the preaching readers. And it surely would not be beyond the wit of the church to provide sermons for them to read in the pulpits.

18 Pop goes the hymn tune

The breakthrough into the use of modern music for hymn tunes and settings of the Eucharist made by Geoffrey Beaumont and the Twentieth Century Light Music Group in the 1950s proved to be no more than a modest beginning for a torrent of new hymnody that poured into all the churches from the 1960s onwards. This consisted of new words as well as new music and the overall standard of both was extraordinarily low. Even more extraordinary was the fact that much of it was published and found its way into new hymn books.

As in earlier revivalist eras, Evangelicals now led the way and favoured material that would raise the emotional temperature of their services. Later, the words would be projected on to screens, thus obviating the need for books. *Mission Praise* became a widely used book in these circles, but gave way to *Complete Anglican Hymns Old and New*, which offered almost 1,000 items in order to embrace all the well-known traditional hymns and a great deal of new rubbish. On the whole, the new Anglican hymn-writers eschewed the emotional, based their work on sound theology and sought to produce suitable hymns. Bishop Timothy Dudley-Smith was the most notable example of this and many of his hymns are now in frequent use.

Hymns Ancient and Modern ventured into the new field with a supplement, *A Hundred Hymns for Today*, which Archbishop Ramsey mischievously recommended to those who wished to study the ancient heresies of the church. The *New English Hymnal* made room for a good deal of new material by weeding out the worst of the old and is generally considered to be the best for use in parish churches that require neither choruses nor gospel songs.

19 *A song and a dance*

Easily the most celebrated among the new breed of Christian musicians was Sydney Carter – a poet and songwriter whose 'Lord of the Dance', written in 1963, was an instant success and went into use by church congregations, school assemblies, folk camps and other religious or semi-religious gatherings throughout the English-speaking world. It became an all-purpose ingredient, though not always appropriate, at weddings, baptisms, funerals and on a multitude of other occasions. This success was owed to two inter-related elements: the words were optimistic and the tune, adapted from an air of the American Shaker movement, was lively, catchy and memorable. The underlying theology was a long way from orthodox.

It was not, however, the work of an amateur. Sydney Carter, a delightful man, gentle, humble and a pacifist who had served in a Friends' Ambulance Unit during the war, was already established as a writer and singer of folk songs in pubs and clubs, then provided material for his friends Michael Flanders and Donald Swann, and finally sang in company with Judy Collins, Pete Seeger and Ewan MacColl. Some of Carter's other compositions were readily incorporated into new hymn books, notably 'One more step along the world I go' and 'When I needed a neighbour were you there?' But not all found universal approval. Enoch Powell, devout churchman and Conservative politician, called for the banning of his poem 'Friday Morning' because of its lines 'It's God they ought to crucify/Instead of you and me', and his song 'The devil wore a crucifix'.

The 1960s gave Carter an environment in which he was entirely at home and many of his poems were sent first to *New Christian* for publication. Once asked at a press conference why he wished to introduce dancing into worship, he explained that it had always been there in the church's ceremonies and that he was simply proposing a different choreography.

20 *Money for old rope*

There is no doubt that it is best for an author to have an unearned income. Quite the best advice to a young literary man would be to take Orders in the Church of England.

Guardian

21 *Choosing bishops and deans*

During the 1950s there was some concern, though not frequently voiced in public, over the long tradition by which the Crown, in the person of the Prime Minister, appointed bishops and deans. It was known that Archbishop Fisher was always consulted and it was assumed that no one of whom he disapproved would ever be appointed. But this was still some distance from choice by the church as a whole and the activities and influence of the Prime Minister's Secretary for Appointments also aroused disquiet from time to time – sometimes even to Fisher. That suffragan bishops were by long tradition selected by the diocesan bishop concerned, even if their appointments were announced in the name of the Crown from 10 Downing Street, seemed fair enough.

The speed with which Geoffrey Fisher's resignation from the Primacy in 1961 was followed by the announcement of his succession by Michael Ramsey – a matter of days – did, however, provoke serious criticism, not because of the choice itself but because it suggested that there had been no serious consultation over the matter, neither had there been time for the church to make it the subject of prayer. As the movement towards hoped-for church unity gathered pace, Free Church leaders also began to ask questions about a method of episcopal appointment that would be totally alien to their own tradition. As for the appointment of deans, the only complaints seem to come from bishops who had never been consulted and were simply informed by Downing Street of the Prime Minister's choice. There was considerable disquiet, however, when, in 1961, the Crown failed to appoint to the Deanery of the new Guildford Cathedral the priest who had been the Provost of its parish church predecessor since 1952 and was largely responsible for its building.

A strong debate about this in the Church Assembly in November 1961 led to a request to the Archbishops, by a large majority, to set up a commission to consider the entire field of Crown appointments in the church. This met under the chairmanship of Lord Howick of Glendale and produced at the end of 1964 an ultra-conservative report which declared fundamental change to be undesirable. The most it could envisage was the introduction of a 'vacancy-in-see' committee in dioceses requiring a new bishop. This would draw up a statement of the needs of the diocese for transmission to the archbishop of the province, and he would have the assistance of an appointments secretary to ensure that he was no less well informed than the Prime Minister about likely candidates for bishoprics and deaneries. The report disclosed, interestingly, that an informal, highly confidential, system of consultation with leading figures in dioceses was already in existence and that the archbishops were encouraged to submit two or three preferred names to the Prime Minister.

Although these proposals were accepted by the Church Assembly, great dissatisfaction was expressed in that forum and more widely with the commission's work. It did not reflect the mood of the moment. Pressure for something different mounted, the new radical reformists being particularly vocal, and the appointment in the autumn of 1966 of a new commission under the chairmanship of Professor Owen Chadwick raised expectations that no reasonable suggestion for change would go unconsidered.

22 Avoiding confusion

Our wise and careful Mr. Macmillan is known to favour more rather than less control in ecclesiastical appointments. These appointments *must* be controlled by the Prime Minister since otherwise all sorts of unsuitable men favouring views contrary to the policy of the Government may become powerful figures in the church and cause much confusion.

Letter in *Church Illustrated*

23 Liturgy and architecture

Although there was a good deal of church building during the decade immediately prior to the 1939–45 war, it is necessary to go back to the second half of the nineteenth century to find a precedent for the scale on which new churches were erected during the 1950s and 1960s. Part of the explanation for this was the need to replace buildings destroyed by wartime bombing, but chiefly it was a response to a massive housebuilding programme that led to the creation of estates on the outskirts of most towns and cities, and of a significant number of new towns. Unlike their nineteenth-century predecessors, the church's leaders now moved swiftly – money was allocated or raised for new buildings and young, enthusiastic priests were appointed to exercise pioneering ministries.

It was unfortunate (some would say disastrous), however, that in the haste to deal with new opportunities no one paused to consider what new churches were really for and how the answer to this question might determine their design. A rectangular structure on the medieval pattern, though without its artistic embellishment, was considered to be the normal requirement, and if this could serve the dual purpose of church and community hall there would be obvious financial benefits.

This did not coincide with the thinking in continental Europe where the growth of the Liturgical Movement started during the early years of the century had led to some notable departures from the layout of Gothic churches. This was now accelerating quickly, with dramatic consequences for church architecture. The High Mass, with the priest celebrating the Eucharist at the east end of a building on behalf of a largely passive congregation arranged in serried ranks until it reached a distant west end, was being replaced by a Parish Mass, in which priest and congregation were united in Offering and Communion, and therefore drawn to worship together in close proximity to the altar. Circular, octagonal, square new buildings, often of spectacular modern design, were the result.

Little of which was noticed by the Church of England, and this for a number of reasons, the first being its insulation from church life in the rest of Europe, the second the uninspiring state of English architecture generally at the time, third the lack of money to finance ambitious projects, but above all else the late development of liturgical thinking in this country. Had it been possible – and it was not possible – to delay the church building programme for ten years the result would have been very different. Or had Dom Gregory Dix published his seminal *The Shape of the Liturgy* in 1935, rather than in 1945, the shape of church buildings in many parts of England would now be far more useful and inspiring.

As the 1950s advanced, however, a small number of architects and a few theologians became increasingly concerned about the problem, and a breakthrough came with the publication in 1960 of Peter Hammond's *Liturgy and Architecture*. The author could hardly have been more blunt in his assessment of the church's efforts: 'The results of all this activity have been depressing in the extreme. It is hard to think of any field of ecclesiastical investment where so much money has been squandered to so little purpose . . . and, as a result, the majority of post-war churches are likely to prove a grave source of embarrassment to those who have to use them in years to come.'

He continued with chapters on the implications of the Liturgical Movement for church planning, a survey of post-war developments in this field in Western Europe and North America, a survey of developments in England since 1945 and a heartfelt plea that theologians, pastors and sociologists should combine to brief the architect of a new church on its functional purpose. Soon after the publication of his book an Institute for the Study of Religion and Architecture at Birmingham University was formed and the shape and layout of churches began to change.

24 *Advance and retreat*

My own experience of church building at Stockton-on-Tees illustrated Hammond's case perfectly. Before my appointment to lead the pioneering mission on the Roseworth estate, before any nucleus of a congregation had been formed, the diocese appointed its own architect to design a church to seat 200 people and at a maximum cost of £15,000. This to be capable of westward extension if the building proved to be too small – which, within four years, it did. The result was a well-mannered, yellow-brick, rectangular building with plenty of windows and a small *flèche* to indicate that it was a church. A single concession to the Liturgical Movement was a small apse at the east end to enable the priest at the Eucharist to face the congregation across the altar. A pair of ambones for the reading of the Epistle and the Gospel reminded us of fourth-century liturgies. Thirty years later the building was too large for its much reduced congregation.

When the Hardwick estate began to be developed at the end of the decade, I was totally immersed in the Liturgical Movement and seized the opportunity to engage a London architect, Martin Smith, who had been responsible for the innovative design of John Keble Church, Mill Hill, in 1936 and some interesting post-war churches in Doncaster, Crawley new town and Cricklewood in North London, which he took me to see. The result for Hardwick was a hexagonal ground plan, with a wedge-shaped structure – the roof sloping from east to west and balanced by a slender tower – not large, but combining intimacy around the altar with uplifting height. Thirty years later, however, the roof had developed structural problems and, for want of local support and adequate diocesan leadership, the church was pulled down, leaving a community of 10,000 council house dwellers with only a Roman Catholic place of worship. Even liturgically appropriate buildings were shown to have their limitations.

25 *Movable church buildings*

A study group set up by the Chichester Diocesan Buildings Committee recommended in 1966 that the diocese should invest in a number of relocatable buildings that could be leased to new housing areas for a period of 5–7 years at a nominal rent and then moved to other sites. The buildings would seat about 100 people and include a small office and a store. It was anticipated that the 5-year period would give local churches an opportunity to gather strength, to consider the usefulness or otherwise of the proposed site, and to plan carefully the kind of build-ing that would best meet the needs of the area. The group, which was made up of architects, engineers and surveyors, and worked in consul-tation with the Institute for the Study of Worship and Religious Architecture, made the further point that, since the 1960s new housing was not expected to last more than 40–60 years, the church should not invest in buildings that might outlive their pastoral relevance. The report was not implemented in Chichester, neither was it taken up by any other diocese, so its title *Buildings and Breakthrough* proved to be over-optimistic.

26 *A prophetic gadfly*

Eric James was one of the most significant figures in the late twentieth-century church. Hugely gifted as prophet, priest, pastor, preacher and writer, we have shared a close friendship extending over sixty years, going back to our student days at King's College, London, and includ-ing partnerships in the Parish and People movement and Christian Action.

He left the chaplaincy of Trinity College, Cambridge in 1959 in order to become Vicar of St George's, Camberwell and join a group of priests invited by Bishop Mervyn Stockwood of Southwark to share in a new attempt to bridge the wide gap between the church and the working class in South London. After five years of experimenting with new forms of worship and pastoral ministry, however, he was pressed to become the first full-time Director of Parish and People and spearhead a move-ment that aimed at wide-ranging reform of the church's life.

Under his leadership the movement prospered and before long had two thousand members, including many bishops, but after five years of speech-making and organizing pressure groups in most dioceses, he was driven to conclude that the Church of England was still far removed from acceptance of the need for reform. So he resigned and became a canon residentiary of Southwark Cathedral, continuing to promote what had become known as 'South Bank religion' and devoting much time to the inner-city riverside parishes of South London.

This ended abruptly in 1973 when he had a serious disagreement with Bishop Stockwood over another issue, and at the invitation of Robert Runcie became Diocesan Missioner of St Albans – a post which included concern for the church's mission in Hertfordshire's expanding towns, but left him with time to pursue his national interests. These included Christian Action, of which he became part-time Director in 1979 before moving back to London as full-time Director in 1983.

The emphasis of the organization had changed since the days of Canon John Collins's leadership, since many other groups were now working in the field of social reform, but over the next 11 years James made his own distinctive contribution in this area. It was at his suggestion that Archbishop Runcie formed a Commission on Urban Priority Areas and he not only serviced the Commission but facilitated the widespread circulation of its report *Faith in the City* (1985). Christian Action was by now providing financial support for many organizations concerned with housing, poverty, racism, sexuality and community development.

For many years James was a regular broadcaster in the BBC's 'Thought for the Day' slot, but there was a year's gap when he had a disagreement with the BBC over what he regarded, with justification, as undue editorial interference with his script. He declared his own homosexuality on television and created some controversy in 1998 with a lecture in Westminster Abbey in which he called for a national debate on the possibility of monarchs being elected. The fact that he was a Chaplain to the Queen made his proposal specially interesting to the media. His qualities as a preacher and pastor made him greatly valued by the lawyers at Grays Inn where he held the office of Preacher for many years. Among his books, the biography of Bishop John Robinson was the most important.

It is a moot point whether or not such a gifted priest should have become a church leader. Certainly he would have made a refreshingly different kind of bishop or dean, though he would probably have been driven crazy by the official demands of either office. His role as a prophetic gadfly probably suited him best and was of most use to the Christian cause.

27 *In defence of Mattins*

By 1960 the evangelical Sunday morning preference for 'A good Mattins, a good Sermon and a good Lunch' had to be defended against the threat of the Parish Communion. Thus Peter Morgan:

> The view that a Family Communion service with simple vestments should be the central service of every Sunday is very widespread and seems to be held by most of the bishops. Those parishes which are happy to continue with the old 8 a.m. Holy Communion, 11 a.m. Mattins, 6.30 p.m. Evensong pattern are often spoken of at best as behind the times or else as being downright reactionary and obstinate. The fact remains that most Evangelical clergy are still quite happy with this pattern, not because they are behind the times but because they see no reason why Mattins should be displaced by a service with a far more limited appeal and with an infinitely more complicated musical arrangement than the simple well-loved chants normally associated with Morning Prayer. Because 'Mattins' or 'surplice and stole' (or scarf) parishes are in a decreasing minority the range of service which Evangelical clergy can give to a diocese is becoming still more limited.

In spite of this plea Mattins continued on its downward path, not least because more and more evangelical parishes came to acknowledge the centrality of the Eucharist in Sunday worship. And when later they recognized the need for a more simple form of worship for new occasional churchgoers they produced informal Family Services, without 'well-loved chants'.

28 *An impossible parson*

A Consistory Court is always the last resort when dealing with the problem of a crazy or a delinquent clergyman and is rarely successful. As the Bishop of Gloucester discovered to his cost when he arraigned one of his parish priests in 1969.

The Revd Michael Bland, a former RAF intelligence officer who was said to have the physical presence of a heavyweight boxer, was instituted to the Rectory of Buckland and Stanton with Snowshill in 1958. All went well for a time, but things soon began to go badly wrong and in the end he was tried on four charges of neglecting his duties: by leaving church before Divine Service ended; refusing to baptize a baby; preventing a parishioner from entering the church to object to his son's marriage at the time the banns were published; and repelling another parishioner from Holy Communion without lawful cause.

Furthermore he was alleged to have written rude letters to six people; made offensive and hurtful remarks to parishioners; indulged in fits of temper in church; and at a parochial church council meeting said in effect that he hated his parishioners. On another occasion he was alleged to have told the Council that on the day he found no one in the church when he arrived to conduct a service he would have achieved what he wanted to do: he could then run the church the way he wanted without the local squire's paid servants and tenants.

The Rector was the first priest to be tried under the Ecclesiastical Jurisdiction Measure of 1963 and was defended in court by none other than Geoffrey Howe, the future Chancellor of the Exchequer and Foreign Secretary whose House of Commons speech delivered the *coup de grâce* to Prime Minister Margaret Thatcher. And he was no less successful in the ecclesiastical sphere, for, although the Consistory Court sentenced Bland to be deprived of his living, its verdict was overturned in 1970 by the Court of Arches which simply administered a formal rebuke and allowed him to return to his parish. The Bishop was left with a legal bill amounting to some £30,000.

But the problem remained unresolved. Bland seemed incapable of establishing cordial relations with his parishioners and, when asked about the angry emotions felt by some of the congregation, he said, 'Quite right. Get the violence off the streets and into the church where it belongs.' For many years Sunday services were attended only by the Rector's housekeeper and the sad situation was resolved only when, shortly before his death in 1988, he was persuaded to accept retirement.

29 *Success at last*

The biggest success story in the church since 1948, said Archdeacon Bean, had been the provision of accommodation for 515 retired clergymen, widows or dependants.

A *Church Times* report of a 1964 Church Assembly

30 *An ex-Gurkhas reformer*

Hubert Madge was in many ways the epitome of a former Gurkhas officer. Short, wiry, brisk and of clipped speech, he served in Mesopotamia in 1918, followed by spells in Salonika, the Caucasus and Turkey. During the 1939–45 war he was commandant of the regimental headquarters, in the rank of Lieutenant Colonel, in the India he loved. When the war ended he trained as a doctor at King's College Hospital, London, planning to set up a tuberculosis clinic in India for Gurkhas who were particularly vulnerable to this disease. But the partition of the subcontinent made this impossible.

Three months working in the casualty department of the Winchester County Hospital was sufficient to convince him that he was not cut out for British medicine, so he became instead Diocesan Secretary at Sheffield. There he became a close friend of the then bishop, Leslie Hunter, and with him saw the urgent need for reform if the church was to get to grips with the problem of a great industrial diocese. When he moved to be Diocesan Secretary at Winchester in 1949 he found different problems, and was among the first to see that the church could not be mobilized for effective action in the dioceses unless certain major reforms were undertaken at national level.

Soon he was elected to the Church Assembly and, strongly supported by Parish and People, of which he was a most diligent honorary treasurer, he initiated in 1960 a debate which ended with a resolution requiring the Central Council for Ministry to 'consider, in the light of changing circumstances, the system of the deployment and payment of the clergy, and to make recommendations'.

31 *Leslie Paul's vision*

The usual response to such a motion is to appoint a commission, carefully balanced to represent the church's different constituents, and to allow it a few years in which to investigate and report. In this instance, however, the Council appointed one man, Leslie Paul, a layman and a sociologist. He toured the country, interviewed laity, priests and bishops, gathered statistics, canvassed opinions and in the astonishingly short space of three years produced *The Deployment and Payment of the Clergy* – the first-ever survey of the Church of England's parochial system – comprising over 300 pages of information and including 62 principal recommendations. These were nothing if not radical and included: the replacement of the clergy freehold by a leasehold of no more than ten years; the formation of major parishes run by a college of clergy, all of whom would enjoy incumbent status; lesser forms of group and team ministries; the raising of the status of the rural dean, making him a 'bishop-in-title' and responsible for the leadership of the church in his deanery; there should never be fewer than two suffragan bishops in a diocese, each with a territorial charge; benefice funds – endowments and the like – to be pooled to create one common stipendiary fund administered by a regional board in accordance with a national scale; a joint staffing machine to be established regionally to supervise all clergy appointments; independent patronage to cease; the laity to form a parochial lay apostolate based on house churches.

It was not to be expected that proposals of this sort would be received calmly and dispassionately. They were not, and in the ensuing controversy the enthusiastic reformers were outnumbered and outmanoeuvred by the horrified conservatives. But consideration of the church's 1,000-year-old pastoral system would never be the same again, and numerical decline combined with shortage of money proved to be more powerful than Leslie Paul's visionary scheme as an impetus for change.

32 'The new morality'

The stir created by John Robinson's *Honest to God* was focused initially on its author's conviction that the Christian God is not to be thought of or related to as a supernatural Being detached from the universe but rather as an infinitely loving presence located 'in the ground of our being'. But there was another chapter in the book which proved to be no less controversial.

Headed 'The New Morality', this called for a revolution in ethics and argued that Christian behaviour is to be determined not by obedience to a set of fixed rules, say the Ten Commandments, but by the application of love to particular situations. 'Nothing can of itself always be labelled as "wrong",' he wrote. 'One cannot, for instance, start from the position "sex before marriage" or "divorce" are wrong or sinful in themselves. They may be in 99 cases or even in 100 cases out of 100, but they are not intrinsically so, for the only intrinsic evil is lack of love.'

This became a matter for heated debate during the rest of the 1960s. Robinson took up the subject again in three lectures given in Liverpool Cathedral, published as *Christian Morals Today* and subsequently developed in *Christian Freedom in a Permissive Society* (1970), and he was at pains to explain that he was not in the least interested in jettisoning law; he believed that morality should be based on something deeper and yet more flexible.

An American theologian, Joseph Fletcher, extended the discussion in a book *Situation Ethics* and Douglas Rhymes, a canon of Southwark, devoted six cathedral sermons to the subject. These were published in 1964 as *No New Morality*, his case being that the situation or contextual approach was more in line with the gospel of love than was an ethics of fixed rules. Later, in an article in *New Christian,* he argued that the church concerned itself too much with *ideal* situations and not enough with *actual* situations. What is more, 'In any given situation the ideal and the actual have to be the same, for the only ideal that is practicable is what is the most responsible and loving thing to do in a given situation.' He concluded that Christians must try to build an ethic in a secular society which is both *real* and *ideal* within the actual world of people who have to make decisions, not in the light of abstractions but in the circumstances of hard reality.

33 Back to bell, book and candle

Quite the most grotesquely unedifying ceremony to assault the sanctity of an English cathedral took place at Southwark on 4 May 1961 when Bishop Mervyn Stockwood publicly deposed ('unfrocked') one of his priests from Holy Orders. Dr Bryn Thomas, Rector of Balham and an erstwhile friend of Stockwood, had previously been arraigned before a Consistory Court and judged guilty of adultery with one of his parishioners. It was a particularly sordid case and when, at the outset of it, Stockwood requested Thomas's resignation to avoid a public trial, he refused. Thus for several days – during Holy Week of all times – the media were given the opportunity to report the salacious details. (It was while he was returning from a sitting of the court that Bishop John Robinson of Woolwich, in whose territory Balham was located, fell and injured his back, this requiring several months of rest, during which he wrote *Honest to God.*)

When the Chancellor, Garth Moore – a leading ecclesiastical lawyer – announced his guilty verdict at the end of the trial, Stockwood lost no time in depriving Thomas of his living, a step which any other bishop would have been obliged to take in the circumstances. The question of his future in Holy Orders now remained to be settled and Archbishop Fisher ruled that resignation was inappropriate since this was intended only for those intending to leave the priesthood for honourable reasons. Deposition by the church was required and this raised the further question of what form, and in what circumstances, this might take place.

There can be no doubt that the necessary legal procedure could, and should, have been transacted behind closed doors. Instead Stockwood chose, on the advice of the Chancellor, to carry it out in the retro-choir of the cathedral in the context of a service. Never one to resist the temptations of drama, he produced a service of gruesome medieval character, with himself processing in carrying a bell, a book and a candle – all witnessed and reported on by an open-mouthed corps of journalists.

The ceremony of bell, book and candle was, in fact, used in the Middle Ages for the wider purpose of excommunication. A bell was tolled, a book closed and a candle snuffed out to symbolize the exclusion of a gross sinner from the sacraments, and sometimes even from any act of worship. It has never had any place in the life and liturgy of the Church of England – nor should it. On this occasion the erring priest was not present, having some three weeks earlier entered a Deed of Relinquishment before the Master of the Rolls in the Court of Chancery, thus rendering the deposition unnecessary. The legal costs of the case ran into many thousands of pounds.

Stockwood came to believe eventually that he had made a serious mistake and sought to excuse himself on the grounds that he had been a bishop for only two years and was acting on the advice of his Chancellor.

34 *Bells beat Old Nick*

Now, after seeming to leave us alone for a while, our adversary is on the attack again and instead of going forward as we should we are having to consolidate the positions we have gained. Past victories, however, encourage us to await a further opportunity to advance. One victory was the restoration of our bells and their augmentation to six in 1967.

Report on Bredgar parish in *Canterbury Diocesan Notes*

35 *The birth, life and death of a radical magazine*

In January 1965 a postcard from Timothy Beaumont dropped through the letterbox of my northern vicarage – would I like to consider the possibility of moving to London to edit a new fortnightly magazine to replace *Prism*? I was already editing a successful parish newspaper and Parish and People's quarterly journal, so this may have explained the postcard, but an ambitious new fortnightly was an altogether different proposition and, in any case, ought I to leave a large and still developing parish for such an enterprise? Obviously not, but after much consultation with my colleagues and talk with Timothy Beaumont I accepted his invitation.

In October of that year *New Christian* was born. Modelled on the *New Statesman*, *New Society* and the *Spectator*, its aim was to convert *Prism* into a journal that was both ecumenical and concerned not just with church matters but with relating Christian thought to political and social affairs. A distinguished editorial board was formed, an assistant editor and a sub-editor recruited, and a team of writers, including Bishop John Robinson, engaged to provide substance during the first 12 months.

In the event the contribution from readers was considerable and, although about half the feature articles were commissioned, the rest simply turned up and it was never possible to publish more than one in ten of the articles submitted for consideration. Over the course of the next five years we were able to publish the work of most of the best theological writers in Britain, together with some of the 'big names' in North America. It was rare for anyone to decline an invitation to write for the paper. We campaigned for Anglican–Methodist unity and every proposal for reform in the Church of England, we castigated conservative bishops and politicians, poked fun at unenterprising clergymen and, having absorbed a lively Roman Catholic newsletter *Search,* seized the opportunity to denounce the Pope for his encyclical on contraception. We also published many serious, but always refreshing, articles on serious theological issues and reviewed hundreds of books. It was enormous fun.

But after five years it died – just like that. We had succeeded in attracting just over 10,000 subscribers, a fair number of them laypeople, including some holding positions of responsibility within the nation, and also the majority of the leaders of the British churches. A circulation of double this number was, however, needed to reach financial break-even point and we lacked the resources for promotion that might have made this achievable. Timothy Beaumont, who had by 1970 become chairman of the Liberal Party and Lord Beaumont of Whitley, was remarkably generous in his subsidizing of *New Christian* and could not have been expected to provide more.

It was also the case that by the time the magazine was established the hope of the reformers was giving way to despair and it was being suggested that the institutional life of the church was beyond renewal. There were indications that filling our pages with stimulating and useful material would become much more difficult. But the closure was more serious than I recognized at the time, since a subscription had provided entry to a 'lonely hearts club for radicals' – a large number of isolated ministers and frustrated curates who were sustained by the sense of belonging to a significant movement within the church and of having a certain kinship with others of their kind who were fighting similar battles. It was very good while it lasted and, with hindsight, it is apparent that I should have tried harder to keep *New Christian* afloat, even if in a much more modest format.

36 *Phoenix at Coventry*

The rebuilding of Coventry Cathedral after its wartime bombing and its consecration on 25 May 1962 caught the imagination of the Christian world and television enabled the superbly executed ceremony to be witnessed by a vast audience. Within a few months of the near total destruction of the beautiful fourteenth-century parish church of St Michael, which had been the cathedral since the formation of the diocese in 1918, a reconstruction committee had been formed. But although the design submitted by the chosen architect, Giles Gilbert Scott, won the approval of the committee, the plans were turned down by the Royal Fine Art Commission. A competition was then held, it being stipulated that the building should be in the English Gothic tradition, and of the 219 anonymous entries that of Basil Spence was a new committee's unanimous choice.

The design, once published, caused a loud public controversy, though the design was, in compliance with the brief, for a deeply conservative building. Good use was made of modern building materials and there were some imaginative touches, but the layout was rectangular with the high altar at the east end and seating for the congregation arranged in equal rows extending to the distant west end. Many architects and most liturgists were highly critical – 'expresso-bar Gothic', one called it and in retrospect it is even more clearly apparent that an opportunity to be truly creative was lost.

There was nonetheless some compensation for this in the extraordinarily high quality of the art incorporated into the building, the credit for which goes to Bishop Neville Gorton, who knew the world of contemporary artists but did not live to see the most notable items he had commissioned. Graham Sutherland's great tapestry of Christ in Glory, Jacob Epstein's sculpture of St Michael defeating the dragon, and John Piper's baptistry windows are major works of twentieth-century art.

And there are many others by important artists such as Elisabeth Frink. The foundation stone was laid in 1956 and the building completed at a total cost of £1,350,000, of which war damage compensation provided £1 million. The response to the consecration was remarkable. Visitors came from all quarters of the globe and long queues formed to gain admission to the building. Four million were admitted during the first 18 months and, although entrance was free, the cathedral's income from sales in its bookshop and restaurant was sufficient to finance a large staff. The services also attracted large congregations.

37 *Shush* . . .

Sir,

A week ago I went to Evensong in Salisbury Cathedral. The usual calm surrounding this aesthetic and very Anglican experience seemed on this occasion to be lacking. From the south aisle behind the choir came such a hubbub of raised voices, laughter, cross-conversations and exclamations that I doubted for a moment that I had come to the right place. Had the vergers, usually so efficient at frightening away any offending plebeian before the beginning of 'Divine Service', gone on strike, or failed for once lamentably in their duty? Or had the Margate Plague come to Salisbury, to wreck the even tenor of their ways I fondly asked. 'Indeed, no,' I was told. 'The Greater Chapter of Salisbury Cathedral is vesting for Evensong.'

May I refer these venerable fathers to Hamlet, Act 1, scene III, line 47?

Yours faithfully,
Brian W. T. Williams
Bristol 6

38 Defrosting the laity – but not yet

When *God's Frozen People* by Mark Gibbs and Ralph Morton appeared in 1964 it made the obvious but long-neglected point that 99 per cent of the responsibility for the church's witness and service in the world rests on its lay members. The paperback became a bestseller. Gibbs was a Manchester schoolmaster and Morton the deputy leader of the Iona Community and their plea was that laity training, which was then beginning to be talked about more frequently, should not be confined to equipping laymen and -women for church-centred ministry – editing the parish magazine, leading Bible study groups and the like – but should, rather, concentrate on enabling them to reflect on their faith in ways that might be applied to issues confronting them in their daily work. New methods of training were needed.

The demand for assistance in exploring further this approach became so great – for a time – that Gibbs abandoned his schoolmastering in order to conduct seminars and to address meetings and conferences on the subject. Eventually he developed strong relations with the World Council of Churches Laity Department (a sharp, far-seeing outfit) and the impressive German Kirchentag Movement. *God's Lively People* (1966) contained many constructive ideas about the form and content of laity education.

For over 35 years Gibbs stumped the country and made as many as a dozen visits to the USA every year to earn money to finance his shoe-string operation – the Audenshaw Foundation. I worked closely with him from the early 1970s until his death from cancer in 1986, chiefly editing his publications, but also, and perhaps more importantly, providing a receptacle for his frustration and anger. There was ample excuse for both. By the time his life and work ended, virtually no progress had been made in the direction to which he had pointed. A mass expansion of lay ministry had been devoted almost entirely to the running of the church and, as money became tighter, most frontier work was closed down. The very danger against which he had warned was not avoided.

39 A miracle in Rome

Although concerned only with the life of the Roman Catholic Church, the far-reaching decisions of the Second Vatican Council (1962–65) had implications for every other church, not least for the Anglican

Communion. The presence of observers from all the other churches, apart from the Baptist, was itself a notable breakthrough. Previously, those outside the Roman fold had been regarded as doubtfully Christian, but now, even though the observers were not permitted to speak in the debates, they were supplied with all the papers and given many opportunities to comment on them. The Anglican delegation was led by Bishop John Moorman of Ripon, an internationally famous Franciscan scholar, and warm and lasting friendships were established with a number of leading bishops and theologian consultants, and most importantly with the Vatican's Secretariat for Christian Unity.

Forty years on, it is not always easy to recall just how great a transformation in the Roman Catholic Church took place during the years of the Council and how this changed its relationships with other churches. The transformation was along the lines experienced by the Church of England and the continental Protestant churches as a result of the Reformation in the sixteenth and seventeenth centuries and required these churches to look with new eyes on the largest of the Christian communions. The possibility of reunion one day could no longer be ruled out. It was a time of expectancy and hope.

40 Archbishop at the centre of a storm

Michael Ramsey was not cut out for controversy and was surprised, though he should not have been, when a few words in a speech at a British Council of Churches meeting in Aberdeen in October 1965 provoked a national outcry. A white, racist minority government in what was then Rhodesia had declared its intention to break unilaterally its few remaining links with Britain. This was being resisted by Harold Wilson's Labour government in Westminster and liberal opinion worldwide, but an awkward question remained: what could anyone do if the rebel regime in Rhodesia carried out its threat? There was talk of military action by British forces but Wilson was not enthusiastic and, in any case, the logistical problems attending an invasion of land-locked Rhodesia seemed insuperable.

In order, as he hoped, to strengthen Wilson's fading resolve, Ramsey spoke at Aberdeen of Britain's responsibilities and concluded that if the government thought it right and practicable to use force to protect the interests of the majority of the Rhodesian people (who were black) 'then I think that as Christians we have to say that it will be right to use force to that end'. A quarter of a century later Owen Chadwick, Ramsay's judicious biographer, wrote: 'Suddenly Ramsey was at the centre of the windiest storm endured by an Archbishop of Canterbury since the revolution of 1688.'

Like all storms, this one eventually died down, force was not employed and the Rhodesian regime continued in ever-increasing repression of the black population until overthrown by guerrilla bands in 1979. Ramsey was tough enough to weather the elements at the time but was deeply hurt by the long-term hostility displayed towards him by a number of members of the House of Lords.

41 *Wigan declares Holy War*

Eight Anglican clergy from the Liverpool diocese have issued a statement declaring that armed intervention in Rhodesia would be 'a justifiable holy war'. They said that the present situation in Rhodesia was 'in the sight of God an intolerable injustice and a denial of human rights'. Among those signing the statement are the Rural Dean of Wigan and the diocesan youth chaplain.

News report, June 1969

42 *New missionary approach proposed*

A conference organized jointly by the British Council of Churches and Parish and People held in Birmingham at the end of April 1966 offered the last opportunity for the churches, still in reasonable strength, to reshape their lives to meet the serious challenges of the second half of the century. Attended by 300 people, mainly Anglican but with a good number from other churches, chiefly clergy but with a significant number of laity, theologians present but also sociologists, it was convened to consider the results of a four-year study by a World Council of Churches group on 'The Missionary Structure of the Congregation'.

The conference was as stimulating to those present as was the report itself which had drawn on the best thinking of the churches of Western Europe. It had two main themes, the first being that the world must set the church's agenda. Instead of the church seeking to impose its traditional forms of belief and practice on the rapidly changing, and increasingly secularized, world, it must become so closely involved in its surrounding social order that it can respond with the resources of the gospel to the real needs of society.

In order to do this (the second theme of the report) there was the need for radical change in the church's own organization. Instead of devoting almost all of its resources to residential communities, it should diversify in order to minister to individuals and groups in their many other spheres of activity – factories, offices, schools, hospitals, universities, social services and so forth. This required a modification of the church's inherited units of administration – parish, diocese, circuit, district – so that boundaries might coincide more or less with those of the secular communities, with 'the human zone', as the report called it.

These radical proposals were hardly questioned in the conference: on the contrary, they were received with excited approval and most of the three days was spent considering how they might be implemented in Britain. A string of resolutions called on the churches to set up pilot schemes involving zonal structures, establish lay-training centres throughout the country, decide what buildings were, or were not, needed for the new approach, reshape their budgets for mission rather than maintenance, and much else. A special issue of the Parish and People magazine which I devoted to the conference sold several thousand copies, but the ears of those who might have done something about it were deaf to the message. Nothing much happened, apart from an increase in the number of specialist chaplains, and most of these were axed when money became tight.

43 Old Theology at Digswell

A report in 1965 on church life in Digswell, an older High-Church parish within the new town of Welwyn Garden City, offered an interesting commentary on the conservative outlook of its Rector. Father Geoffrey Ford belonged to the Church of England's Catholic wing and lost no opportunity in the Church Assembly and elsewhere to denounce 'those intellectuals of the Cambridge school of theology who undermine the Faith and destroy the truth'; also, for good measure, 'the "with it" clergy and writers who are emptying the church with their gimmicks'.

His own church was far from empty on Sunday mornings – about 50 at the 8 o'clock Holy Communion, 350 adults and children at the 9.30 Sung Eucharist, two dozen at the children's Sung Eucharist at 11.15 and about one dozen at Evensong. Over the previous 7 years 220 adults and 150 children were confirmed, while 350 adults, including some lapsed, received instruction. There were 11 groups of Baden Powell organizations, 2 youth clubs, 2 women's fellowships, and an old people's club attached to the church. A do-it-yourself stewardship campaign had raised the current parish income from £600 in 1958 to £4,500 in 1965.

By the end of the century these statistics would seem remarkable, but in a socially mixed, developing community of 15,000 people, lacking any other churches, and served by a hard-working rector and two curates, they could be matched in many other parishes of this sort – even in those served by Cambridge-influenced, 'with it' priests.

44 Putting asunder and putting together

In January 1964 Archbishop Ramsey appointed a group to consider whether a new kind of divorce law might be devised such as would be free from the most unsatisfactory features of the current law and yet would not weaken the status of marriage in the community. The group, which met under the chairmanship of the Bishop of Exeter, Robert Mortimer, was as high-powered as might be imagined and made up of distinguished moral theologians, lawyers, psychiatrists and sociologists. It was made clear that their task was to consider only the secular law and not to trespass on the territory of church discipline.

The report *Putting Asunder* was published in 1966 and proved to be one of the finest and most influential ever produced by the Church of England, notable also for the quality of its prose. Its chief proposal was that the doctrine of matrimonial offence, requiring one or other of the parties to be proved guilty of a serious breach of the marriage commitment – cruelty, adultery and prolonged separation – should be replaced by a doctrine of marriage breakdown, requiring firm evidence that the relationship had in fact ended, with no realistic possibility of it ever being revived. The report's other proposals were all related to the operation of this new approach, which was quite quickly adopted by Parliament and became the basis for divorce in England. It was disappointing, however, that the group's recommendation of new provisions for seeking to effect reconciliation before a court appearance was not adopted.

While the report emphasized over and over again that it was dealing only with secular law and not with the church's discipline, the new doctrine of marriage breakdown served to undermine the church's stance on the indissolubility of marriage. For once it is acknowledged that marriages can and do break down irretrievably, how can it be asserted that they still exist and that the inauguration of another union is impossible, or at least so undesirable that the church will not preside over it? Three more decades would be needed before the only valid answer to this question came to be recognized by the Church of England. Meanwhile the temporary excommunication of those who remarried after divorce (a practice widely imposed during the early years of my own ministry) ceased and the (at first) discrete blessing of remarried couples became common.

45 A missed opportunity at Weymouth

The spectacle of the Sands Mission was impressive enough, the tall commanding figure of the Bishop of Salisbury carrying a simple shepherd's crook attended by three servers. A bevy of clergy and a colourful assembly of local choirs received instrumental reinforcements from the Salvation Army Band. A congregation of many hundreds stood on the promenade above and craned for a better view, their ears assaulted by the shouts of local bloods and their noses by the smell of fried onions. They listened attentively to a sonorous voice delivering a rambling discourse nearly half an hour long. I wonder what they thought? The Bishop embraced the whole range of Christian belief from the Creation to the Cross, but the effect was neither religious instruction nor exhortation, the other definition which the dictionary gives to the word sermon. The supporters from the local churches no doubt followed what it all meant, but a sermon which included quotations from the Greek and the story of the ride of Roland from Ghent to Aix (a popular reading for bingo players?) will not get the holidaymakers off the promenades and into the churches where they belong. An opportunity had been missed.

Edward Salmon in *Prism*

46 Women priests – no progress

The Anglican Group for the Ordination of Women, formed in 1930, enjoyed the support of the distinguished liberal theologians Charles Raven, Master of Christ's College, Cambridge and Walter Matthews, Dean of St Paul's, but its membership remained small and many regarded it as tiresomely eccentric. Thus by 1950 deaconesses and women parish workers were still unable to take part in the leading of Mattins and Evensong in parish churches, and when Janet Lacey, the dynamic Director of Christian Aid, went to St Paul's to speak about the needs of the underdeveloped world she had to await the end of Evensong before starting her address and was not permitted to occupy the pulpit. Shortly before his retirement in 1961 Archbishop Fisher said that the ordination of women was 'unthinkable'.

A Church Assembly report, *Gender and Ministry*, published in 1962, recommended no more than better deployment and conditions of service for deaconesses and parish workers, but was strongly attacked in a maiden speech by Bishop John Robinson of Woolwich who argued that the most urgent need was to give them much greater responsibility. An Archbishop's Commission on *Women in Holy Orders*, published in 1966, stated the pros and cons for women priests, said there were no conclusive reasons against their ordination, but produced several pragmatic reasons why they should not be ordained. The Church Assembly debated this report twice in 1967 and again in 1968, but in spite of some impassioned speeches from women members, no progress was made. In retrospect it seems strange that in the major programme of reform that many of us in Parish and People were battling for in the 1960s, the issue of women priests was not on our agenda.

47 A sensitive writer and a vigorous campaigner

Monica Furlong, a close friend for almost forty years, was the most interesting Church of England writer of her time. Her range encompassed biography, church affairs, spirituality, poetry, fiction, feminism and travel – all expressed in books and journalism and, for a short time, as a BBC radio producer. But there was nothing slapdash about her writing. She used to say that a writer's task, in contrast to that of a journalist, is to turn a torrent of words into an attractive stream. Everything she wrote was very readable and, like her religious faith, of a deeply personal character, making considerable use first of Jungian, then of Freudian insights.

She had the capacity to penetrate beneath the surface of events, often with uncomfortable and sometimes devastating results for the evaluation of individuals and the institutions they served. An unfulfilling marriage and some other personal disappointments gave her a special sensitivity to suffering and enabled her to give wise and tender counselling to many others in distress. A formative influence in her Christian journey was Joost de Blank, the notable Archbishop of Cape Town and outspoken opponent of apartheid. In her late teens she attended St John's, Greenhill in North London, where he was the Vicar and enlivening the parish.

A pronounced stammer, later more or less overcome, precluded certain forms of employment, but a gift for words took her into journalism where she enjoyed great success, first on the *Spectator*, then on the *Daily Mail*. In the early 1960s she became involved in the reforming movement in the church, writing regularly for *Prism*, then *New Christian* and establishing friendships with Bishop John Robinson and other leaders of the movement.

Her first book, *With Love to the Church* (1965), was a sharply critical evaluation of the ecclesiastical policy of that time and went on to outline her own vision of a liberal church open to all, including homosexuals, for whose acceptance by both church and society she always pleaded. Of the many books that followed, a sympathetic but not uncritical biography of *Thomas Merton* (1980) – a remarkable Trappist monk – was the most widely acclaimed on both sides of the Atlantic. Three books concerned with the interaction of prayer and psychology, *Travelling In* (1971), *Contemplating Now* (1971) and *The End of our Exploring* (1973), were probably the most widely read, and her final book, *C of E: The State It's In* (2000), the most substantial.

From 1980 until her death in January 2003 Monica was a leading figure in the Movement for the Ordination of Women (MOW), though she had no wish to be ordained herself, then in campaigns to abolish 'flying bishops' and to secure the recognition of women as suitable for high office in the church. She was Moderator of MOW from 1982 to 1985 when her leadership was sometimes challenged by those who did not favour demonstrations and other bold methods. She wrote and edited several books on the subject and, although confined to a wheelchair, with her leg in plaster following a walking accident, she was among those who celebrated outside Church House, Westminster in 1992 when the result of the General Synod vote was announced. *A Bird of Paradise* (1995) was the title of her revealing autobiography.

48 A sorry tale at Sheffield

Bishop Ted Wickham often made the point – still not recognized by many – that unless experimental work in mission is built into the organizational structure of the church nationally, it will be at serious risk of ending once its pioneer leader has moved elsewhere. This truth could not have been demonstrated more clearly or more tragically when in 1959 Wickham himself left the leadership of the Sheffield Industrial Mission to become Suffragan Bishop of Middleton – a move that in itself made little sense, since there was urgent need for someone to spearhead industrial mission nationally.

He was succeeded in the leadership by Michael Jackson, an able, thoughtful priest who had already worked on the shop floor in Sheffield and been an ordained member of the team for the last four years. At the time of transition it was assumed by everyone – clergy and laity – that policy would continue to be developed in line with Wickham's original vision. And so it was, for a time, but by 1963 it was apparent that Jackson was no longer in sympathy with the established approach or with its underlying theology. Moreover Bishop Leslie Hunter – a strong but by no means uncritical supporter of Wickham – had retired and been replaced by Francis John Taylor, a man of evangelical convictions and autocratic disposition who had no sympathy with the Wickham approach. He and Jackson formed a close alliance and were determined to change the Mission.

They believed it had become too closely identified with the mores of industry and, although concerned to raise moral and social issues and examine them in the light of the biblical revelation, lacked the distinctiveness derived from a firm commitment to preaching the gospel in such a way as to secure conversions and new members for the church. A sharp and painful debate followed among members of the Mission, leading to the dismissal of two chaplains by Jackson who proved to be no less authoritarian than his new bishop. Their departure was soon followed by the resignations of other chaplains and within a short space of time the largest and most radical expression of industrial mission in the world had been effectively dismantled.

At the time of Wickham's leaving there were 8 chaplains covering 18 steel and engineering companies in Sheffield and Rotherham, as well as some departments of British Rail. Besides 250 lay groups, there were regular consultations and conferences on particular issues relating to the workplace, and frequent celebrations of Holy Communion away from the mills and factories. It was estimated that the Mission was in touch with about 43,000 of the 70,000 workers and managers employed within its sphere of influence. The dramatic change of policy created deep concern locally and nationally. Canon Gerald Hollis, a member of the diocesan advisory committee on the Mission, moved and secured a vote of no confidence in the Bishop. Relations between the diocese and the other participating churches, who had not been consulted, hit rock bottom. Archbishop Coggan of York appointed a committee to look into the situation, but this proved to be so weak in composition that it was unable to produce a credible analysis.

Jackson gradually formed a new team to implement the changed policy, but the chief lay groups collapsed in an atmosphere of disillusionment. Meetings now began with prayer and a sermon-like talk by a chaplain and the previously open lay groups were renamed study groups. The importance of research was stressed. But the trust between the Mission and industry patiently built up over the years was destroyed and financial support greatly reduced. Out of the wreckage some good came inasmuch as the chaplains of the Wickham era dispersed to other dioceses where they initiated new industrial work. Following the departure of Jackson to become Vicar of Doncaster in 1969 and the death of Bishop Taylor a year later, some reconstruction became possible, but this continued to be church-based, rather than industry-determined. By this time the leadership of the Wickham-inspired approach had passed to Bill Wright of the Teesside Industrial Mission. He had been a member of the Sheffield team in the 1950s and on Teesside created a large-scale ecumenical project in different industrial circumstances and with a flexibility that enabled it to meet the demanding changes of the 1980s.

49 Sent to Coventry

When in 1965 my close friend Lawrence Jackson consulted me about an invitation he had received to become Vicar of Holy Trinity, Coventry, I strongly advised him to decline. This glorious church, hardly a stone's throw from the rebuilt cathedral, had fallen on hard times. The congregation was small and, with the life of the cathedral still burgeoning, there appeared to be not the remotest chance of making any significant improvement.

I had reckoned without the flair of my friend – one of the most entertaining of preachers and after-dinner speakers – who was at the time ministering to a crowded St James the Greater, Leicester. He accepted the invitation and, being himself of a decidedly conservative outlook, discerned that a church devoted to the 'old religion' – Book of Common Prayer, Authorized Version of the Bible and so forth – might provide for the citizens of Coventry a welcome alternative to what was on offer at the go-ahead cathedral.

There was the added factor that the national and international reputation of the cathedral had left the same citizens feeling sorely neglected.

Lawrence set to work – enlivened the worship, preached his own in-imitable sermons and spoke at countless clubs and dinners to provide a taster of what could be enjoyed every week at Holy Trinity Church. And it worked. Before long the church was full and exhibiting a vibrant life. The Bishop made Lawrence an honorary canon of the cathedral but it was perhaps hardly surprising that his relations with its Provost were never more than formal.

50 A pre-nuptial ring from Rome

Michael Ramsey's visit to Pope Paul VI in Rome in 1966 was the first official visit by an Archbishop of Canterbury since the Middle Ages. Geoffrey Fisher's visit to Pope John XXIII in 1960 had been informal and unofficial. At first Ramsey was reluctant to go, since he heartily disliked the Vatican's attitude to the Anglican Communion, but the recently concluded Council promised better things and the visit proved to be a considerable success. The two leaders got on well, finding common interest in serious theology, and after an end-of-visit service in the basilica of St Paul-without-the-walls, in which both shared, the Pope took from his finger the episcopal ring, studded with emeralds and diamonds, which had been presented to him by the citizens of Milan when he was archbishop there, and placed it in Ramsey's hand. Ramsey put it on his own finger. This was an extraordinary happening and when later at a press conference a journalist asked him, 'Does this mean that Rome is tacitly recognizing the apostolic succession in England?', he replied, 'Not at all, but what it does betoken is the official recognition of the Church of England as an official church with its rightful ministers. That from Rome means a great deal.' It was also agreed to set up a joint commission of theologians (later known as ARCIC) to consider such matters as the Eucharist, the ministry and authority in the church.

51 Bishops, bombs and battles

It would be worth doing anything, even to destroy humanity, rather than run the risk of Communist enslavement.

Robert Stopford, Bishop of London in a speech at
Coventry in 1961

A new idea in religious instruction in the Army was announced from Colchester Garrison last night. Troops of the Prince of Wales Own Regiment are to study Old Testament battles as a serious military exercise. The first lesson today will be on Gideon's fight against the Amalekites in 275 BC.

Eastern Daily Press

The decision of the Bishop of Chester, Gerald Ellison, to conduct a service at the launching of the second Polaris submarine *Renown* at Birkenhead in February 1967 was not universally welcomed. While the service was being held in the shipyard, there was an act of witness in protest and a service of penitence at the central Methodist Church.

52 *Evangelical turning point*

I attended the 1967 Keele National Evangelical Conference as a reporter, albeit in a sceptical liberal frame of mind. But I was mightily surprised by what I encountered. Michael Ramsey was most warmly welcomed as 'our Archbishop' and not as a High-Church heretic. When John Stott gave the keynote address it was apparent that he at least (and many of his followers regarded him as infallible) had moved some distance from the biblical fundamentalism which had for so long characterized the conservative evangelical approach. There was, of course, no welcome for demythologizing, nor much for other current New Testament scholarship. It was more an embracing of biblical theology – 'the Bible interpreting itself in the light of the Bible' – but this represented significant movement. Among the many younger clergy present there was also a distancing from the Calvinism proclaimed by James Packer, a leading figure at the Conference, whose star seemed to be waning. Last but not least there was wide recognition that high regard for the Bible required no less regard for its ethics – social as well as personal. That seemed like progress and in my report I suggested that Keele 1967 might well turn out to have been a turning point in the history of twentieth-century Evangelicalism. So it was, though I was not myself converted.

53 *Desperate measures*

Yarm Fair will be held on Friday, Saturday, Sunday and Monday of October 18–21. The Rector of Yarm will celebrate an evening service with the choir and congregation on the dodgems on Sunday.

Middlesbrough Evening Gazette

The Dean of St. Paul's, the Very Revd. Martin Sullivan, leapt from the roof of his cathedral yesterday and, aided by soldiers of the Parachute Regiment manning a cable, landed unharmed.

Daily Mail

So many people are stealing books and pamphlets on religion and morality from a bookstall in Southwell Minster that the Provost and Chapter have closed down the stall, which has operated for twenty-four years.

Church Times

54 *Multi-faith Commonwealth*

The multi-faith Observance of Commonwealth Day, started at St Martin-in-the-Fields in 1967, was something of a breakthrough. So much so that the Bishop of London forbade a repeat performance the following year. Since the Commonwealth embraces all the major faiths, it seemed obvious that any shared religious occasion should not be exclusively Christian. St Martin's was packed to capacity, the Queen and the Duke of Edinburgh were there, along with all the High Commissioners and a good cross section of Commonwealth citizens in London. It was hoped that the description of the service as an Observance, rather than as an act of worship, would mollify those Christians who believed that sharing must inevitably involve 'dilution of the one true faith'.

Not a bit of it. The matter was raised and deplored in the Church Assembly, Archbishop Michael Ramsey was unhappy, and the usual suspect parties expressed their horror that different nations had the effrontery to bring their hopes and aspirations to God together. The Observance was therefore banished to the secular setting of the Guild-hall in the City of London. But the Queen didn't like this and after a couple of years asked Eric Abbott, then Dean of Westminster, to have it in the Abbey. This was an astute move, since the Abbey not only has strong links with the Commonwealth but is also a royal peculiar and therefore quite outside the jurisdiction of archbishops, bishops, synods and other authorities in the Church of England. No one can ban it, neither can anyone besides the Dean of Westminster be held responsible for it, and if the Queen wished it to be held in the Abbey, who was he to deny her?

I attended the event just about every year that I was at the Abbey and never failed to find moving the presence of so many people from so many different races, cultures and religions affirming their belief in God and their solidarity (such as it is) within the Commonwealth. But as an act of worship, which it did not pretend to be, it could never have been made to work. The different languages used and the very different understandings of God expressed in the readings and prayers seemed to me to militate against any corporate spiritual atmosphere. So it never 'took off'. But it was well worth doing then, and must be even more so now in these multi-cultural, multi-faith days.

55 *The conscientious homosexual*

When in February 1967 Norman Pittenger, who had for many years been Professor of Apologetics at the General Theological Seminary, New York, and was now residing at King's College, Cambridge, submitted to *New Christian* a 1,500-word article headed 'A Time for Consent' I realized immediately that this was something of a scoop. It was the first time, in Britain anyway, that a professional theologian had produced a Christian case for the acceptance of homosexual behaviour. It was at the time still a crime and in the eyes of the overwhelming majority of churchgoers certainly a heinous sin.

The article was a gentle piece in which Pittenger, who was himself 'gay' though he did not say so, spoke of what he called 'the conscientious homosexual'. This was someone whose only hope of finding *any* sexual life was with someone of their own gender. Such persons, he agreed, could not be expected to 'give up sex' altogether. And if, he went on, it happens that one is dealing with a couple who, so far as one can see, deeply and truly love one another, it is pretty close to spiritual homicide to separate them, or to try to do so, just as it is death-dealing tactics to demand that they shall never, in any way, give physical expression to their love. He concluded by declaring that he had known a number of homosexual couples whose relationships 'Our Lord himself, as Love enmanned, has been ready to bless'.

The article aroused much interest among *New Christian* readers, most of it by no means unsympathetic, but the secular media's handling of it created an uproar and the enterprising SCM Press got the author to expand it into a paperback which became an immediate bestseller.

56 *An anxious archdeacon*

In the following issue of *New Christian* we published, under the headline 'On the Fringe of Society', a personal account of a homosexual's background and attitudes in the hope that it would stimulate a new appraisal of the ethical issues involved. It provoked a large and interesting correspondence, including the following letters:

You will know that *New Christian* is read in the theological colleges (and not impossibly in the upper forms of public schools). I submit that the article 'On the Fringe of Society' with its strong emotional content does grievous disservice to young men, and the assumption that it is quite normal for public schools to be honeycombed with vice is gratuitous. This article can but disparage those who strive after personal purity, and would shrink from the very idea of corporate sex orgies to say nothing of sodomy.

(Archdeacon) T. Dilworth-Harrison, Newark

Archdeacon T. Dilworth-Harrison reproaches you for publishing the article 'On the Fringe of Society' on the grounds that we, the innocents in theological colleges, may be incited to bouts of homosexual activity. Let me report, Sir, on the situation in Leeds!

Because of the Easter holidays we found two issues of *New Christian* awaiting us. Within minutes of reading the first, latent passions were aroused, and a mad glorious frenzy of sex orgies and sodomy was enacted. Satisfied at last, we then turned to the current *New Christian* and read 'Cheaper than Alcohol'. O the bliss! Within minutes we had dragged out our pipes and were having a marijuana session in the common room. The next issue is awaited with eager, excited anticipation – what further thrills lie ahead.

John E. Roberts, Wesley College, Leeds

57 *A fast runner at Woolwich*

Nicolas Stacey, one of my close friends, offers the perfect example of the dynamic young priest of the 1960s. Fired by a vision of how both church and society might be improved, he forsook what promised to be an outstanding career in the Royal Navy and was ordained in 1953. While at Oxford he had taken up athletics and, besides winning a Blue, competed in the European Games held in New Zealand and represented Britain in the Olympic Games at Helsinki in 1952.

He had an acute analytical mind, enormous energy and the gifts of a brilliant communicator, but his impatience with the church's inability to change and the church's impatience with his widely publicized outspoken views brought his clerical career to an end when he was only 40. After a brief spell as Deputy Director of Oxfam he became Director of Social Services, first for the London Borough of Ealing, then for Kent County Council. There his innovative schemes for the care of troubled children and adolescents and the support of frail elderly people strongly influenced government policy and permanently changed practice.

After a curacy in Portsmouth and two years as chaplain to Bishop Leonard Wilson at Birmingham, Stacey accepted an invitation from Bishop Mervyn Stockwood to become Rector of Woolwich and join the band of able priests who were being recruited to tackle the seemingly intractable problems facing the church in South London. It was a daunting task. The Georgian parish church, designed to seat 700, had a congregation of no more than 50. The interior was dark, dank and decaying; rats and mice were found scurrying around the unused galleries. Two other churches in the parish had even smaller congregations and there was no doubting that the church had ceased to count for anything in the community.

Over the next nine years (1959–68) Stacey moved heaven and earth to remedy this situation. He recruited a team of gifted curates and embarked upon a massive programme of activity, mainly of social work, that attracted widespread publicity. A regular column in the London *Evening News* and much television work helped to pay the curates, as did Bingo in the church hall and a bar in the crypt. A branch of the Samaritans was formed, along with a housing association, and the closure of one of the smaller churches released money for the reordering of the parish church, the aisles of which became offices and the galleries a coffee bar. The local Presbyterian church joined in to make it an ecumenical enterprise.

But Stacey was not satisfied with the progress and in 1965 wrote a blunt article for the *Observer Colour Supplement* under the title 'A Mission's Failure'. He reasoned that although they had at Woolwich 'pulled out all the stops' the congregation had grown to only 150 and, given the capacity of the church, they had failed in their mission, as indeed had most other churches in the country. Something altogether more radical was therefore needed. The response of the church's leadership was swift and severe. The Archbishop of York accused him of 'rocking the boat', other bishops charged him with defeatism, and his own bishop warned him that he would not be offered another job 'for many years to come'.

Two years later, and with no other church appointment in prospect, he resigned from Woolwich and, like others of his sort, began a career in the secular sphere. This was a serious loss to the church but not, as it turned out, for the furtherance of the Kingdom of God, and it is doubtful whether his gifts would have been effectively employed in the leadership of a cathedral or a diocese. The harnessing of a racehorse to a heavily laden but dilapidated wagon would hardly have been good for either horse or wagon.

58 *Standing firm*

Parishioners will welcome the assurance, if news of changes and experiments has come their way, that no such changes are contemplated in this parish church; they will not be used as guinea pigs for liturgical experiments. The form used at their weddings and at the baptism of their children will be exactly the same as it has been for centuries.

There have been changes in the world around – especially perhaps in the Victorian era, which we are pleased to think of as solid – but human needs are very constant and those who study it will find that the Book of Common Prayer, compiled from ancient sources in the sixteenth and seventeenth centuries, meets those needs in a manner more realistic than more contemporary efforts in this direction. It is difficult for instance to discover any need in 1966 which is not fittingly brought to God in the 400 year old words of the Litany. So the motto for our public transactions with Almighty God in the churches of our parish will be 'Business as usual'. If any declare that we stick in the mud, we retort that by loyalty to the Prayer Book we stand on a rock.

Beeston Parish Paper

59 *A popular German import*

The Christingle was introduced into England in 1968 by the Children's Society and became immediately and lastingly popular. Imported from Germany, where it was initiated by the Moravian Church on Christmas Eve 1747, it is usually held in English churches on the Sunday before Christmas. An orange represents the world and a candle inserted into its centre represents Christ the Light of the World. Fruits and sweets skewered on four cocktail sticks, also inserted into the orange, represent God's good gifts – the fruits of the earth and the four seasons. A red crêpe paper frill at the base is a reminder of Christ's passion or, if white paper is used, of the purity of Christ's life as an example to us all. In the context of an imaginative pre-Christmas family service, the candles of many Christingles are lit in a darkened church, symbolizing the truth that in the darkness of the world a great light has shined. The children then present offerings for the work of the Children's Society and in return are given a Christingle, after which they sing the traditional Moravian carol 'Morning Star, O cheering sight'.

60 *Sharing opportunities not taken*

After several years of agitation the Church Assembly passed, in 1969, a Sharing of Church Buildings Act, which permitted new churches to be erected on a shared basis by the Church of England and any other church wishing to be involved in such an ecumenical enterprise. It also allowed existing Anglican churches to be used by other denominations. The need for such a development was clearly demonstrated by the fact that in 1965 Crawley new town had 36 buildings open for public worship, Basildon and Hemel Hempstead each had 35, Harlow 32 and the rest of the new towns figures ranging from 9 to 25. Virtually every other new housing development had several new churches, providing salutary evidence of the neglect of the plea of the 1952 Lund Conference of the World Council of Churches that their member churches should 'act together in all matters except those in which deep differences of conviction compel them to act separately'.

This had been taken up in 1964 by a Faith and Order Conference held at Nottingham, which urged the churches 'to make every effort to promote the common use of church buildings, and to set up whatever machinery is necessary to implement this'. The Archbishop of Canterbury responded quickly by appointing a commission to investigate the matter and make recommendations. This met under the chairmanship of the Bishop of Leicester, Ronald Williams, a notably conservative figure, and its report published in September 1966 sought to explain why the Church of England could not become involved in sharing arrangements with other denominations.

Fortunately its recommendations were so manifestly out of tune with the ecumenical aspirations and practical necessities of the time that they were largely ignored. Three years later the sharing of buildings was authorized, though legal reasons were advanced to preclude parish churches from becoming jointly owned. The way was now clear for sharing in new areas, though by this time much of the church building had already taken place. In inner-city areas, where the churches were struggling to survive, there was some coming together into one building, but by the end of the century the extravagant waste of human and financial reserves caused by the existence of too many separate churches had still to be tackled.

61 A commanding bishop

By command of the Right Reverend Father in God, Charles Robert, by Divine Permission Lord Bishop of Blackburn, I hereby require you and each of you personally to be and to appear before the said Lord Bishop in the Parish Church of St. John, Preston, at 3 o'clock in the afternoon of Saturday 14th day of December in the year of our Lord One thousand nine hundred and sixty eight there to answer by name and undergo a visitation of the said Lord Bishop.

Letter to Readers in Blackburn Diocese

62 Clergy training in decline

A Church Assembly debate on the reorganization of the theological colleges held one Thursday afternoon in November 1968 saw the Church of England at its most deplorable. The subject, affecting the training of all future clergymen, could not have been more important, nor the crisis with which the church was faced in this area of its life more serious. The plain facts were that of the total of 1,314 places scattered over 24 small independent colleges, only 940 were occupied. Capital grant to these colleges over the previous eight years, based on over-optimistic estimates of likely recruitment, had totalled £713,128 – a huge sum in today's values. But it was not just a question of money.

In February of that year a report produced by a small group, meeting under the chairmanship of Sir Bernard de Bunsen, a distinguished educationalist, had pointed out that the colleges were not only financially ruinous but also educationally inadequate for the modern age. Located in cathedral closes or other far-off places, most were a long way from university or other centres of theological learning. Their teaching staffs consisted of no more than a principal and perhaps two, or at the most three, young priests who, while undoubtedly bright academically, could not be expected to cover the wide ground required by their students. The Oxford and Cambridge theological colleges might be prospering but elsewhere there were problems of varying degrees of seriousness. De Bunsen recommended fewer and larger colleges (about 120 strong), all located near universities.

Such a seriousness and sensibility did not inform the debate, which was taken up almost entirely by the stubborn defence of entrenched interests. No bishop wished to lose the college in his cathedral close, none wished to see the demise of one of which he had once been the principal, no protagonist of an evangelical or Anglo-Catholic interest could bear to contemplate the extinguishing of the beacon of truth that colleges of these parties still carried. In the end it was agreed that, while the situation was obviously serious, the solution was best left in the hands of those who knew best – the principals of the theological colleges.

Shortage of money eventually compelled action and ten years after the debate the number of residential colleges had been reduced to 14 by means of amalgamations and closures. This would be reduced further to 11 – 3 in Oxford, 2 in Cambridge, 1 each in London, Durham, Bristol, Nottingham, Birmingham and Mirfield – but by then there were 30 local training schemes and the academic requirements for ordination had been significantly lowered.

63 *Anomalous analogies*

In the same year the Church Assembly accepted a report on intercommunion. This was 7 years after 32 prominent Anglicans, mainly teachers of theology led by Professor Geoffrey Lampe, had signed an open letter to the Archbishop of Canterbury urging the Church of England 'to admit, without let or hindrance, to the Communion at Anglican altars all persons who (although not episcopally Confirmed) are recognised as full members of their own churches and who desire to receive the holy sacrament at an Anglican celebration of the Eucharist'. Another open letter, signed by 53 lay members of the Assembly opposed this.

The debate at Church House, Westminster was marked by extensive use of analogy. Already familiar ones about pre-marital sex and wall-papering over cracks were followed by more startling inventions. Someone likened inter-communion to skin-grafting and this encouraged a woman – presumably from a rural diocese – to speak of treating deep wounds in horses, with the consequent problem of proud flesh. A former naval commander saw inter-communion in terms of one of Her Majesty's ships anchored off Eastbourne and holding a cocktail party to which only socialists were invited; he thought this would cause distress in certain parts of the town. Most extraordinary was the suggestion of a leading Anglo-Catholic priest that Free Churchmen only wished to receive communion in Anglican churches because 'the apples in the next door garden always look tempting'. It was unfortunate that no one asked him whose apples he believed them to be. In spite of all this, the report passed into law soon after the inauguration of the General Synod in 1970.

64 Instant baptism

Efforts to rescue baptism from its place as a private Sunday afternoon ceremony to become a Sunday morning congregational event, preceded by preparation meetings for parents and godparents, were rarely popular with non-churchgoing parishioners.

Please I want the baby done,
She muttered at the door,
She's nearly two years old, you know
We've had no time before.
We want her doing Sunday
We've got the cake and all
There'll be thirty-seven coming
And can we have the hall?
We thought perhaps you would have come
And done it long before
Ask you? But you ought to know
It's what they pay you for.

You want to talk to Jack and me
About a thing or two?
But Sunday's only three days off
We've far too much to do.
Other children? Yes, we've two
Of course they've both been done.
To Sunday School? Well no, you see,
They're both too highly strung.
We say they ought to wait and see
(Kids have no need to pray)
If then they want to take up church
We won't stand in their way
We promised when they both were done
That as they older grew
That they would learn about the Church
And what they ought to do?
We never! Or at any rate
The parson never said.
Our fault that they know nowt of God?
You must be off your head.
And so, our mam, I told him strait,
I did, I cut up rough,
We want our Linda doing soon
Without that sort of stuff.
And then, I'm dashed, he smiled and said
With no harsh words at all,
'All right, I'll do it Sunday
And you can have the hall'.
Another parson in the house
Who looked a different sort
Had talked about some kid called Grace
And 'Contract of a sort'.
If you ask me it's rather daft –
They don't know where they are.
I think this talk of promises
Is taking it too far.
The verger at that other place
Where we had done our Dawn
Just gave a form which we filled in –
The same when Roy was born.
But still they have their little ways;

They've little else to do
'cept services one day a week
But try some scheme or two.

Peter Malton

65 Divided on unity

A survey of attitudes to church unity among Yorkshire churchgoers was published in the 1969 edition of *A Sociological Yearbook of Religion in Britain.* It invited a sample of 600 laity and 16 ministers to respond to 3 statements current at the time in the realm of ecumenism – unity is the will of God; unity leads to mission because of improved efficiency; unity can be achieved without 'take-over'. Only 10 per cent of the laity and 14 per cent of the ministry thought that unity was the will of God; on the issue of unity creating effectiveness, 21 per cent of the laity and 36 per cent of the ministry thought that unity would make little difference to the problems facing the church; 26 per cent of the laity and 6 per cent of the ministry felt that 'Methodism would be swallowed up in Anglicanism'. The researchers from Leeds University remarked dryly, 'It would appear that at the grass roots of the church the present language of ecumenism does not receive unqualified support.'

66 Collapse of an experiment

Within two years of my leaving Stockton-on-Tees in 1965 the pioneering work which I had been responsible for leading in Rosework since 1954 had virtually collapsed. So fragile was its structure. In order to maintain continuity it was, correctly, decided that John Williams, the next senior member of the team, with special responsibility for the ministry in Hardwick, should take over the leadership and exercise this from his Hardwick base. The bishop produced another priest, who had been ordained late in life, to lead the work at Rosework. All went well for a time but difficulties over co-operation arose in 1966 and in the following year the new priest, with the support of the archdeacon, and he said that of the Rosework congregation, made a unilateral declaration of independence.

Two separate parishes were created, the team ministry was disbanded, John Williams left to become Diocesan Social Responsibility Officer for Teesside, no more assistant clergy were recruited and the area was left to the ministry of two single-handed vicars. This was hopelessly inadequate for the social challenge that soon followed. As the supply of private housing on Teesside increased, so the church's lay leaders moved away from their council house homes in Rosework to their own property in more leafy suburbs. The excitement of the pioneering days was over, the church's presence in the streets disappeared, youth work was abandoned, the parish newspaper closed and rapid decline in church attendance and influence followed.

The position in Hardwick was even worse. The estate had been built to house those affected by slum clearance in central Stockton but, although the new council houses were superficially more attractive than those in the back streets, they were of poor construction and the overall urban design, marked by lack of amenities, made it an unattractive alternative to the intimate community life experienced in the town. Few wished to move there, many of those that did became unhappy and during the 1970s and 1980s the estate displayed all the grim signs of social disfunction. The church was now helpless, lacking any of the resources necessary to meet a rapidly deteriorating situation. By the end of the 1990s the borough council was boarding up empty houses to prevent further vandalism.

In the following year properties in the central area were demolished. High unemployment and low educational attainment were further signs of deprivation and the estate was classified as one of the worst 10 per cent in the country. Plans were announced for the demolition of 615 dwellings and a housing-led regeneration scheme to be carried out by private developers and a housing association. The Church of England had responded to the crisis by demolishing the church erected in 1961 and incorporating the estate into an established town parish. The Rosework estate was returned to the distant parish from which it had been carved in 1954. The congregation now numbered about 20.

67 Thirty-five years in a new town

The experience of the church in the north-east new town of Peterlee over exactly the same period offers a valuable comparison. Started in the late 1940s and named after a legendary Durham miners' leader, Peterlee was intended to provide coal miners with a modern form of urban community from which they would commute daily to their long-established pits. But not many of them wished to leave the close community life of the mining villages. Some rebelled against the prospect and before long the total collapse of the coal industry in Co. Durham resulted in the large-scale migration of the miners to coalfields elsewhere.

One of my Stockton colleagues, Keith Woodhouse, became a young Vicar of Peterlee in 1964 and stayed until his retirement in 1999. The population was 15,000 at the time of his arrival and was expected to increase to 30,000; there had been a previous vicar, a fairly large church, St Cuthbert's, had been built and there was a healthy, outward-looking, pioneering congregation. Keith, who had spent a couple of years as a youth specialist in a Manchester inner-city team ministry after leaving Stockton, adopted for Peterlee virtually the same policy he had helped to create while working with me on the Rosework estate – Parish Communion, daily services, parish meeting, public baptism, house church, parish newspaper, intensive confirmation preparation, collaboration with other churches, much involvement in the life of the community. Thirty-five years later the parish was still flourishing. Seventeen curates had been trained there, six men from the parish had been ordained, and when in 1999 the new town was fifty years old this was celebrated by the development of a new park named Woodhouse Park – a fitting tribute to a great priest and a remarkable ministry.

Why was this so different from the Rosework and Hardwick experience? The dedicated and extraordinarily long stay of Peterlee's vicar was an obvious factor, as was the regular supply of curates to infuse new life. But most significant was the social make-up of a new town which its development corporation had designed to embrace variety. People from very diverse backgrounds lived side by side – a doctor next to a refuse collector, a miner next to a registrar. The plentiful supply of houses ensured a cosmopolitan character, with people moving in from many other parts of the country, bringing new ideas and style. In a population of 30,000, in a clearly defined and well-planned community, there was therefore sufficient of the sort to whom the Church of England usually appeals, an adequate supply of lay leadership and the possibility of maintaining a vibrant form of church life to which others might be drawn.

These favourable factors were exploited to the full and Keith Woodhouse, unmarried, had time enough to serve as rural dean for 26 years, to tutor a Durham County Council youth leadership course for 21 years, and to serve for several years as chairman of the district Council of Voluntary Service. The Stockton grain of wheat that died produced much fruit elsewhere.

68 A *new way of killing prophets*

Hebrew prophets were often put to death by stoning; the Church of England killed two of its outstanding 1960s' prophets by overwork. Joe Fison, who became Bishop of Salisbury in 1963, was an original theologian who was never afraid to think new thoughts and say new things, but he was never likely to be able to cope with the increasing pastoral and managerial demands of a huge rural diocese caught up in massive social change. He died in office in 1972 aged 66. Ian Ramsey's appointment to Durham in 1966 seemed at the time to be an inspired move, and he achieved much, but it proved impossible for him to combine the demands of a diocese undergoing traumatic social change with those of the wider church which needed his special gifts and with his vocation as a scholar. He died in office after only seven years, aged 57.

Earlier, the retirement of Archbishop Geoffrey Fisher in 1961 led to anticipated translations of Michael Ramsey from York to Canterbury and of Donald Coggan from Bradford to York. David Say had gone to Rochester the previous year and being only 47 and, not subject to the compulsory retirement age for clergy introduced in 1975, became a pillar of the community in north Kent and of the councils at Westminster for the next 27 years. George Reindorp took lively pastoral experience and a much welcomed sense of humour to Guildford in 1961. When his fund of stories was finally exhausted by over-use he was translated to Salisbury where he dealt effectively with pastoral reorganization.

The appointment of the little-known Stuart Blanch to Liverpool in 1965 was so surprising that, wearing my editorial hat, I asked for the press release to be checked. But he proved to be popular on Merseyside and it might have been kinder to him and to the greater advantage of the church if he had been allowed to stay there, though this would have prevented David Sheppard from exercising his gifts in that special region. Robert Runcie's appointment to St Albans in 1969 seemed just right and much good resulted from it. The other episcopal appointments of the decade were unremarkable, though the return to England of Leslie Brown enabled a great Archbishop of Uganda and Rwanda to be translated to St Edmundsbury and Ipswich in 1966.

69 *Radical reform proposals rejected*

The Paul Report on the Deployment and Payment of the Clergy was essentially a discussion document, the work of one man, and its radical recommendations were inevitably controversial. When the furious debate about them had subsided a little, it became necessary to determine what action should be taken and a commission under the chairmanship of the Vicar of Leeds, Canon Fenton Morley, was set up to make specific proposals. There appeared to be general agreement that the Paul idea of major parishes and group and team ministries was the right way forward.

The commission's report, published in 1967, went very much further than this. Having confirmed Paul's diagnosis of the problem, it recommended that the clergy should lose their independence as parish freeholders and be taken on to 'the strength of a diocese'. Private patronage would thereby cease and a diocesan ministry commission would assume responsibility for all appointments. It was envisaged that these would be made for a term of years on a contractual basis, though no priest could remain in office beyond the age of 70. A central ministry commission would determine overall policy and ensure co-ordination of diocesan decision-making.

The haphazard method of paying clergy stipends from endowments, glebe fees and various other sources of income would be replaced by a central stipends authority, that is, the Church Commissioners, who would take over responsibility for all these funds and remunerate the clergy on an agreed scale. The clergy would also have much stronger pastoral care – and oversight – from suffragan bishops and archdeacons.

These were bold proposals, made possible by the fact that the commission's membership was heavily weighted in favour of some of the church's most able reformers. This was its strength, but also its weakness for when the report was presented to the Church Assembly it ran into strong and articulate opposition led by the Bishop of Chester, Gerald Ellison. He argued that the proposals would undermine the very basis of the Church of England's life in the parishes and he produced a pamphlet of his own, *Progress in Ministry*, containing alternative proposals. In the subsequent debate Bishop George Reindorp of Guildford remarked that the Bishop of Chester, being a rowing man (he had for some years umpired the Boat Race), could only conceive of progress being made by facing backwards.

The proposals were remitted to the dioceses for further opinion and it soon became clear that they stood not the slightest chance of acceptance. It was agreed, however, that a more rational method of clergy payment was needed and that a modification of patronage was needed, so that parishes might have some say in the choice of their priest. Steps were eventually taken to secure these reforms and a Pastoral Measure, already making its way tortuously through the Church Assembly, made provision for the reorganization of adjoining parishes and the setting up of group and team ministries.

It was widely believed that Fenton Morley's robust advocacy of the report – he stumped the country speaking about it – made him enemies in high places and deprived him of an expected bishopric. He was one of the church's most able and experienced priests, with strong leadership gifts, and was appointed Dean of Salisbury. This was good for Salisbury but a considerable loss to the wider church.

70 Reformers abandon their struggle

The resignation of Eric James from the directorship of Parish and People in March 1967 signalled the ending of the movement's attempts to bring about substantial reform of the Church of England. It was a sudden death and whether or not it was premature remains an open question.

The merger of Parish and People and the Keble Conference Group in 1963 released a surge of reforming energy and hopes ran high. But the more James travelled about the country and the more bishops and parish clergy he met, the more he became convinced that the spirit of reform was confined to the relatively small membership of the movement he was leading. There was, in fact, stiff resistance to most proposals for change, instanced by the hostile reception accorded to the Paul Report, followed by the rejection of the Anglican–Methodist unity proposals and the Morley proposals for the deployment and payment of the clergy. Soon the election for the new General Synod, on which much hope had been pinned, would confirm the depressing situation by returning a considerable conservative majority.

James suggested, therefore, to the council of Parish and People that the basis on which he had been appointed in 1964 was a false one. There was no great reforming desire awaiting dynamic leadership. The council could only agree and the question to be resolved therefore was future policy. James had himself already accepted a canonry of Southwark Cathedral and wished to resign from the directorship, though he agreed to continue in an honorary capacity until the end of the year. I indicated that my work as editor of *New Christian* left me without time to remain editor of the Parish and People journal, and Peter Whiteley, the Treasurer, said that, because of increased business responsibilities, he would have to reduce his commitment. More seriously, Nick Stacey and some others argued that time devoted to overcoming the reactionary forces in the church was time wasted. Service of the Kingdom of God now demanded effort for the creation of a better social order.

Further meetings of the council led to a decision to cease the pursuit of institutional reform and to concentrate on the creation and linking of small ecumenical cells, united by sharing in informal eucharistic celebrations, with or without the presence of an accredited minister, and a commitment to social action. Negotiations with the renewal groups in the Free Churches, all of which were feeling equally disenchanted by the slow pace of progress in their churches, found a ready response and a new organization ONE for Christian Renewal, with a full-time executive secretary, was launched in 1970. It was designed to be an underground movement and prospered as such for some years, but never grew large enough to become truly subversive.

71 Explosion at Lambeth

The 1968 Lambeth Conference followed almost immediately after the Fourth Assembly of the World Council of Churches in Uppsala and seemed something of an anticlimax and almost provincial by comparison. The World Council had, as it turned out, been at the peak of its strength and influence, and the experience of its handling of international as well as church issues was exhilarating.

But Lambeth had its moments – including an Indian-created explosion. The style was different from that of its predecessors. Besides the 462 bishops present (150 more than in 1958) there were, after the example of Vatican II, 24 consultants and 76 participating observers from other churches. Size required the conference to be held in the circular assembly hall of Church House, Westminster and, for the first time, the press were admitted to some of the plenary sessions. Much of the discussion took place in 15-strong groups, which facilitated participation, though there were still complaints that the English bishops seemed to regard themselves as a superior breed.

Early in the conference the Pope's recent encyclical prohibiting artificial methods of birth control was rejected and the more positive judgement of Lambeth 1958 reaffirmed. An attempt to get the bishops to agree that there were no theological objections to the ordination of women to the priesthood failed but they were united in urging the conservation of the sea bed. The most heated debate involved the proposals for Anglican–Methodist union and when Bishop Eastaugh of

Peterborough, a leading opponent of the English scheme, tried to get the conference to abstain from passing judgement on its details, the Metropolitan of India, the aristocratic Lakdasa de Mel, exploded, 'A little more of this behaviour and the Anglican Communion will get such a magnificent reputation for double-talk that we will become utterly disreputable. Our very honour will be challenged.' Earlier he had accused some bishops of 'supporting church unity right down to the last Indian' – contrasting their approval of unity schemes in North and South India with their refusal to accept anything of the sort on their own territory. There was an uproar. Bishop Trevor Huddleston described de Mel's attitude as 'utterly un-Christian' and some other bishops declared themselves unwilling to attend the closing Eucharist at St Paul's Cathedral at which he was to be the preacher. But in the end they were persuaded to go and only six bishops voted against a resolution supporting the English scheme. The subsequent failure of the Church of England to accept could not have demonstrated more clearly the Lambeth Conference's limitations.

72 Alf the scapegoat?

The churches should protest at the proposed return of the BBC TV programme 'Till Death Us Do Part'. On 13 February the word 'bloody' was used sixteen times and 'Gorblimey' five. On 27 March there were horrible remarks like 'Take off yer drawers.'

Letter in Home Words, parish magazine inset

The interesting thing to explore in the Alf Garnett saga is the curious response he gets from the audience. There are times when he is pretty pathetic but generally speaking he presents as a person in which there is nothing to admire: a bigoted, obstinate, dogmatic, selfish nit blowing off about the coons, the RCs, the Bosch, the long-haired and the Socialism lot; a deplorable being, with whom we would not want to identify ourselves – overtly. Yet there are bits of each of us which correspond with something in him. We would be too ashamed to admit it, but if he exposes it, that's all right. Have we here a slice of very primitive religion? Do we, in our imagination, sacrifice Alf, and let him get rid of our latent prejudices? How else can you explain him? Bloody humiliating, innit?

Review by Vernon Spraxton of the film Till Death Us Do Part

3

The Reactionary Seventies

The creativity and excitement of the 1960s was succeeded by a decade of disillusionment and disappointment and, once more, the life of the Church of England reflected much of the character of the national trends. The defeat of Prime Minister Harold Wilson in 1970 and the replacement by the Conservative Edward Heath, a committed Anglican, marked the beginning of a long period of economic recession, rising unemployment, hyper-inflation and industrial unrest. The return of a Labour administration four years later did nothing to arrest this, but paved the way for a right-wing Conservative government led by Margaret Thatcher. By this time 15 per cent of the population was living below the poverty line and the divorce rate in England and Wales was the highest in Europe.

These dismal figures were more than matched by those of the church. In 1960 baptisms were still running at about 70 per cent of the population, by 1970 they had fallen to below 50 per cent, and by 1980 to 40 per cent. Confirmations standing at 191,000 in 1960 were down to 96,000 in 1977 and continuing to fall by an average of well over 2,000 every year. In 1961 there were 26 theological colleges educating 1,663 students, in 1977 there were 15 educating 769. In 1963, 636 deacons were ordained, in 1976 only 273. Church attendance showed similar decline and it was apparent that since 1945 the numerical strength of the Church of England had almost halved.

That all the other churches in England apart from the Roman Catholic (which was temporarily insulated from the general trend) had experienced similar decline indicated that deep changes – some said in the direction of secularization – were taking place in the mores of society. Particularly serious for the Church of England was the fact that, with the demise of its 1960s reforming movement, there were now few who were willing to face the implications of the catastrophic decline and even fewer who were ready to respond to it realistically and constructively.

The failure, at the second time of asking, of the Anglican–Methodist unity scheme effectively ended serious unity negotiations for the remainder of the century. The premature death of Bishop Ian Ramsay in 1972 was a serious blow to the whole church, as well as to his diocese of Durham, and when Archbishop Michael Ramsey retired in 1974 he had no obvious successor. Donald Coggan was translated from York to act as a caretaker for a few years, but then none of the eligible bishops wished to move to the northern primacy.

The new General Synod's rejection of proposals for the ordination of women priests in 1975 was greeted with an anguished cry from the public gallery, 'They gave us a stone', and this seemed to express the dashed hopes of many others, extending to almost every part of the church's life. Archbishop Coggan's subsequent 'Call to the Nation' did nothing to restore them, but there were still things to cheer in the parishes.

1 A playground for bureaucrats or bores

Synodical government was seen by the 1960s radicals as an important plank in their reform programme. It was expected that the bringing of the laity into the central government of the church, on equal terms with the bishops and the priests, would lead to more dynamic leadership in a Christian community renewed for mission. There was the further point that if control of doctrinal and liturgical matters was to be wrested from the state it would need to be vested in a credible church organization. In the event a Synodical Government Measure passed through the Church Assembly quite easily – the only obstacle being created by the clergy who wished to retain their ancient Convocations – and Parliament was not inclined to stand in the way of what looked like an advance in democracy.

The elections for the first five-year session of the new body were therefore fought with considerable vigour and when the General Synod assembled in 1970 in the presence of the Queen (who declared it open), the Prime Minister and other members of the political establishment, it was noted that a significant number of reformers had won seats. The future offered the promise of lively debates and legislation to effect much needed change at every level of the church's life. And so the debates during the first year or two turned out to be. The fact that the inauguration of synodical government had been achieved so easily should, however, have served as a warning. Machinery for effecting change can just as easily be used to prevent change, especially when elements of democracy are involved, and it soon became apparent that the newly elected reformers were outnumbered by the newly elected conservatives. What is more, it was gradually realized that the bishops, who might have been expected to lead the way to at least some new arrangements, were now hemmed in by the need for two-thirds majorities to be secured in the Houses of clergy and laity. Further formidable obstacles to be overcome were provided by the extension of the synodical process to the dioceses and deaneries, to which all proposals for significant change must be referred.

The first casualty was the scheme for uniting the Church of England and the Methodist Church which led the revival of party divisions – catholic, liberal, evangelical – which had been thought to belong to the

Church of England's past. Further reversals followed, including proposals for the ordination of women in 1978, the acceptance of women
priests from abroad in 1979, covenanting with Free Churches in 1982,
the remarriage of divorced people in church in 1973, 1978 and 1985. It
was for the reformers a sorry tale. But too much had been expected of a
structure which, while embracing some parliamentary principles, lacked
a government with power and required a degree of consensus appropriate to the conciliar tradition. In an episcopal church, however, space
would sooner or later be needed for apostolic-style leadership.

Within two years of the Synod's inauguration, Bishop Mervyn
Stockwood of Southwark was complaining in his diocesan newsletter:
'I regard it as a disaster, a playground for bureaucrats or bores. Worse
still is the time wasted on endless chatter and the money wasted on
cascades of memoranda and minutes, stamps, envelopes and secretarial
expenses.'

2 A good decade for appointments

During the 1970s no fewer than 37 of the 45 dioceses required episcopal replacements (3 of them twice) and it was not to be expected that
every one of these would create excitement. The translations to
Canterbury and York in 1974 were in fact disappointing. Not so the
appointments to Chichester and Winchester made in the same year. Eric
Kemp's elevation had been delayed for several years by an unduly opin-
ionated and over-powerful Secretary for Appointments at Downing
Street and was therefore all the more welcome when it came, though he
overdid things by remaining at Chichester for 28 years until he was 86.
John V. Taylor leapt directly from the General Secretaryship of the
Church Missionary Society to Winchester and what he lacked in pastoral skill was more than compensated for by his prophetic vision.

Ronald Bowlby's appointment to Newcastle in 1972, followed shortly by John Habgood's to Durham, brought two Old Etonians together
to form a fruitful partnership in the North East in a time of social and
economic stress. Douglas Feaver (described by the ever-charitable Eric
Abbott as 'the rudest man in the Church of England') was contemplating retirement when invited to go to Peterborough in 1972, but he put
this off and, being always his own man, entertained and exasperated the
people of Northamptonshire for several years. The episcopates of David
Brown, who went to Guildford in 1973, and Stuart Hetley Price, who
went to Ripon in 1975, were both cut short by early deaths, thus depriv-

ing the church of two gifted leaders. Stress was said to be the explanation. Kenneth Woolcombe, whose appointment to Oxford had been welcomed in 1970, resigned in 1978, not long after the death of his wife.

Two tough guys were Kenneth Skelton, who returned from Rhodesia to take on Lichfield in 1974, and Stanley Booth-Clibbon, a descendant of the founder of the Salvation Army and also with strong African experience, who flew the flag of Christian socialism in Manchester from 1979 onwards. David Sheppard, the former Test cricketer with socialist inclinations, began what was to be a notable ministry in Liverpool in 1975. In the same year, John Tinsley's appointment to Bristol replaced some of the bench's recently lost intellectual weight and two years later Peter Walker took a good, liberal mind to Ely. The only publicly controversial appointment of the decade was that of Hugh Montefiore to Birmingham in 1978. His espousing of 'green' issues and questioning of the future of the motor car worried those involved in the already ailing Midlands motor industry and he proved to be an admirably controversial bishop for the next nine years. All in all, a good decade – crowned at the end by the announcement of Robert Runcie's translation to Canterbury.

3 More new ideas

The Revd. Raymond Dean answers questions through a loudspeaker in a model Dalek after preaching at Lyngford Parish Church, Somerset. The seating capacity has been enlarged to take bigger congregations.

Daily Mail

Vicars who feel their parish life is becoming stale were advised yesterday to join the Army for three months. Canon Peter Wansey, Vicar and Rural Dean of Darlington, recommended the 'cure' after trying it himself.

Guardian

A rector is thinking of putting a coffee vending machine in the chancel of his church. The Revd. John Stone, of St. Mary's Church, Woodham Ferrars, Essex, thinks it would be 'symbolic of Christ feeding the 5,000'. The Bishop of Chelmsford, the Right Revd. John Tiarks, is to have a talk with him.

Huddersfield Examiner

4 *Not cricket*

There was something essentially English in the fuss and fury over the planned visit of the South African cricket team to Britain in the summer of 1970; the members of the team had been selected on racial grounds, all were white. Having tolerated an appalling amount of discrimination against the coloured immigrants on their own doorsteps; having accepted without much unease a situation in Rhodesia where 4 million Africans were being held in thrall by 20,000 white settlers; having agreed to the exclusion from their country of Asian refugees from Kenya, the English people suddenly became angry about a game of cricket. The British churches played an important part in the campaign that led to the cancellation of the tour, and the leadership of the former Test cricketer, David Sheppard, at that time Bishop of Woolwich, brought an element of authority and integrity to it. No longer could it be discussed as the sole preserve of students and rowdies.

5 *Archbishop meets racist thug*

Shortly before retiring to bed in Cape Town on 27 December 1970, Archbishop Michael Ramsey told his chaplain, 'The worst day of my life is over.' Earlier in the day he had had a 40-minute encounter with the South African Prime Minister John Vorster, and this had been a bruising experience. He told the Bishop of Pretoria, 'It was like a meeting between heads of states of two nations at war.'

Vorster started the conversation by accusing Ramsey of not caring to protect South Africa from Communism, which Ramsey naturally denied and went on to express his belief that in some parts of Africa the identification of white supremacy with discrimination against Africans put men off Christianity and made them more vulnerable to Communist propaganda. Responding to Ramsey's remark that the Anglican Church, in co-operation with other churches, was undertaking much work – in hospitals and schools – that was uncontroversial and likely to create good will among all races, Vorster responded aggressively, 'I do not agree. The Anglicans meddle in politics and condemn our policy.'

So the conversation continued without any meeting of minds. Back in England, Ramsey told Prime Minister Edward Heath that Vorster was very grim throughout and the most totally rude man he had ever met. It had been a unique experience and he was at the time deeply upset, but the morale of the South African churches was raised by his visit and strong stance, and he lived to see Vorster ousted.

6 Combating racism – surprising opposition

Michael Ramsey's stance on race matters was generally impeccable. He spoke frequently against all forms of racism, was invited by the government to chair its National Committee for Commonwealth Immigrants, and strongly supported the government's opposition to the racist regime in Rhodesia, even to the point of indicating that it might be right to use armed force against the regime. But he baulked at support for the World Council of Churches' Programme to Combat Racism announced in 1970. Developed from the long discussions on racism at the WCC's Church and Society Conference in 1966, its Uppsala Assembly in 1968, and a more recent consultation at Notting Hill, the programme aimed to provide support for freedom fighting movements in Southern Africa by means of modest grants for welfare work among widows and children of victims of white racism, medical programmes, scholarships for students, together with information programmes about the nature and effects of white racism in the territories concerned.

The Archbishop's opposition, voiced on several occasions and at some length in his presidential address to the General Synod, had three strands. He alleged that the WCC had not faced 'the serious questions about what a just war or a just rebellion would involve'. Next, the Programme seemed to 'confine itself to white racism' whereas Christianity should decry every harshness of a state towards either a majority or a minority of its population. Third, the church must confine itself to the stating of ethical principles, rather than venture into the realm of specific action, otherwise it cannot conserve 'that role of reconciliation which is one of its highest functions'.

These lines of argument, largely supported by the British Council of Churches, were puzzling. The WCC, by no means lacking in competent theologians, had discussed the doctrines of the just war/just rebellion endlessly. The Programme specifically stated the wider context in which racism needed to be tackled, but there were in fact no organizations tackling black racism that required support. Furthermore, it seemed impossible to draw a moral distinction between the Programme's humanitarian aims and the unqualified support which the Church of England had lent to the prosecution of the 1939–45 war.

The only explanation of Ramsey's position seemed to be that, as in other startling innovative actions – and the support by the church of black freedom fighters certainly fell into this category – he needed time to assimilate the basis and consequences of the proposal. There was the further point that in common with some of the British Free Church leaders, he had no love of the World Council even though, by virtue of office, he was a member of its presidium. Its method of doing theology was not his, and amid the hustle and bustle of its assemblies and conferences, he always appeared to be uneasy, unsure of his position now that he was outside a familiar hierarchical structure. This should not have influenced his judgement, but non-theological factors can sometimes have surprising effects.

7 Of mosques and missions

Can a Christian church ever become a mosque? The Turks evidently thought so when they took possession of the great cathedral of St Sophia in Constantinople, but in 1972 the diocese of Wakefield thought not. The church in question was the 70-year old St Mary's, Savile Town, in Dewsbury, which had been declared redundant four years earlier. It was thought then that the building would be demolished and the site sold for housing or commercial purposes, but the local Pakistani immigrant population approached the Church Commissioners towards the end of 1971 with a proposal that they be allowed to buy the building and convert it into a mosque.

The Commissioners were generally in favour of the sale and received a paper from the Church Missionary Society which expressed the view that the gospel did not need to be protected from competition. But they had failed to reckon with local opinion. About a hundred Christians claiming a former association with the building wrote letters of protest. Three hundred other residents of the area expressed dismay. The Bishop of Wakefield, Eric Treacy, said that the conversion of the church into a mosque would 'make nonsense of the Christian missionary movement'. A considerable local controversy ensued and the Commissioners became divided over the issue. In the end it was resolved ungenerously by demolishing the church and allowing the Muslims to buy the vacant site.

8 Insights from other faiths

More than anyone else in the twentieth century, Kenneth Cragg, still going strong at 93, helped Christians to a deeper understanding of and wider sympathy for the religious faiths of Muslims and Jews. For a short time, 1970–74, he was an assistant bishop in Jerusalem archbishopric, responsible for the pastoral oversight of the small Anglican communities in Egypt, but for most of his life he was a distinguished academic and a prolific writer – over 40 books in all. At various times he held university appointments in Beirut, America, Cambridge and London's School of African and Oriental Studies.

His studies, combined with long experience in the Middle East, gave him a profound knowledge of the Arab world and his sympathy for both Islam and Judaism took on added significance when it was realized that he had been nurtured in an evangelical tradition which believed that there was nothing to be learned from other religious faiths. *The Call of the Minaret* (1956) and *Sandals at the Mosque* (1959) broke new ground with their sympathetic interpretation of Muslim spirituality, while *The Dome and the Rock* (1964) offered a new perspective on Jewish–Christian dialogue. His insights were, however, admired yet largely neglected during most of his long lifetime, but by the end of the century terrorism and other forms of violent conflict had made interfaith dialogue and co-operation the most pressing item on the political as well as the religious agenda.

9 Jesus in musical guise

The British rock opera *Jesus Christ Superstar* and the American musical *Godspell* made considerable impacts on London's West End stage in the 1970s and seemed to indicate that although the church might have difficulty in attracting young people, Jesus still had plenty of followers among them. Both were based on the gospels' accounts of his life, though *Jesus Christ Superstar* omitted the resurrection, and both provided twentieth-century settings and used modern lyrics – all of high quality. *Superstar* opened at the Palace Theatre in London in 1972 and ran for eight years, becoming the world's longest-running musical at the time. A film adaptation was released in 1973 and the musical version continues to be produced by amateur, usually church, groups. *Godspell*, which opened off-Broadway in New York in 1971, enjoyed similar success when it moved to London in the following year and also had a film version and amateur production popularity. Archbishop Ramsey, who saw both on the West End stage, declared that Jesus was presented because of *Godspell*'s approach and in spite of *Jesus Christ Superstar*'s approach.

10 *A sermon 'of sadistic length'*

The consecration of Robert Runcie as Bishop of St Albans in Westminster Abbey in February 1970 was not essentially different from that of any other new bishop. But no one who was present will ever forget the length of the sermon. Runcie entrusted this to an old friend, Harry Williams, who had taught him when he was a student at Westcott House, Cambridge, and was now a monk of the Community of the Resurrection at Mirfield.

Williams was, by common consent, one of the finest preachers, so the choice of him for the consecration sermon was sound. He began by saying, 'It is difficult to know what to say at the consecration of a bishop,' but went on to demonstrate that in fact he had not the slightest difficulty, for, having been briefed to occupy no more than 12 minutes, he spoke for 40. Very good material, too, about the nature of a bishop's authority in the light of the resurrection, but miles too long. On three occasions Archbishop Ramsey touched his mitre and prepared to stand, believing that the preacher had finished, but still he went on. Lunch engagements involving other participating bishops were broken; one of them, his old headmaster, wrote him a letter of reproof and Williams himself admitted later that the sermon had been 'of sadistic length'.

11 *A shorter sermon of sadistic content*

This was preached by the Precentor of Lincoln Cathedral, Canon David Rutter, on the day – somewhat later than elsewhere – that the Series 2 Holy Communion Service was introduced into the cathedral's worship.

> Dean Dunlop, the man of taste rejected this service.
> Dean Peck, the man of prayer, rejected this service.
> It has remained for the present Dean to introduce it.
> In the name of the Father, and of the Son,
> and of the Holy Ghost. Amen.

Considerable conflict with the Dean, the Honourable Oliver Twisleton-Wykeham-Fiennes, and the rest of the Chapter followed.

12 A misunderstood sermon

Shortly before leaving St Martin-in-the-Fields, I mounted once again its high pulpit to preach on the Pauline text from Galatians: 'Christ set us free to be freemen.' The main theme of the sermon was Jesus the liberator – the man who came to set men and women free from all that enslaves them, politically, socially, economically, sexually, racially and psychologically. The church (the community of Jesus) was, I said, a society placed in the world as an embodiment of and agency for freedom. The theological basis of the sermon was presented in terms of the remembrance of Jesus of the past, the awareness of his liberating power in the present, and the hope of that deliverance which he promised at the end of time. All reasonably coherent and not, I thought, all that difficult to understand.

At the end of the service a very tall, distinguished-looking member of the congregation shook me by the hand and declared the sermon to be the best and most helpful he had ever heard. His only regret was that the worship surrounding the sermon did not attain the same high level. I warmed to this as I had for some time felt the Sunday morning service to be rather dull, but there was no time for a discussion of the subject in the draughty portico of the church in Trafalgar Square, so the impressive gentleman promised me a letter on the subject.

Within a few days the letter arrived from the Army and Navy Club. Its sender was a naval commander, a member of a Scottish aristocratic family. Again the virtues of the sermon were extolled, but then came the suggestions for adjusting the worship to accord more closely with the spoken message: 'You should not allow that black man to carry the cross at the head of the choir procession, and you should have the National Anthem at the close of the service.'

13 Changing services and choosing bishops

The Archbishop's Commission, appointed in the wake of the disappointing Howick Report on Crown Appointments to Bishoprics, was given a far weightier membership and had the task of considering the issue of appointments in the wider context of church and state relations.

It had 29 meetings under the chairmanship of Professor Owen Chadwick, and its report, published in 1971, was generally considered to be a first-class piece of work.

On the large question of the church's 'establishment' the Commission, with three dissenting voices, favoured no significant change. It argued that the severing of the historic links between church and state would be 'impracticable in the present state of public opinion . . . the people of England still want to feel that religion has a place in the land, and they are unlikely to be pleased by legislation which might suggest that the English people as a whole were going unChristian.' The report added, however, that members of the Commission would not shrink from the acceptance of disestablishment if the state decided it to be either wise or politically necessary.

On two specific matters its proposals were nonetheless radical. The first was that in matters relating to worship and doctrine the final authority should lie with the General Synod and not with Parliament, subject to certain safeguards concerning the status of the 1662 Book of Common Prayer and the requirement that changes in forms of worship must be approved by two-thirds majorities in each of the three Houses of the General Synod. The second was that bishops should be chosen by a committee or electoral board representing the dioceses concerned and the church at large. Names would be submitted to the Crown through the Prime Minister or, alternatively, directly to the Sovereign.

Both proposals were subsequently accepted by the General Synod and by the state and, since it is constitutionally impossible for the Sovereign to be approached directly, it was acknowledged that the Prime Minister must continue to be involved in the appointment of bishops, albeit with less influence. The report contained no recommendations concerning appointments to deaneries, Crown canonries and livings and was content to leave these for further consideration by the General Synod.

14 Responding to the Spirit

In 1971 the parish of St Hugh, Lewsey in Luton experienced what later became known as a charismatic revival. The recently arrived Vicar, Colin Urquhart, was aware of what he believed to be a special influence of the Holy Spirit in his personal life and he shared this experience with the congregation of his church. Some of its members also began to have similar experiences, receiving 'gifts of the Spirit'. These included 'speaking with tongues' (a form of unintelligible speech) and 'prophecy' (the ability to preach the gospel, usually in New Testament terminology), healing, and increased openness in prayer. Within the congregation there was a sense of excited expectancy, a new concern for evangelism, a desire for less formal forms of worship, a new love of the Bible and a deeper experience of community, which led eventually to 50 people sharing a common purse, pooling income and, wherever possible, sharing houses. News of all this spread and, besides attracting more people from its own locality, the church became a magnet for others further afield.

Similar developments were taking place in other parts of the country, most notably at St Michael-le-Belfrey, York, where, under the dynamic leadership of David Watson, a church on the verge of redundancy was transformed into a place seething with intense religious activity, including a full-time theatre company. At St John the Baptist, Harborne, Birmingham a mid-week prayer group grew from about 20 to 300, with as many as 200 more involved in smaller prayer groups. The average weekly collection increased from an average of about £50 to £1,500 a week. Substantial increases in church income on this scale were not uncommon, and the forming of house churches in various parts of a parish was integral to the new approach.

During the 1970s similar responses to the Holy Spirit's prompting were taking place in many different parts of the world and were closely related to longer-standing and much more extensive developments in Africa and Latin America. Although the origins could be traced in Europe and North America to evangelical influences the manifestations were soon expressed more widely – in Roman Catholicism, where Cardinal Suemens, the Primate of Belgium, became its leading advocate, and across the Church of England's different traditions. A significant feature of the Anglican experience was its containment within the more traditional framework of parish life, but a serious problem in many places was the division created by those who had been 'baptized in the Spirit' and those who had not. By the end of the decade the house churches had, in some areas, taken on a life of their own and, crossing denominational boundaries, formed a movement with over 50,000 members in several hundred cells. This movement and also the less sectarian elements in the charismatic renewal continued to grow during the rest of the century.

15 *A charismatic experience*

My own encounter with the charismatics was, apart from welcoming their large diocesan group to Winchester Cathedral for tediously repetitive worship, confined to a short visit to the Netherlands. When I accepted an invitation to preach in the British Embassy church at The Hague the chaplain arranged to meet me at Schipol airport. My flight arrived at 4 p.m. but there was no sign of the chaplain until more than an hour had passed. When eventually he turned up he expressed the hope that he was not late, explaining, 'I have no watch as I'm a charismatic.' It was perhaps fortunate that my sermon at the traditional Sunday morning Mattins was patient of a charismatic interpretation.

16 *The cloth cap episcopal philosopher*

If in the sphere of the eternal there is, after Plato, the model of the ideal Bishop of Durham, then Ian Ramsey, who was there from 1966 to 1972, was its most accurate shadow. He was the last but one twentieth-century professor to become a bishop and combined the gifts of a distinguished philosopher with those of an acute social analyst and a warm-hearted pastor. He was greatly loved as well as widely admired and at his London memorial service Archbishop Michael Ramsey said, 'It will not be surprising if history comes to remember Brooke Foss Westcott and Ian Ramsey as the two bishops who made the biggest impact upon the Durham community.'

When Maurice Harland retired from Durham in 1966 it was all too evident that Archbishop Fisher's insistence on the diocese having a purely pastoral bishop, after a long sequence of scholars, had not been wise. To be fair to Harland, he had no desire to move from Lincoln to Durham and I am bound to acknowledge that during my time in Stockton-on-Tees I could not have received stronger episcopal support, though I was never convinced that he really understood what I was up to.

The demand in the diocese therefore was for a return to the scholar tradition, yet, although I was by this time in London, I do not recall any suggestion that Ian Ramsey might be the appropriate choice. The day, even then, seemed past when an Oxford professor would leave his chair for the rough and tumble of a northern diocese whose social and economic fabric was soon to enter a deep crisis. But Ramsey was invited and, to great rejoicing, accepted. Characteristically he went to

Buckingham Palace in a cloth cap to pay homage. This did not, how-ever, indicate a low estimate of the significance of the occasion, for when the ceremony was over he went into a philosophical and theological dis-cussion with the Queen on the problems created by a recent disaster at Aberfan, South Wales, in which many schoolchildren were killed by a moving coal-mine spoil.

He was that sort of man. Short of stature and with a Lancastrian accent, the initial impression was of an affable north-country rural dean. He was kind, warm, approachable and genuinely interested in ordinary people. Yet, as Nolloth Professor of the Philosophy of Religion at Oxford for 15 years (he was only 36 when appointed), he had stoutly defended Christian truth against the sustained assaults of the fashion-able linguistic philosophers, and broken new ground with his first book, *Religious Language* (1957). This was followed by several more in which he developed the idea that, while the visible world and human life must be open to rigorous scientific analysis, there are experiences – he called them 'disclosure situations' – which go beyond the visible and require both their own language and personal commitment.

At his enthronement in Durham Cathedral he declared his hand by devoting part of a somewhat overlong sermon to an evaluation of a recent report of the Northern Economic Planning Council. But he was soon deeply involved in the life of the parishes and, although his sermons were not always fully understood, his insistence on shaking hands with everyone at the end of the service and spending time in the church hall talking over the refreshments with elderly women about their families won the hardest of hearts. Industrial mission and other manifestations of 'frontier' ministry claimed much attention. But it was too good to last.

The width of his interests and the extent of his high skills caused him to be drawn into a multitude of responsibilities outside the diocese. Every bishop is expected to undertake some of these, but Ramsey simply could not say 'No'. Among other things, he held the chairman-ships of the Church of England's Doctrine Commission, of a commis-sion on the future of religious education, of the Institute of Religion and Medicine, of William Temple College, and of the Central Religious Advisory Committee on religious broadcasting. On most Wednesdays when Parliament was sitting, he travelled to London to attend the House of Lords, in which he spoke frequently on social and moral prob-lems. During the last quarter of 1971 he prepared 57 original talks and sermons besides the normal quota of confirmation addresses.

On Easter Eve of the following year he suffered a heart attack which

put him out of action for several months and one of his first engagements after returning to duty was to address a large gathering of church
leaders, at which I was present, in Birmingham. It was an astonishing,
unforgettable experience: although the time allocated to him was 45
minutes, he spoke at breakneck speed for 75 minutes – stimulating, edifying, a tour de force – yet it seemed to be like an express train that was
out of control. Before long he had another heart attack, this time fatal,
immediately after chairing an all-day meeting at Broadcasting House in
London. Michael Ramsey concluded his memorial service address: 'He
was living in a whirl of mental and physical movement. The whirl
became a whirlwind which swept Ian, like Elijah of old, to Paradise.'

17 *Doctrinal priorities*

It was passing strange – more candid commentators said it was outra-
geous – that when the Archbishops of Canterbury and York broke new
ground by establishing a standing Doctrine Commission and recruiting
to its membership 18 high-calibre theologians, the most urgent task they
could set before it was the old issues of clerical assent to the 39 Articles
of Religion and prayer for the departed. On the first, the Commission
recommended that in future the clergy should be required to do no more
than assent to the Articles as one among several of the church's historic
formularies, and on the second it devised forms of prayer that it hoped
would be acceptable to all. It was recognized, of course, that most
Christians prayed for their departed loved ones and friends without any
aid from a commission, and in a letter to the archbishops, printed at
the beginning of this report, the chairman, Bishop Ian Ramsey, asked
gently but firmly for different priorities:

> As we say in paragraph 11 of our report, we are conscious of being 'in
> a cultural situation where the very existence and nature of God are
> subjects of lively controversy, and urgently demand the attention of
> Christian thinkers.' That is not to deny the importance of Christian
> prayer and the Christian hope for human destiny, of which this
> subject is a limited aspect. Nevertheless, many members of the
> Commission incline to the belief that the doctrinal responsibility
> which it is anxious both to practise and to foster ought to be exercised
> in relation to more urgent and important issues than traditional rival-
> ries in areas of speculative theology, whose notoriety largely derives
> from their divisive power in days past.

The point was taken. The next task given to the Commission concerned the nature of the Christian faith itself and its expression in holy scripture and the creeds, but before its work on this was completed the chairman had joined the departed – and was being prayed for.

18 *All creatures great and small*

The Rector who prayed in church with a cat on his shoulder was not pleasing himself but bringing a little animal before God. We should not grudge God's blessing to any of His creatures.

Home Words parish magazine inset

People in England are such animal lovers that one of the best ways of making friends is through my horse. Quite often people only speak to the horse to begin with, but once the ice is broken I can talk to them and get to know them.

The Revd D. P. Jones, quoted in the *Guardian*

Annual Animal Service: Bring your Pets for the Blessing of the Church. The famous dog Goldie will speak to the congregation on Biblical matters in his own way.

Church Times

19 *A brief glimpse of new life in East and South London*

Two notable London suffragan bishops – Trevor Huddleston of Stepney and David Sheppard of Woolwich – convened a working party in the early 1970s to consider 'Local Ministry in Urban and Industrial Areas'. Viewed in the light of Bishop Ted Wickham's work in Sheffield and Manchester and the worker-priest experiment, not to mention the extensive work of the World Council of Churches, this seemed a little late in the day. But individuals, especially bishops, often have to learn for themselves and different problems may sometimes require different solutions.

In this instance the working party's report proposed the creation in London of cadres of Christian people – ordained and lay – drawn, but not separated from, the working-class milieu in which their mission would be exercised. Nothing specific about the character of this mission was mentioned but it was emphasized that it would involve totally different concepts of leadership, ministry, education and theological reflection from those based on the outlook and needs of the professional classes. An experiment, involving the training of six indigenous priests, was reported to be well advanced in East London.

There could be no objection to any of this or to the stated requirement of long-term experiment. After all, the seemingly intractable problem of Christian mission in long-alienated areas of East and South London was not going to be solved overnight. But what became of the experiments? Three years after the publication of the report David Sheppard moved to Liverpool and three years after that Trevor Huddleston moved to become Archbishop of the Indian Ocean. And since the experiments were not incorporated into the structures of the dioceses of London and Southwark neither their long-term continuity nor their careful evaluation was ever possible.

20 *Anglican–Methodist unity debacle*

The death knell in 1972 of the scheme to unite Anglican and Methodist after some 17 years of negotiations was a sad reflection of the Church of England's own divisions, and also of its unwillingness to take bold steps that might enable a united church to prosecute the Christian mission more effectively in England. Conversations between representatives of the two churches began in 1955 and, although an interim report published three years later made no specific proposals, it clearly envisaged their full union after an initial period during which they would have unified ordained ministries yet continue to exist side by side.

This was accepted by both churches and led to further conversation and a definitive report in 1958, which proposed unity in two stages. First there would be a 'Service of Reconciliation' designed to express the union and at the same time integrate the ordained ministries of the two churches. The Methodists would have bishops consecrated in the historic succession and all future Methodist ministers would be ordained by bishops. Arrangements would be made for the two churches to undertake common action and formulate common policies, while retaining their own distinctive ethos and style. Stage two would, at some unspecified date and in some unspecified manner, complete the integration process and create full union.

It was recognized that there were no fundamental doctrinal differences between Anglicans and Methodists (the division in the eighteenth century had not been over doctrine), at least none that were not already in existence within the two churches and had proved to be containable. The sticking point was the Service of Reconciliation which was perceived by some to be too ambiguous. Did it, or did it not, propose to remedy a specific deficiency in Methodist ministerial orders? Some Anglo-Catholics in the Church of England believed it was not sufficiently precise on this point, while many Evangelicals believed the attempt to integrate the two ministries was unnecessary, since the Methodists were already ordained and any ceremony of the sort proposed could only cast doubts on their authenticity. The same objections were lodged within the Methodist Church, but on a much lesser scale.

Further conversations were initiated to secure greater clarity on certain points and another report was published in 1968. By this time the opposition forces had gathered strength and, astonishingly, included in their number the former Archbishop of Canterbury, Geoffrey Fisher, who considered the scheme to be unnecessary. Michael Ramsey, on the other hand, supported it strongly, though it was felt by some that he had declared his hand too late and not been sufficiently active in promoting something of major importance.

When on 8 July 1969 voting took place, the Methodist Conference approved the scheme by a majority of 76 per cent, whereas the Convocations of Canterbury and York failed to reach the 75 per cent majority required because of the opposition of their Lower Houses of Clergy. The bishops of both provinces were in favour by 38 votes to five. The scheme was resurrected in May 1972 in order to be judged by the new General Synod, in which the laity had a voice and a vote. By this time, however, it was shown to have insufficient support in the dioceses and, although the bishops again gave strong support (85 per cent), the clergy mustered fewer votes than before and the laity reached only just over 62 per cent. The Methodists, of whom the greater change was required, felt badly let down and the cause of institutional Christian unity in England never recovered from the blow during the remaining years of the century. Those who had favoured the scheme did, however, pursue local unity with increased vigour and some further collaboration ensued.

21 *Apostolic succession*

The Revd. Karl Lundberg, Rector of Ropsley, near Grantham Lincolnshire, who delivers fish to parishioners to raise money for his church, has upset local fishmongers. Mr. Ernest Cribb, a Grantham official of the National Federation of Fishmongers, said last night: 'If he had told his supplier at Grimsby that his church was financially embarrassed to that extent, I am certain that same supplier would have made a weekly donation.'

The Times

22 *In Constable country*

Least affected by the general decline in churchgoing during the second half of the twentieth century were the county town parishes. A medieval church, standing in an identifiable community with a sizeable middle class, and served by a diligent, enterprising parson continued to attract largish Sunday morning congregations and often a reasonable number at Evensong.

When 'Johnnie' Johnston, one of 36 nominees, became Vicar of Dedham in Essex in 1950 the parish was living up to its name. His predecessor had been in office for 44 years and church life was at a low ebb; a major work of renewal was needed. Johnston had left school early and as a young journalist secured a notable world-exclusive scoop in 1936 when he was first to report the divorce at Ipswich of Wallis Simpson, an action that left her free to marry the future King Edward VIII following his abdication. Soon afterwards he struggled through academic problems and family responsibilities to respond to a call to the priesthood and after a short wartime curacy in the heavily bombed Tilbury docks area and a notable RAF chaplaincy, for which he was Mentioned in Despatches, he turned round a weak parish in Colchester which the Bishop of Chelmsford was on the point of suppressing.

It was on the strength of this that he was appointed to Dedham and within months attendance had increased considerably. At festivals the large church – painted by Constable – was filled to overflowing. The Harvest Festival, which extended over two Sundays and included five afternoon services, attracted hundreds of people from far and wide, and large-scale Nativity and Passion plays involved the whole village. The Royal Philharmonic Orchestra and the choir of the Temple Church gave performances in the church, and the building was gradually fully restored, its interior beautifully renewed.

Johnston stayed for 21 years, until driven by sudden ill-health into early retirement in 1971. His ministry was inspired by a traditional faith, a deep spirituality, a compassion for individuals, as well as a vigorous desire to get things done. He also had considerable flair as a communicator and played a leading part in community life, most notably in a local and national outcry that saved Dedham Vale from despoliation by developers who planned to use part of it for London overspill housing. In retirement he looked after the beautiful Suffolk parish of Kersey on a voluntary basis for five years, before settling in Bury St Edmunds, where he died in 1997.

23 *The importance of images*

The ability of a person to give a good television performance influenced the viewing public greatly, said Tim Brinton, former television newscaster now doing freelance work, to the Churchill Tea Club at Whiteleys yesterday. 'I believe that the present Archbishop of Canterbury is jolly good at appearing on television because he is physically absolutely right for the part he plays, almost a cross between Moses and Father Christmas,' said Mr. Brinton.

Huddersfield Examiner

24 *'Expect anything, and be surprised by nothing'*

Austen Williams, who was Vicar of St Martin-in-the-Fields from 1956 to 1984, was firmly in the tradition of Dick Sheppard who, during the 1914–18 war and afterwards turned a church attended by only a handful of people into a refuge for the lonely, the unwanted, the homeless and the disturbed. He shared many of Sheppard's gifts – a burning love of Jesus, a style of preaching that suggested a personal conversation with each individual in the congregation and an openness to all comers. He spent most of the 1939–45 war in a German internment camp, having been captured while working for Toc H with the army in France, and found this a perfect preparation for his ministry at St Martin's:

> There are people who smell in some way or don't use the right language. They are a threat and a bore and a mess. But you can't exclude them. You live with, you get fed up with – and you live with getting fed up with – them, and you just go on. There is no getting away.

That he was able to sustain such a ministry for 28 years – these including a period of recovery from a cardiac arrest – was truly remarkable.

But there was a shyness in his make-up that enabled him to distance himself from the fray when the pressure became too intense, and his wife Daphne, a former sergeant-major in the wartime ATS, could, when necessary, protect him from the over-demanding. I was privileged to be able to lend him a small hand during my London years in journalism and never ceased to be amazed at the scale of the church's activities. As many as 7,000 young people, most of them runaways from home, came to the crypt every year for help; upwards of 1,000 bowls of soup were served to down-and-outs every Sunday morning and 17 social workers, assisted by 100 volunteers, were fully stretched in meeting the demands made of them.

Austen warned me when I first met him in his Trafalgar Square vicarage, 'Expect anything, and be surprised by nothing', and before long I discovered what he meant. Celebrating Holy Communion at 8 a.m. one weekday, with a congregation of about ten, I became aware, midway through the service, of movement within the altar. Soon a dishevelled figure appeared, having been awakened from his night's sleep, and a pause was necessary while he moved off. He returned a little later to collect his cap. It was an odd experience but, at St Martin's, easy to make the connection between the Christ of the altar and 'the Son of Man who has nowhere to lay his head'.

25 Call to the North

On his return to Merseyside after the 1968 Lambeth Conference the Bishop of Liverpool, Stuart Blanch, called a meeting of the other senior church leaders in the region to talk about mission. It was agreed that something fresh was required of all the churches and, early the following year, Archbishop Coggan readily agreed to chair in York what turned out to be a remarkable meeting of church leaders from every part of the North of England. An ecumenical mission under the title 'Call to the North' was planned and after substantial preparation this was launched in Holy Week 1973 by the reading in every church and chapel of a letter signed jointly by Coggan, the Roman Catholic Archbishop of Liverpool and the Chairman of the Northern Free Church Conference.

A feature of the Call was the lack of prescribed methods of evangelism and of imported missioners. Every district, diocese and local church was left free to choose its own activities. Outdoor meetings (Cardinal Heenan addressed a huge crowd in a Sheffield football stadium), lunchtime meetings in factories, and many other initiatives extended for well over a year. It was intended that the Call should mark the beginning of continual mission, but it gradually fizzled out and, while there had been church revival in some places, it was agreed that the most significant outcome had been the marked improvement of ecumenical relations throughout the North of England.

26 Donald Coggan

Donald Coggan did not wish to become Archbishop of Canterbury (who would?) and almost certainly should not have been translated to the Primacy in 1974. Which is not to say that he was lacking in gifts or that he had not been an outstandingly good diocesan bishop at Bradford (1956–61). There could be no doubting that he was devout and patently sincere in the best sort of evangelical tradition, that he was a scholar and that he was a top-class preacher and teacher. Moreover he was energetic: Archbishop Fisher who hoped that Coggan would succeed him in 1961 said he was 'like a man with a wheelbarrow, however much you pile on him he goes on pushing'. And besides his labours for the Church of England, there was the considerable achievement of having chaired the joint committee for the New English Bible. In a former age he would have been a Puritan.

Wherein, therefore, lay the problem? It was quite simply that his years as Archbishop of York (1961–74) had demonstrated that in spite of his many gifts and considerable experience, his outlook on life and his understanding of the church's mission was not what was required in a late twentieth-century leader of the Church of England. He was popular among laypeople and seemed altogether more down to earth and practical than Michael Ramsey, his predecessor, who had delayed his own retirement for as long as possible in the hope that Coggan would by then have been considered too old for appointment. The Queen could understand him and liked him since he strongly upheld traditional values, and many found his highly skilled expositions of the Bible comforting and reassuring as well as challenging. But his approach belonged to an era now past and he seemed insulated by his faith from the complex influences of modern society

He was nonetheless more open to change in the church than either his predecessor or successor. Lacking their high doctrine of the priesthood, he had no difficulty in advocating the ordination of women some years before most joined the campaign. He was the first chairman of the Liturgical Commission charged with revising the services. He was an ardent advocate of church unity and bold enough to suggest in Rome that the time had come for inter-communion between Anglican and Roman Catholics. He devoted much time and energy to the fostering of good relations between Christians and Jews.

Yet he did not perceive that the time had come for a radical reshaping of the church's life and a reinterpretation of its message if the gospel was to be proclaimed with power in a new era. Even the best of the old wine was no longer palatable. In any event his six years at Lambeth were far too short a time for anything to be achieved in this direction and he proved to be, perhaps inevitably, an ageing archbishop in a hurry, taking numerous initiatives – not always well thought out and usually without consultation. Had Robert Runcie succeeded Michael Ramsey these six years might well have been more profitably used and Runcie, enabled to retire somewhat earlier, could have left space at Lambeth for John Habgood.

Coggan's retirement years were spent in Winchester where he became greatly loved and where his sermons and lectures, generously offered, attracted large audiences. Living in a tiny flat just outside the cathedral close, he and his wife Jean, who always played a full part in his ministry, took over a small plot in the Deanery garden, thus enabling me to claim to be the only Dean to have a former archbishop as his gardener.

27 Confronting Old Nick at Hampstead

For about thirty years, from the mid-1950s to the mid-1980s Hampstead boasted two clergymen who specialized in the handling of occultism, hauntings and apparent demon possession. Both wrote books on the subject and both attracted a great deal of publicity arising from their activities, though much of their ministry was undertaken privately and they were serious pastors.

Jack Wellman went to Emmanuel Church Hampstead in 1956 after service as an RAF chaplain. His healing services attracted troubled people from far and wide, and he was sometimes called on to exorcise houses that were believed to be demon-possessed. When successful, a dark shape was claimed to have been seen slithering away. Once, at a funeral, as he was turning away from the coffin, he felt a blow on the shoulder which almost sent him reeling – later he learned that the deceased had been strongly opposed to Christian burial. More happily, he once told his wife on the morning of Derby Day that he had had a vision of a newspaper headline 'Troy wins', and the horse duly romped home.

Christopher Neill-Smith became Vicar of St Saviour's, Hampstead in 1959 and four years later felt himself to have been 'invaded by a spirit'. This was while laying on hands for healing on a man who turned out to be an unfrocked priest who had been dabbling in black magic. He sought the advice of a highly regarded exorcist priest, Gilbert Shaw, who detected in him a psychic sensitivity. After several years of training he was licensed by the Bishop of London to minister as an exorcist; he was also a trusted confessor and counsellor to people of all ages.

But his occasional use of exorcism sometimes had dramatic consequences. After he had laid hands on the high priestess of a witches' coven she fell unconscious before the altar and had to be revived with holy water. Sometimes he was thrown across the floor of the church in the course of an exorcism and it was not uncommon for the church furnishings to vibrate. Ghosts and paranormal phenomena encountered in haunted houses were frequently expelled and he once attempted, for the benefit of a radio audience and surely unwisely, to exorcise a man who had been charged in court with causing grievous bodily harm. Listeners heard the sound of the accused 'wrestling with the spirit'. Within a year of the publication of his book *The Exorcist and the Possessed* (1973), Neill-Smith had carried out 1,000 exorcisms and become a minor celebrity, but his parishioners did not appreciate this aspect of his ministry and he retired in 1989 broken in health.

28 Militant here on earth

A somewhat gloomy Monday morning weatherwise was enlivened by the news that the Revd. Jack Wellman chased an intruder from his vicarage with a full-dress sword. The hearts of many must surely have been uplifted by this splendid piece of evidence that the church upon occasion has not lost its ability to be 'militant here on earth'.

Letter in *The Times*

29 Hawking an archbishopric around

Following the translation of Donald Coggan from York to Canterbury in 1975 the question obviously arose as to who would succeed him in the northern archbishopric. This, as it turned out, was the last occasion on which an archiepiscopal appointment was made without the involvement of the Crown Appointments Commission, though it is known that the Prime Minister, Harold Wilson, consulted widely before making his nomination.

In the event, no one seemed to want the job. First choice was John Howe, who had been Bishop of St Andrews in Scotland before becoming a highly effective Anglican Communion executive officer, but he pleaded ill-health. Then the offer went to Patrick Rodger who claimed priority for his work in Manchester and went three years later to a more relaxed life in Oxford. Robert Runcie was, apparently, attracted to the idea of returning to the North of England where he had had a rewarding curacy, but his wife was unhappy at this prospect. So the lot fell eventually on Stuart Blanch of Liverpool after an unprecedented hawking around of the Church of England's second senior appointment.

Blanch had by this time spent nine years at Liverpool where his leadership had been popular and largely successful. He was a modest man whose chief gifts were as a pastor and an expositor of the Bible. But he lacked the wide range of gifts necessary for discharging a national role with distinction. He had little skill in political and public affairs and, while able to translate his biblical insights to the personal realm, he was without the theological and philosophical background required to deal with the moral aspects of corporate decision-making.

Moreover, he was vulnerable to stress after sustained periods of hard work. This vulnerability became increasingly evident after his appointment as Archbishop and sometimes put him out of action for long periods. Nationally, he was hardly known. None of which was his fault: he was a good man who had no real desire to be Archbishop of York and only accepted the post under pressure when the leading candidates had declined. Both he and the church suffered as a consequence.

30 *From fighting to selecting*

Colonel Alec Salmon was Chief of Staff to Lieutenant-General John Glubb 'Pasha', commander of the Arab Legion from 1950 to 1953, and went on to command the 1st Battalion, the Highland Light Infantry before he became Assistant Adjutant General of the Army in 1962. His wartime exploits included service with the BEF in France in 1939 and escape from a prisoner-of-war camp after capture by Germans during heavy fighting on the Greek island of Leros.

Different but hardly less resource was needed in a civilian post involving the placing of clergymen in appropriate parishes. On leaving the army in 1963 Salmon became Assistant Ecclesiastical Secretary to the Lord Chancellor and the Prime Minister, with an office at No. 10 Downing Street. His task was to advise on the appointment of clergy to parishes under the patronage of the Crown and the Lord Chancellor, the Secretary dealing with the more senior appointments to bishoprics and deaneries. A lifelong churchman, married to a daughter of a former Bishop of Guildford, Salmon was ideally suited to the post.

He travelled extensively, consulting churchwardens of several hundred parishes, getting to know local needs and interviewing potential rectors and vicars with sensitivity and skill. Often he would keep in touch with incumbents in a semi-pastoral role, after presenting them to the bishop at the service of institution, and was unfailingly thoughtful and courteous in offering advice. As the clergy became fewer in number and the amalgamation of parishes became more common, bishops also came to regard him as an invaluable source of information about clergy and parishes. His contribution to the life of the Church of England over 13 years was enormous.

31 *Those parsons*

While passing through a small Hertfordshire town during his years as Bishop of St Albans, Robert Runcie noted a leg of pork hanging in the window of a butcher's shop. He asked his driver to stop and to enquire of the butcher whether the bishop might purchase this item. 'Yes, of course,' was the butcher's reply, 'and tell him that he can have the whole bloody pig if he will rid us of our rector.'

32 *The irrepressible Algy*

Algy Greaves was one of Westminster Abbey's most colourful characters as Dean's Verger from 1953 to 1975. The head of a team of 12 vergers, he had a key role in the day-to-day running of the 'floor' of the Royal church, and made a vital contribution to the managing of many great ceremonial occasions. He was involved in the Coronation in 1953 and in the weddings of Princess Margaret, Princess Alexandra and Princess Anne. A dapper figure who moved unobtrusively, he was always in the right place at the right time, and often corrected a ceremonial slip so that it appeared to be part of the prescribed ceremonial. He could also remove the tension from solemn occasions, as when a nervous new Legal Secretary, about to take part in the installation of a canon, was handed the order of service with the comment, 'Here is the race card.'

Greaves was an irrepressible character and some found his sense of humour difficult to accept until they realized that it concealed a heart of gold and that his remarks were usually made with tongue in cheek. But he was perfectly serious in his reply to a BBC interviewer who asked him what he was doing at the moment of the Queen's crowning: 'I was in the crypt,' he said, 'having a Guinness.' This was true since he had no particular duties to perform at that point in the service and popped out for a break.

When during the late 1960s the tourist boom significantly increased the number of visitors to the Abbey, the Dean, Eric Abbott, convened a press conference at which he spoke with his usual eloquence of the deeply spiritual character of the Abbey's welcoming ministry. Next to speak was the Dean's Verger who told us how earlier that morning he had been standing at the Great West Door talking to the Receiver General when a jumbo jet passed overhead. 'There's another 300 buggers on the way, I said.' He added, 'We have about 6,000 persons a day, and about 3,000 at night – the latter being much quieter.' It took the slower journalists a few seconds to realize he was referring to those in their graves in the Abbey.

Unlike some members of his staff, however, Algy was in fact very welcoming to visitors and keen to further the Abbey's role as a tourist attraction as well as a place of worship. He was frequently consulted by those interested in the Abbey's great number of monuments and memorials, and was the last holder of the ancient and long redundant office of Butler to the Dean. On his retirement he vowed never again to set foot within the Abbey walls, believing that his successors should work without his interference. Before he became an Abbey verger his early years were spent as a shoemaker and he was in the wartime Royal Air Force.

33 *May I have your attention, please*

In an attempt to affirm the primary spiritual purpose of their buildings, many cathedral chapters, especially those receiving large numbers of visitors, introduced a brief act of prayer at hourly intervals – less frequently where fewer leaders were available. This proved to be controversial, for a time, since it was argued that the imposition of prayer on so motley a gathering, which included atheists and others who were visiting for no more than historical or artistic reasons, was likely to be unwelcome. I was myself very hesitant about the practice until I went to Westminster Abbey and took a turn on the 'hourly prayers' rota. The experience soon brought me to a more positive assessment. A single sentence of welcome, followed by one prayer, usually for some current human need, then the recital of the Lord's Prayer, a blessing and 'I hope you will enjoy your visit to Westminster Abbey'.

Brevity – no more than two minutes at most – was essential if attention was to be held, and often there would be a word of thanks from visitors who had valued the opportunity to share in the Abbey's work of prayer. A considerable problem arose whenever Victor Pike, a former Chaplain General to the Forces, then Bishop of Sherborne, came for a week's Visitors Chaplaincy duty. A dear man, brimming over with Irish blarney, he often sought to engage the visitors for up to ten minutes, thus leading to a fair amount of chaos when they got on the move again well before his final blessing.

34 Two missionary statesmen

Canon Max Warren was one of the outstanding figures of the twentieth-century church and a missionary statesman of international reputation. Having taken a first in history and theology at Cambridge, he had intended to devote his life to missionary work and went to northern Nigeria in 1927. But within a year he had been struck down by a virulent form of tuberculosis and further overseas work became impossible. During the 1930s therefore he exercised a notable ministry as Vicar of Holy Trinity, Cambridge – the leading evangelical presence in both town and university – but in 1942 he was called, against his initial inclinations, to become General Secretary of the Church Missionary Society.

Wartime travel restrictions made overseas travel virtually impossible, so the next three years were spent in reflection and on the planning of a new post-war, missionary strategy that would enable the CMS and, through Warren's influence on Archbishop Fisher, the Anglican Communion as a whole, to meet the demands of emerging forms of nationalism. Thus it became possible, once the war ended, to encourage and support the development of indigenous, autonomous churches some time before Prime Minister Harold Macmillan discerned 'a wind of change' blowing through Africa. He made extensive annual journeys to these churches where his arrival was eagerly awaited and his wisdom fully employed.

Under Warren's editorship the monthly *CMS Newsletter* provided a substantial contribution to Christian thinking on world affairs and its wide readership extended to the Foreign and Commonwealth Office, overseas embassies and other agencies with international concerns. On his retirement from the CMS in 1963 he spent ten years as a canon of Westminster – an ideal base for an elder statesman of the world church.

It might have been thought impossible to find someone of his calibre and experience to succeed him at the CMS, but there was in fact a ready-made successor within the Society's own organization. John Vernon Taylor, another first-class scholar, had seen missionary service in East Africa and, since 1959, been African Secretary and effectively Warren's right-hand man. He had shared fully in the implementation of the post-war missionary strategy, contributed much new thinking of his own, particularly in a classic book *Primal Vision* (1963) and moreover was equal to the challenge of the *CMS Newsletter*. Thus, under his leadership – he had a quieter, more gentle personality than his predecessor – the CMS continued to adjust to new overseas situations and to offer prophetic insight into the demands of mission in Britain.

On reaching the age of 60 in 1975 Taylor left to become Bishop of Winchester and the first priest to be appointed directly to this senior see since the Middle Ages. He took with him not only his wide vision of the church's missionary role but also the gifts of a preacher, a poet and an actor. He wrote and produced an acclaimed passion play which was broadcast from Winchester Cathedral on television and the missionary spirit never left him. It was therefore regrettable that the management demands of a late twentieth-century diocese inhibited its fullest expression during his ten years at Winchester, though he was an invaluable contributor to the deliberations of the bench of bishops.

35 *A call that went unheeded*

In October 1975, just nine months after his enthronement as Archbishop of Canterbury, Donald Coggan surprised everyone with what he described as 'A Call to the Nation'. This was, he said, addressed to 'all men of goodwill' and it asked individuals and groups to study two questions – What sort of society do we want? What sort of people do we need to be in order to achieve it? At a press conference to launch the campaign, he commented that the country seemed to him to be 'drifting without an anchor' and, since materialism could not halt this, moral and spiritual matters must be considered. A pastoral letter along these lines and signed by himself and Archbishop Stuart Blanch of York was read out in all the churches on the following Sunday.

The media coverage of the Call was enormous and for several days it seemed that Coggan had managed to take control of every television and radio station in the country. By the end of the year he had received 27,000 letters, most of which he read. A team of volunteers at Lambeth Palace despatched a prayer card to all who asked for one – 75,000 in total, since some asked for several copies:

> God bless our nation,
> Guide our rulers,
> Give us your power,
> that we may live cheerfully,
> care for each other,
> and be just in all we do.

Then, almost as quickly as the Call had been prepared for sounding it was over. There seemed nothing substantial for any of its hearers to act upon. In truth, the preparation had been hasty and inadequate, and, apart from Archbishop Blanch, no one had been consulted. He had simply gone along with it. The British Council of Churches was up in arms that such an initiative should have been taken without ecumenical consultation. The Bishop of Southwark, Mervyn Stockwood, somewhat curiously chose to voice his criticism of the Call in the Communist daily newspaper the *Morning Star*.

Besides the lack of preparation and consequent follow-up, the Call presented two problems. The first lay in the fact that if, as the Archbishop said, the nation was 'drifting without an anchor', most people did not wish to hear his questions, but rather his answers: what was to be done about it? The second, pinpointed by Stockwood, related to the fact that complex social, political and economic problems will not be solved by an improvement in individual behaviour ('What sort of people do we need?') since human beings are themselves formed, at least in part, by their social environment. Does the Archbishop have any ideas about the kind of structural changes in society that might be called for?

This futile exercise was an almost classic example of an older-style evangelical approach to life that is not really sensitive to what is happening in society and sees the solution to every kind of problem only in personal categories.

36 Women priests – 'They gave us a stone'

A certain amount of progress towards the ordination of women took place in the 1970s, of which easily the most significant was the decision by the General Synod in July 1975 'that there are no fundamental objections to the ordination of women to the priesthood'. The Lambeth Conference had passed a similar resolution seven years earlier and catholic-minded Archbishop Michael Ramsay had reached the same conclusion. There remained a few High Churchmen who believed, and said, that it was no more possible to ordain a woman than it was to ordain a horse, and some Evangelicals insisted that the Bible forbade women any position of leadership in the church. But, for the most part, the theological debate was over.

The Synod had, however, a second resolution before it in July 1975: 'that legal barriers should be removed and legislation brought forward'. This was rejected, largely on the grounds that 'the time is not ripe for action', by which was meant 'we are fearful of causing division in the church'. The acute disappointment caused by the Synod's apparent volte-face was heightened when in 1978 another attempt was made to bring forward the legislation necessary for the opening of ordination to women and this also failed. When after a tense debate the result of the voting was announced, Una Kroll, a leading advocate of women priests, broke the regulations by calling out from the public gallery of Church House, Westminster, 'We asked for bread and you gave us a stone.' There was shocked silence and some hostility, but television cameras and newspaper photographers carried around the world pictures of a courageous, middle-aged woman, clad in a tee-shirt, making her stand and thus becoming an icon for the growing number of impatient and often angry supporters of her cause.

37 'Success' and circumstances

St Mary's, Ware, the Hertfordshire parish in which I spent just over four happy years (1971–76) and with which I had what Robert Runcie, then Bishop of St Albans, described as a 'love affair', was a good example of the circumstances in which the Church of England could then flourish – and 30 years later still does. An old market town, sitting astride the London-to-Cambridge road, it had a thirteenth- to fourteenth-century church at the end of the High Street which a significant number of local residents had known since their earliest years. Post-war expansion had not fractured the community and ease of access to London had injected into it a good number of middle-class professionals ready to be involved in the life of the church and other town activities.

My predecessor, John Whitley, an able and dynamic priest, had capitalized on this in his rousing of a small, somewhat somnolent congregation to become as lively a Christian community as might be found anywhere. The Parish Communion, a still-strong Evensong, a choir capable of leading cathedral worship, house churches, strong young people's and children's work, close ecumenical relations, good-neighbour schemes, exceptional involvement in the life of the town. It was all there when I arrived and, for a few years anyway, made my own heavy involvement in journalism and broadcasting quite feasible.

At the other end of the town was Christ Church, a powerful evangelical centre which had been a breakaway from St Mary's in the nineteenth century when the wearing of surplices was introduced. Although the combined congregations represented only a small proportion of the total population of abut 5,000, the church's influence extended wide and its ministry was welcomed by many more at baptisms, weddings and funerals, at Christmas and Easter, and on community commemorations and celebrations. A Festival of the Arts attracted thousands. All of which emphasized, yet again, the significance of circumstances in the discharging of the church's mission.

38 Confusion at Winchester

Not since the Middle Ages had there been an appointment to a cathedral chapter such as that which took Emmanuel Armand de Mendieta to Winchester in 1962. He was a Belgian and for most of the past 30 years had been a Benedictine monk of the Abbey of Maredsous, at the time a leading stronghold of Roman Catholicism in Belgium. Moreover, he was a world-famed authority on St Basil of Caesarea, a fourth-century Father of the Eastern Church. He had had, however, an unhappy relationship with his abbot and this problem was dealt with by permitting him to travel widely in pursuit of his studies. It was while attending the first International Conference on Patristic Studies at Oxford in 1951 that he first encountered the Church of England. Christ Church Cathedral, the college, the University Church and the Bodleian Library cast their spell over him, and they were to be enjoyed without interference by abbot or pope, or by a demand for celibacy. In the summer of 1953 he met a young Parisian woman, Ginette, and by June 1956 they were together in England, married, and he a priest of the Church of England.

But how was such a priest – considered by Archbishop Fisher an important 'catch' – to be employed? A spell at St Augustine's College, Canterbury, a recently established Anglican staff college, proved to be useful and further time was bought with a three-year bye-fellowship at Gonville and Caius College, Cambridge. When this ended, however, a more substantial decision as to his future could be delayed no longer, and Fisher persuaded the Bishop of Winchester, Falkner Allison, who was chairman of the church's Foreign Relations Council, to appoint him to a vacant canonry of Winchester.

At first sight this seemed an admirable solution. What could be more appropriate than the presence of a learned former Benedictine in the Close at Winchester? The only difficulty was that, although de Mendieta was fluent in many languages, he knew little English and seemed incapable of improving what he had. His cathedral sermons over the next 14 years were virtually incomprehensible and his particular field of study was so specialized and technical that no more than a few scholars in the entire world might have understood what he was talking about. His inability to distinguish between numbers, such as ten, one hundred and one thousand, and his unworldly ignorance of the realms of administration and finance limited his contribution to chapter meetings and sometimes caused confusion.

His reading of lessons at the services was perplexing and often a source of amusement – 'Joseph's bruzzers vent on zheir own vay. Joseph 'owevair, reemained in goal', or, on the first Easter Day, 'Ze disciples came to ze empty tum'. The announcement of hymns could be no less bewildering: ''ymn numberre two sousand and one eleven [i.e. 211]' or 'ze 'ymn is one souzand and elephant [i.e. 111]'. Nonetheless, the eminent scholar, always deeply engrossed in his books, was much valued and admired by the cathedral community. The portly – eventually almost spherical – figure, known to have an extreme fondness for Dubonnet and milk chocolate, won the affection of many by his geniality, kindness and good humour. His wonderful singing of the Exultet at Easter was worth travelling miles to hear and when in 1976 the tolling of the cathedral bell marked his death in office, there was an awareness that at Winchester the age of Barchester had ended – well, almost.

39 *Turning a blind eye to an illuminating report*

The fourth report of the Doctrine Commission, published in 1976 under the title *Christian Believing*, was worth waiting for. The Archbishops had asked the Commission to look into 'The Nature of the Christian Faith and its Expression in Holy Scripture and Creeds' and it employed an unusual method. It was evident from the start that among the 17 distinguished theologians who constituted the Commission there were some sharp differences of belief. The report which all were prepared to sign was therefore confined to just 42 pages, but these contained important material. On the nature of religious language there was the reminder that language about God or about religious experience cannot adequately express the realities to which it claims to refer. On the Christian and the Bible it was pointed out that right from the very beginning of Christianity, as demonstrated by the New Testament, there was pluriformity of faith, just as there had been in the faith of Israel before it. Moreover, 'the New Testament itself handed on to the church a volume of unfinished business'. On the creeds was the comment that the Christian pursuit of truth has a dynamic character, so that it looks to that which is given, and yet at the same time is ever open to new possibilities of understanding.

There was nothing particularly new about any of this, but it was certainly unusual to find it in an official church report. Faithful to affirmations of pluriformity and openness to new understanding, the report was followed by a series of essays by individual members of the Commission and to which they alone were committed. These contained some very interesting material, not least the contributions from Professors Maurice Wiles, Denis Nineham and Geoffrey Lampe. So interesting that Archbishop Donald Coggan, who had succeeded Michael Ramsey after the Commission was convened, ensured that it was never submitted even for consideration by the General Synod. The church has still to take it seriously.

40 *Myth and belief*

The publication of *The Myth of God Incarnate* in the following year created the kind of furore that is normal whenever someone attempts to say something interesting about Christian doctrine. The book itself consisted of ten essays by a group of professional theologians, all of them Anglican apart from the editor John Hick. Their general concern was to question the traditional language of the doctrine of the incarnation and some suggested that it was best understood in mythological terms. To the theologically uneducated – the vast majority of the interested public – this was taken to mean that the writers believed it to be *untrue*.

The press conference, held in the Chapter House of St Paul's Cathedral, was stormy and it was fascinating to see the hacks of the secular media defending the Nicene Creed, both then and in their headlines the following day. The *Church Times* described the book as 'a notably unconvincing contribution to the cause of unbelief'. The Moderator of the General Assembly of the Church of Scotland called for the resignations of the authors, while the Greek Orthodox Archbishop in London issued a letter accusing them of 'falling prey to an opposition of demonic character'. The Archbishops of Canterbury and York managed to prevent an emergency debate in the General Synod and suggested, not unreasonably, that time was needed for the book to be read. Thirty thousand copies were sold.

41 *New use for rectory gardens*

A row is going on between the Church Commissioners and the Rector of St. Luke's, Tiptree, Essex, because a public convenience has been built in the rectory garden with a plaque which says 'To the Glory of God for the Needs of Man'. Says the Rector, the Revd. Christopher Candler: 'They wouldn't have complained if it was a bus shelter.'

Daily Mail

42 *Coggan in Rome – a plea for inter-communion*

Archbishop Coggan's visit to Pope Paul VI in April 1977 was thought by some observers to have been marked by much less enthusiasm in the Vatican than that accorded to Michael Ramsey 11 years earlier. There was a suggestion that the Anglican Church's growing interest in the ordination of women to the priesthood explained this. But the visit went well enough. The private conversation between the two leaders lasted one hour and twenty-three minutes, which was longer than that with Ramsey and also the talk between Pope John XXIII and Archbishop Fisher. Later they signed a common declaration affirming the work of the International Theological Commission and urging that its reports be considered more widely so that both churches 'may be led along the path towards unity'.

The controversial moment came a few hours after Coggan's meeting with the Pope when he preached at a service in the American Episcopal Church in Rome. The sermon was devoted to the importance of evangelism, which had been discussed at the meeting, and towards the end of it Coggan suggested that joint evangelism might well be seriously weakened 'until we are able to go to that work strengthened by our joint participation in the Sacrament of Christ's Body and Blood'. He added that inter-communion was already common in some places and was likely to increase, therefore in the search for truth 'we can no longer be separated at the Sacrament of Unity. We are all sinners in need of the forgiveness and strength of our Lord. We will kneel together to receive it.'

This was variously interpreted. Some – the media, especially – saw it as a call for immediate inter-communion between the two churches, and there were those who praised the Archbishop's courage in voicing his convictions in Rome. Others believed him to have been naive and tactless, and, in the context of ecclesiastical diplomacy, it was certainly remiss of him not to inform the Vatican in advance of what he proposed to say. A year later Coggan repeated his plea in a sermon in Westminster Cathedral and a month later, in an address to the General Synod (the first ever to be made by a Roman Catholic), Cardinal Basil Hume explained why his church could not accept such a development.

43 A new religious presence in Britain

Between 1955 and 1962 some 260,000 immigrants from the Caribbean entered the United Kingdom, 71,000 of them in 1961 alone. They came by invitation of a government desperate to remedy a labour shortage in largely unskilled, low-paid occupations. But the flow did not cease once the problem had been solved. In spite of legislation – much of it harsh and unjust – designed to control immigration, there were in Britain by the end of the century over 1.1 million people with Caribbean or African antecedents, 2.3 million with Asian, 0.5 million with mixed and 0.6 million with Chinese and other oriental, in total 7.7 per cent of the entire population. In some parts of the country, mainly London and the big cities, this led to a transformation of the make-up of local communities.

The Church of England and all the mainstream churches had a good record in opposing restrictive legislation and defending the rights of ethnic minorities. They were, however, singularly unsuccessful in integrating members of these minorities into their own church life. There were a few exceptions to this and in many places it was possible to find a handful of black faces in congregations, but in general the immigrants, and later their children born here, although usually deeply religious, remained as isolated from the church as from society as a whole.

There were several reasons for this. Those of Asian origin were, apart from a tiny minority, Muslims, Hindus or Sikhs and would eventually establish their own places of worship. The West Indians and Africans included many devout Christians but the Church of England's services, and even those of the Methodist and Baptist churches, seemed to most of them to be unattractive and congregations lacked the warmth of fellowship they had known in their homeland churches. Another factor was that nearly all the mainstream churches were extremely weak in those run-down areas where the immigrants were obliged to settle.

But the newcomers did not leave their faith behind them when they came, neither did they allow it to fade. Instead they planted on British soil upwards of eighty new religious denominations, many of them with exotic names, such as the Mount Carmel True High Way Church of the Apostolic Faith and the Church of Cherubim and Seraphim. Many were Pentecostal, fundamentalist, exceedingly lively, warm and friendly. Before long they outnumbered their local, long-established congregations and became an important Christian presence in areas where churches had previously counted for little.

After some initial problems, the British churches recognized that the new Christian communities had come to stay and that collaboration was called for. This found expression in October 1978 in a joint conference in London of members of black-led and white-led churches, followed by a service in St Paul's Cathedral attended by several thousand people. The sight of a new Dean of St Paul's, Alan Webster, dancing in the central aisle with an exuberant woman from the West Indies suggested that a new era had dawned.

44 On the front line at Brixton

One of the best multi-racial projects in Britain at the beginning of this decade was located in Brixton, South London, which had, and still has, the largest concentration of West Indians in Britain. In poor housing conditions, with unemployment among young blacks as high as 50 per cent and relations between West Indians and the police hostile, urgent action was essential.

St Matthew's Church, built in 1824 as the parish church of Brixton, is a huge neo-classical edifice designed to seat 2,000 people – one of a series of churches erected to commemorate victory at the Battle of Waterloo. By the 1960s the congregation had dwindled to about a hundred who then decided to turn the building into a meeting place for the community as a whole. Twelve other groups, besides St Matthew's, became its joint landlords on a 99-year lease, with a representative management committee to administer the property and the activities taking place within it.

Among those involved at the outset were a foundation for helping the homeless and unemployed black youth, a West Indian women's group, a unit offering alternative schooling for boys, a Pentecostal church, and a community relations council that campaigned for racial justice and equality of opportunity in the area. The entire building soon became a hive of activity and about £500,000, much of it provided by government urban aid, was spent on the adaptation of the building for multi-purpose use. The inspiration for the project came from the Vicar of St Matthew's, Bob Nind, one of the Church of England's most able priests who had spent some years in the West Indies before returning to England to no less important Christian ministry.

45 *Oriental warmth*

When I joined the staff of St Martin-in-the-Fields it never occurred to me that one of my duties during the next six years would be to preach every few weeks to a congregation of about a hundred Chinese Christians. Two years earlier the Revd S. Y. Lee had moved from Hong Kong to London to start a specialist ministry among the Chinese restaurant and laundry workers in Soho, but also with nurses, students, clerks and a handful of tailors. He soon found plenty to do, since his help was needed for a wide variety of social work, including court appearances in the role of interpreter for those in trouble with the law – all based on St Anne's, Soho.

The Sunday afternoon gatherings in the crypt of St Martin's were, and doubtless still are, full of warmth and joy, and wedding banquets of 14 or more courses were specially memorable. The services were conducted in Cantonese and my address was patiently interpreted line by line to the congregation by S. Y. Lee. He had the religious outlook of a nineteenth-century Protestant missionary and I was never wholly convinced that they were allowed to hear what I actually said.

46 A salvo from the Right

Until the closing months of 1977 the name of Dr Edward Norman was hardly known beyond a fairly small circle in Cambridge, where he taught history and was Dean of Peterhouse. But his six Reith Lectures, broadcast at weekly intervals by the BBC, attracted a degree of publicity that no churchman had enjoyed since the days of *Honest to God*. Now it was the turn of an ultra-conservative pietist to capture the headlines.

Norman's basic thesis was a simple one. Religion, he alleged, had been politicized inasmuch as there had been an internal transformation of the Christian faith itself, so that it was now defined in terms of political values. It had substituted social morality for 'the ethereal qualities of immortality' – the temporal had superseded the spiritual. The main agents of this process of politicization, he went on, were the clergy who had allowed themselves, some eagerly and many others unwittingly, to define their religious values according to the categories and references provided by 'the compulsive moralism of contemporary intellectual culture'. As a consequence, 'The Christian religion has lost its power, and also the confidence to define the areas of public debate, even in moral questions. Instead it follows the definitions made by others.'

Most of the lectures were given to demonstrating the supposed truth of this thesis by reference to the situations in South Africa, where he appeared to excuse the government's apartheid policy; in Latin America, where the discontent of the poor was, he believed, attributable to the importing of subversive ideas from Europe and North America; and in the Soviet Union, where the dissidents were dismissed on the grounds that they had been led astray by 'Western liberal concepts of human rights'.

This polemical material, and the naming and denunciation of churchmen who had erred and strayed from Norman's misunderstanding of the Christian faith was well publicized by the BBC. Volumes of essays, courses of lectures and services, radio programmes and special issues of magazines were prepared in order to 'answer' him and it was all very exciting. It also served to allay the fears of those who had heard it rumoured that Norman was soon to be appointed to the Regius Chair of Ecclesiastical History at Oxford. Instead he had to be content with a post at a College of Education in Canterbury, followed by a canonry of

York. He celebrated his retirement from the canonry by announcing that York Minster was an architecturally inferior building and that he intended to become a Roman Catholic, but he had second thoughts about this intention.

47 Anglican–Roman Catholic agreement – so far, so good?

The three agreed statements published by the Anglican–Roman Catholic International Commission – on the Eucharist (1971), the Ministry (1973) and Authority (1976) – were remarkable, not only for the degree of unity expressed, but also, and perhaps chiefly, for the fact that they had been produced at all. Fifteen years earlier they would have been inconceivable and, naturally, their appearance was greeted with enthusiasm and gratitude. Some said that the first was the most important statement since the Reformation for the two churches, and perhaps it was, but it could not be overlooked that the Eucharist was not the primary cause of the original division between them.

The heavyweight theologians who comprised the majority of the Commission ensured that the discussions concentrated on fundamental issues and were not sidetracked by historical developments since the Reformation. This was doubtless responsible for the large measure of agreement reached. They did leave open, however, two particular issues which would be regarded by many as matters of secondary importance, yet these have divided Anglicans and Roman Catholics for centuries and will continue to do so until they are resolved.

The first concerns the status of Anglican Holy Orders: are they valid ministries of the church or are they, as Pope Leo XIII declared in 1896, 'null and utterly void'? The other relates to papal authority, and the agreed statement on this subject not only acknowledged that the Pope would provide the headship of a united church, but went on to declare that he, as well as church Councils, had the authority to define dogma. Moreover, the Councils were protected from error. This was surprising and I wondered if the Anglican members of the Commission were having a siesta at this point in the deliberations.

48 Woman priest breaks the rules

The visit of two American women priests to England in 1978 attracted a good deal of publicity and, in the case of the first of them, some controversy. The Revd Alison Palmer, of Washington DC, not only preached in various places but also presided at celebrations of the Eucharist in a Manchester parish church and in the University Church at Newcastle-upon-Tyne. This was irregular on two counts: she had not been authorized to officiate at the services by the bishops of the two dioceses concerned and, indeed, could not have been so authorized since the Church of England had refused to ordain women to the priesthood.

The Archbishop of Canterbury and the Bishops of Manchester and Newcastle – all of whom wished to see women ordained – issued statements recognizing the strong feelings of the churches concerned but deploring the breaking of the law and lack of respect for the mind of the Church of England as a whole. With less delicacy the *Church Times* drew a parallel between the priests involved and some German terrorists who were at the same time holding 86 people hostage on an airliner in the Middle East, while the editor of the *Church of England Newspaper*, unrestrained by Christian charity, described Alison Palmer as 'a cow in a china shop'. Others used her actions as an excuse for a general denunciation of all who wished to see women ordained.

Many of those who favoured women priests believed that her presidency at the Eucharist had been a tactical mistake, but the council of the University Church in Newcastle, which held three meetings, including one with the bishop, before deciding to extend an invitation to Alison Palmer, faced the question of what would have been appropriate action had the Church of England maintained a rule forbidding a black male priest from presiding at the Eucharist? There seemed to them to be only one possible answer.

49 A first at Westminster Abbey

Mary Michael Simpson, an ordained nun and a canon of the Cathedral of St John the Divine in New York, declined an invitation to preside at a Eucharist in a Cambridge college chapel, but her acceptance of my invitation to preach in Westminster Abbey drew massive media attention, she being the first woman priest to preach there. Her sermon was unremarkable inasmuch as she chose not to preach about the ordination issue and instead delivered what proved to be a first-class sermon on the nature and meaning of God's love. Her appearance in the Abbey's pulpit did, however, create a little local difficulty. When the possibility of her preaching was first mooted this related to a Sunday when Bishop Edward Knapp-Fisher was Canon-in-Residence and he, strongly opposed to the ordination of women, did not feel able to extend the necessary invitation to her. Then, for totally unrelated reasons, her visit to England was postponed, and the new date turned out to be within my month of Residence, and I, deeply involved in the Movement for the Ordination of Women, naturally offered her the pulpit. My freedom to do this was readily acknowledged in Chapter, though my freedom to allow television cameras into the Abbey was questioned. The occasion was, in fact, hardly controversial, since even laypeople were allowed to preach in the Abbey and there was no reason to exclude a woman priest.

50 Remarriage in church of the divorced – long delays

By the mid-1970s pressure was on the Church of England, from both inside and outside its own active ranks, to modify its attitude to the remarriage in church of individuals who may have had a previous marriage legally dissolved. The divorce rate in Britain had risen dramatically – from 25,000 in 1961 to 121,000 in 1975 – and was still rising. Yet the Church of England still had the most rigorous marriage discipline in Christendom. The Orthodox Church had for centuries been prepared to remarry the divorced, so had the British Free Churches and, although the Roman Catholic Church taught the indissolubility of marriage, it often found ways of applying its nullity procedures to 'deserving' cases. The Church of England lacked any means of mitigating its uncompromising stand and there were those who argued that in circumstances of wholesale marriage breakdown it was more than ever necessary for the highest standards to be upheld. It was this argument that led to the rejection by the General Synod in 1973 of the proposals of a commission headed by Professor Howard Root which would, in certain carefully controlled circumstances, have permitted second marriages in church.

The subject would not, however, go away. Parish clergy were in increasing numbers finding it intolerable that in their pastoral dealings with those embarking on a second marriage, sometimes members of their own congregations, they could do no more than offer a simple and almost secret service of blessing after a civil ceremony or refer them to one of the local Free Churches. Laypeople who increasingly experienced divorce in their own families or among their friends were unable to understand why the church should refuse its ministry at a point where there was both need and opportunity. There was also the fact that the clergy had the right, in civil law, to officiate at the marriages of all, including the divorced, who were duly qualified and, although this was frowned on by bishops, there were clear signs that many more would exploit this freedom if the church did not change its rules.

A new marriage commission was therefore set up by the Archbishops of Canterbury and York in 1975, this time under the chairmanship of the Bishop of Lichfield, Kenneth Skelton, who in the previous decade had fought a courageous battle against the racist rebel Smith regime in what was then Rhodesia. This reported in 1978 and endorsed more or less the recommendations of the earlier Root Commission, namely that a divorced person should, with the permission of the bishop, be allowed a second marriage. What is more, the custom of excommunicating the divorced who remarried until the bishop authorized their readmission to communion should be brought to an end, and a bishop should have the discretion to ordain a man who, having been divorced, remarried or who had married a divorced woman.

All of which would involve radical changes of policy, and the General Synod again rejected the proposals, though this time by a much smaller number of votes. It was not until the 1990s, and after much pressure from Archbishop Runcie throughout his time at Canterbury, that the church's rules were revised along the lines recommended by the two reports. By this time the blessing of civil marriages, often in forms barely distinguishable from the authorized marriage service, had become commonplace. The annual national divorce rate was now in excess of 150,000.

51 *Mind who you kiss*

I find the Revd. E. J. Edmundson's protest about footballers kissing each other very amusing in view of the fact that the Archbishop of Canterbury kissed in public both His Holiness the Pope and His Beatitude the Patriarch of the Romanian Orthodox Church.

Letter in *Ipswich Evening Star*

52 *Lambeth Conference does no harm*

The 1978 Lambeth Conference was held in Canterbury rather than London and, also for the first time, was residential. This helped to create a closer sense of identity and common purpose and Archbishop

Coggan saw to it that the Bible study was of high quality. Unfortunately he took much less trouble over the preparation of the Conference and the lack of an input of substantial material meant that the bishops did not get to grips with any of the major theological and ethical issues of the day. The hymns at the services were accompanied by the Archbishop on a piano.

The most important issue on the internal agenda concerned the ordination of women to the priesthood – an issue over which there were still differences of belief and practice. As they were assembling, the bishops found themselves faced with a barrage fired by the Cardinal Archbishop of Westminster, the Patriarch of the Russian Orthodox Church and a representative of the Greek Orthodox Church, all of whom said, with varying degrees of politeness, that if the Lambeth Conference approved the ordination of women, or facilitated the ordination of more of them (there were already upwards of 100 in the United States, Canada, New Zealand and Hong Kong), this would damage relations with their respective churches.

Most of the bishops regarded this as unwarranted interference, rather than as honest comment, and in the final stages of the Conference a proposal that there should be a 'pause' of five years before any more women were ordained in the Anglican Communion was rejected by about two to one. Instead, they agreed that differences of belief and practice should not be allowed to destroy the underlying unity of faith and worship – a sound Anglican position.

They also agreed that war and violence were bad things and in an 'Appeal to the World' urged greater justice and generosity in matters relating to the development and distribution of the world's resources. A strong call for greater Anglican involvement in the life of the World Council of Churches, and a positive encouragement to Anglican provinces to enter into unity schemes with other churches wherever this might be possible, both went unheeded. And nothing came of an informal suggestion that the next Conference should be held outside the British Isles.

53 A country scholar-parson

Arthur Tindall Hart, the twentieth century's foremost historian of the English clergy, was one of the last of their number who could find fulfilment in the ministry of a country parson and at the same time pursue the vocation of a scholar. Having been ordained to a curacy in

Herne Bay by Archbishop Cosmo Gordon Lang in 1932, the remainder of his ministry was spent in small rural parishes in Northamptonshire, Oxfordshire and Sussex. He died in 1993.

His particular skill as a historian lay in an ability to unearth contemporary accounts of the clergy – many of them highly entertaining – and relate these to the broader movement of events in the church. *The Nineteenth-Century Country Parson* (1954) was a joint work with Edward Carpenter of Westminster Abbey, and marked the beginning of a series of books on the clergy of each of the post-Reformation centuries written by himself.

The Curate's Lot (1970) was a subtle mixture of humour and sadness and, although he made much of the eccentricities of the clergy, he was always quick to point out that the overwhelming majority of them in every period exercised quiet, diligent ministries which were an influence for good in English society. He had, however, a much less exalted view of bishops and, unsurprisingly, deplored the development of rural group and team ministries when they first appeared in the late 1950s.

54 *The Coventry evangelist*

The retirement in 1976 of Cuthbert Bardsley from the bishopric of Coventry, which he had occupied for 20 years, removed from the bench its most personable member. Tall, handsome, always immaculately turned out, a rich voice, great enthusiasm and every inch an Old Etonian, his was at one time a household name. During his time as Suffragan Bishop of Croydon he had been a popular radio broadcaster and his key role in the consecration of the rebuilt Coventry Cathedral in 1962 – seen by millions on television – proved ample, some thought too much, scope for his sense of theatre.

Of the significance of his contribution to the renewal of the life of that cathedral and its diocese there cannot be the slightest doubt. By the time he succeeded the godly eccentric, Neville Gorton, in 1956, Basil Spence's new building was rising from the ashes of the old and a new Provost and Chapter would also be required. In a masterstroke he appointed Bill Williams as Provost, Joseph Poole and Edward Patey as canons, then Simon Phipps as Industrial Chaplain and Stephen Verney as Diocesan Missioner.

This brilliant team created a new expression of cathedral life which soon influenced all the other English cathedrals and some overseas. Meanwhile, he concentrated his attention on the diocese and led a programme of preparation for the consecration which enlivened the parishes. Earlier, after an unfortunate spell on the staff of Moral Rearmament that ended in a breakdown, he had been a notable wartime Rector of Woolwich, the youngest-ever Provost of Southwark Cathedral, where he encouraged the teenage Eric James to seek ordination, and a hugely popular Bishop to the Armed Forces. He was 'good with men' and took over the chairmanship of the Church of England Men's Society during the final phase of its existence. Following his retirement, this soon closed down.

Although Bardsley forged close links with the industries of South London during his ministry, had good contacts with Midlands industrialists, and often spoke about social affairs, his faith and preaching were of the personal sort and there was something of the Puritan about him. Old-time evangelism was his highest priority and he conducted many crusades and missions in England and overseas. He was one of the few bishops who supported Billy Graham's Greater London Crusade in 1966 and called on a crowd of 100,000 at Wembley Stadium to 'thank God for raising up a man who has shown us how great are our capacities as a nation to respond to the challenge to live and work for God and the service of others'.

In the cause of journalism I twice attended his own 'Call to Mission', which packed Coventry Cathedral for ten nights and was relayed by closed-circuit television to other churches in the city in 1968. The Provost pointedly absented himself from the whole enterprise. There was, however, none of the extravagance of a Graham Crusade, though we were subjected to interviews with famous cricketers and actors before the bishop's address.

I treasure a cutting from the *Guardian* relating to an encounter in November 1967 between Bardsley and Godfrey Winn, a sickeningly sentimental and hugely popular journalist of the time:

> Godfrey Winn sat there blowing kisses to some of his admirers – the ballroom at the Dorchester was full of titled and hyphenated ladies – and chatting with the Bishop of Coventry, Dr. Cuthbert Bardsley, who later said Mr. Winn followed the example of Jesus Christ and was very important as a prophet of the fact that all was not yet lost.

4

The Confrontational Eighties

Standing on the doorstep of 10 Downing Street following her election victory in 1979, Margaret Thatcher incongruously recited a prayer wrongly attributed to St Francis – 'Lord, make me an instrument of thy peace. Where there is hatred, let us sow love; where there is injury, pardon; where there is discord, union . . .' Her prayer was not answered and she became the most confrontational, divisive, socially injurious Prime Minister of the twentieth century. And throughout the 1980s she dominated the British political scene by a combination of personality and courageous determination. It was the 'Iron Lady's' belief that the country's economic and social woes owed everything to the adoption by successive post-war governments of a moderate form of socialism that had inhibited enterprise and discouraged personal responsibility. Recovery demanded therefore a radical change to marketplace economics, less state involvement in industry and the utilities and more enterprise all round. In retrospect this is widely recognized as having been a necessary revolution, but the cost at the time was heavy for many individuals and communities – over four million unemployed, many communities in the North East and Merseyside destroyed, leaving their citizens without hope and public services starved of funds.

It was because the church was more aware than most of the price being paid that it mounted what became a serious critique of government policy. The weakness of the Labour Party throughout the 1980s gave this a greater significance than it might otherwise have had and in the end rendered a notable service to the nation. Robert Runcie, who was at Canterbury throughout this decade, was not a natural politician, but made a number of important statements, as did the analytically minded John Habgood of York. David Jenkins became the mouthpiece of the suffering Durham mining community, while David Sheppard, working in partnership with his Roman Catholic colleague, spoke for Merseyside. The Board of Social Responsibility produced several first-

class studies that were largely ignored, but the report of an Archbishop's Commission Faith in the City *attracted massive attention as well as the great displeasure of the government. Besides all the spoken and written words there were in the worst affected areas important church projects dealing constructively with local problems.*

Within the church itself differences of opinion were becoming no less sharp, particularly over the issue of women priests. The machinations of the Bishop of London, Graham Leonard, who led the opposition to them, were not helpful to rational debate or unity. It was often suggested that many thousands of clergy would leave the Church of England if women were to be ordained, and although this proved in the end to be no more than sabre-rattling (only a few hundred left) it was an ugly threat at the time. The rise and growing confidence of the evangelical movement also exposed the existence of divisions, not only over various ethical matters, of which homosexuality was the most pressing, but also over biblical interpretation and broader theological insights. The Evangelicals did not, however, threaten to walk out of the church, and the memory of Pope John Paul II's presence in Canterbury was a cheering reminder that there is no place for the word 'impossible' in the Christian vocabulary.

1 *Robert Runcie*

Of the five Archbishops of Canterbury of my 50-year ministry, Robert Runcie was the one I knew best and the one for whom I had the greatest sympathy in his tackling of what has long been acknowledged to be an impossible job which nonetheless someone has to undertake. He was in a sense the first modern archbishop, for he was not ordained until 1950 – we were both curates in the North East at the same time – and his ideas and presuppositions were those of the post-war era. Although he laid no claim to deep theological learning, having read classics at Oxford, he was highly intelligent, urbane, witty, inclined to be disparaging about himself without really meaning it, and exceedingly good company.

I said in a radio interview on the morning of his appointment in 1980 that he was the best of a poor field. Which was more unkind than untrue, because during his decade in office he stood head and shoulders above most of his contemporaries on the bench. It was his great misfortune (and he knew it) to be called to the archbishopric at a time when the Church of England was rent by serious divisions and when relations between church and state were at a low ebb. Thus his leadership was frequently rejected by factions in the church and his opinions were often attacked by people with political axes to grind, not least in the Cabinet led by Margaret Thatcher. The media, becoming increasingly hostile to all traditional institutions, gave him a rough time and during his early months at Lambeth singled out his wife Lindy for specially cruel treatment.

Had he been a churchman of strong prophetic views and of a crusading spirit all this might not have greatly troubled him. Had he been a churchman of detached spirituality the criticisms would have been absorbed or scarcely noticed. But he was in fact a moderate leader of pragmatic disposition who lived in a constant tension between the demands of a liberal mind and a conservative heart: a thoroughly Christian man who did not lack courage, as his wartime army record convincingly demonstrated, but who liked to be liked, and who deep down preferred the quiet life to the rough and tumble of public affairs. He found most appreciation and tranquillity when visiting the other churches of the Anglican Communion, where he was much admired.

The major church issue of his Primacy concerned the ordination of women to the priesthood. He took the line that, while there were no theological reasons against women priests, it was not expedient for them to be ordained until the main branches of the Christian church had reached a common mind on the matter. This greatly displeased the growing number of supporters of the move to ordain women, who accused him of advocating a delay that might last for centuries, but it can be argued that he held the Church of England, and indeed the whole of the Anglican Communion, together at a critical time. When under the influence of his successor, George Carey, the General Synod voted in favour of women priests in 1992, he declared himself converted to the cause.

Two high points of his Lambeth years were the *Faith in the City* report and the visit of Pope John II to Canterbury, and two low, painful points were the *Crockford's* affair, for which he had not the slightest responsibility, and the detention in Beirut of Terry Waite, whose exploits he became unable to control. A serious mistake was made a few weeks before he laid down the burden of office in 1991 when he invited Humphrey Carpenter, the son of a former Bishop of Oxford and a professional writer, to undertake his biography. Instead of the expected carefully researched volume, Carpenter resorted to the tape recorder and reproduced from interviews with Runcie a good deal of indiscreet material, including revelations of private conversations with the Prince and Princess of Wales, which had never been intended for publication.

There was a violent public storm when the book was published, instalments having appeared in *The Times* on five successive days, and he felt badly betrayed. On seeing the completed work he told Carpenter, 'I have done my best to die before this book is published,' but he lived on until 13 July 2000 and served as an honorary assistant bishop in his former diocese of St Albans where some of the happiest years of his ministry had been spent.

2 *What might you being doing here?*

On Mayday 1980 Robert Runcie came to Westminster Abbey to preside over the consecration of some new bishops and, since it was his first appearance in the Abbey, he was taken first into Jerusalem Chamber where, in accordance with custom, the Dean and Chapter formally protested at his coming. The origin of 'Protest' goes back to the Middle Ages, when the Pope exempted some of the major Benedictine abbeys in Europe from local episcopal jurisdiction and made them answerable to himself alone. At the sixteenth-century Reformation Henry VIII allowed Westminster's exemption to remain, the only difference being that the

Abbey henceforth related directly to the Crown, rather than to the Pope. Hence the official description of the Abbey as a Royal Peculiar and its continuing independence of any ecclesiastical jurisdiction. The 'Protest' asserts this freedom.

It is obviously now something of an anomaly, since relations between the Abbey and the Archbishop are invariably cordial, though it has its uses, as for example on Commonwealth Day and once when permission to consecrate a 'flying bishop' was refused. For Runcie we decided to remove the bleakest phraseology of the 'Protest' and follow it with an expression of warm welcome. But he seemed distinctly unamused, though this may have been no more than irritation at the diversion from a more solemn event.

3 Welcoming an authorized interloper

The appearance of the Alternative Services Book in 1980, this being the first entirely new Church of England liturgical volume since the 1662 Book of Common Prayer, was in a sense a non-event, since all the material in it had been widely used, experimentally, in booklet form for several years. The significance of its appearance lay in the fact that the period of experimentation was now officially ended, and the separate services bound together with hard covers. Although the price of the 1,293 pages was by no means cheap, half a million copies were sold between the beginning of November and the end of the year, with the printing presses struggling to meet a rising demand.

But not everyone was equally enthusiastic. As was to be expected, quite a lot of people preferred the Book of Common Prayer and, although there were few parishes where this was not retained in some form – usually at the 8 a.m. Holy Communion and almost always at Mattins and Evensong – anguish and anger sometimes led to the accusation that the new book was being foisted on a reluctant laity by a dictatorial clergy.

Some of the opponents were nothing if not articulate, and when Professor David Martin collected over six hundred signatures for a petition addressed to the General Synod, expressing concern that the Book of Common Prayer might disappear, he was supported by a substantial part of the English cultural establishment, including a number of avowed atheists. A Prayer Book Society was formed to keep this issue alive and remains active, though its membership is small and predominantly elderly.

4 *The verger's lot*

The lot of the verger improved considerably, though not in most places sufficiently, during the five decades, and the work of the Guild of Vergers encouraged a professionalism and an increased pride in one of the church's key lay ministries. At the same time a very large proportion of the smaller parish churches lost the services of a verger, the position having for so long been undervalued and underpaid. So the verger's duties were taken over on an ad hoc basis by churchwardens and other members of the congregation, and often enough on weekdays, by the vicar. But the loss was much more than functional.

THE VERGER

Blackgowned, he hands out books and rings the bell
   At set times changes
Frontals and hymn boards, keeps the ewer well
Refilled for Baptisms, brings up the rear
Solemnly, at altar-rail often arranges
   Twin hassocks where
The wedding couples kneel; collects the fee
At funerals; is so diligent that he's
Been you might think, a pillar all his life
   Of this small place.
But when he turned landlubber for his wife
He scarce recalled the boy who left for ever
Home by its firs and fiords for wider space,
   A Viking rover.
Oceans and ports became his lesson-book.
Much scanning taught the unastonished look
That still inhabits bleached and rheumy eyes,
   Has carved a face
Figure-head, almost, calm, beyond surprise
Or passion: far too old now to expect
Anything new, he goes his steady pace,
   And all respect
His dogged independence, being one
By nature who best finds himself alone.
Soon from this placid harbour he will make
   One voyage more.
As he speeds others so he too must take
That final journey in a strange craft, ride

Folded and silent towards a foreign shore
  On a dark tide,
Whose voyages not even he who's so
Familiar with all seven seas can know.

Sybil Birch

5   Controversy over London and Durham – all quiet elsewhere

Of the 36 episcopal appointments to English dioceses during the 1980s only 2 attracted much attention and both caused some controversy. The translation of Graham Leonard from Truro to London in 1981 involved what appeared to be a good deal of skullduggery and his tenure of this important bishopric proved to be less than happy. David Jenkins's appointment to Durham caused little comment when first announced but his remarks on the Virgin birth and the resurrection in a television interview soon afterwards caused a sensation.

The vacancy at Durham was created by the translation of John Habgood (who should have gone to London) to be Archbishop of York – a post he later described as 'the best in the Church of England'. Another theologian who became a bishop was John Austin Baker who went to Salisbury in 1982 and, besides his chairmanship of the Doctrine Commission, proved to be a surprisingly radical commentator on social and political matters.

Two years earlier Ronald Bowlby, with whom I worked closely on Teesside, was translated from Newcastle to Southwark as successor to Mervyn Stockwood. The contrast could hardly have been greater, but Bowlby's diligent and sensitive pastoral approach became greatly valued in a diocese soon to be enlarged by the incorporation of Croydon, which had previously been in Canterbury diocese. He was also a leading figure in the Movement for the Ordination of Women. In 1984 Keith Sutton, another godly bishop with much African experience and enough scholarship to be Principal of Ridley Hall, Cambridge, was translated from the suffragan bishopric of Kingston-on-Thames to Lichfield. In this large and most demanding of dioceses, the long and severely disabling illness of his wife made his 19-year stay both remarkable and heroic.

In 1987 Richard Harries began another long ministry – at Oxford – and became a much respected authority on a number of social questions, particularly in the expanding field of medical ethics. He was also the longest-running contributor to the BBC's 'Thought for the Day' radio feature and never became stale. Sadly, there were again a number of casualties: Geoffrey Paul, a devout and learned Evangelical at Bradford, and Stuart Cross, former BBC producer, hymn-writer and pastor at Blackburn, both died in office. Michael Whinney, a great-great-grandson of Charles Dickens and an Evangelical, was driven by stress to resign from Southwell after only three years in office. He recovered later to become an assistant bishop in Birmingham diocese.

6 Getting 'em to church

Our new oil-fired central heating system is now installed and working well. Our new motto must now be, 'Go to church, save fuel.'

Contact *parish magazine*

Whenever you are going by the church, open the door and walk in. If you can sit there for five minutes, so much the better. It is more than likely that what you do will be pointless, but in fact it may well be just what is needed to frighten away potential thieves and vandals.

Wirksworth Parish Magazine

7 A dynamic and compassionate nun

Helen House, the internationally famous children's hospice, was founded by Sister Frances Dominica, a dynamic and compassionate nun who was born into a middle-class professional family, went to Cheltenham Ladies' College, then trained as a nurse at Great Ormond Street Hospital for Sick Children in London. Soon after the completion of her training, however, she went on a parish pilgrimage to the Marian shrine at Walsingham and while there felt called to the religious life.

Against the strongly expressed wishes of her parents she entered the Society of All Saints Sisters of the Poor, Oxford, and in due course was professed as a member of the order founded in the nineteenth century for, as its name indicates, work among the poor. It now has a drop-in centre for the homeless, a home for the elderly, in which Archbishop Michael Ramsay spent his last days, and facilities for retreats and conferences. Soon after her election as Mother of the convent in 1977, she was approached for help by the mother of a child named Helen who was in the Radcliffe Infirmary with a massive brain tumour and not expected to live for long. In the event she survived, but required constant care at home.

In February 1980 Mother Frances Dominica conceived the idea of a special hospice for respite care for very sick children, small enough to reproduce as closely as possible the atmosphere of a family home. She raised £1 million and in November 1982 Helen House, with eight beds, was opened on spare land in the grounds of the convent. This aroused wide interest and, besides her involvement in the work of the hospice, she spoke about the concept in medical circles in other parts of the country. By the end of the century some forty similar hospices had been established, and later Douglas House – a hospice for young people over the age of 16 – was built in the grounds of the convent.

Once Helen House was fully established, she relinquished responsibility for its day-to-day running and, while visiting a rudimentary children's hospital in Ghana, encountered Kojo, a 10-month-old boy who had been abandoned by his mother, and, weighing no more than just over 8 pounds, seemed unlikely to survive. Frances arranged for him to be flown to England and to her convent. There, having ceased to be Mother in 1989, she moved into a separate house across the road, cared for him, eventually adopted him and now combines the religious life with that of a different kind of mother.

8 Women priests – the long haul

Following the General Synod's adverse decision about women priests in 1978 a Movement for the Ordination of Women was formed to begin what was to be a long and increasingly influential campaign to secure a favourable vote. I served on its interim committee but, once established with Stanley Booth-Clibbon, Bishop of Manchester, as Moderator, and Margaret Webster as General Secretary, it was evident that the scale of activity required was incompatible with my other commitments. Over the next 14 years a wide variety of imaginative activity was created – demonstrations, lobbying, literature, local groups, regional and diocesan meetings, vigils, protests and always close contact with the media. More bishops became members and the recruitment of substantial numbers of laymen and priests ensured that it could not be dismissed as 'merely a women's movement'.

In July 1980 Monica Furlong, always a leading member and the second Moderator, went with seven other members to the Petertide ordination at St Paul's Cathedral and held up banners asking for women's ordination. Despite their silence and general decorum they were driven out of the cathedral and one of them was struck repeatedly by a sidesman. The resulting publicity was invaluable and the event was evidence of a tension which always existed in the movement between those who, as in the Women's Suffrage Movement 70 years earlier, favoured robust action and those who favoured a more subtle approach to the changing of hearts and minds in the General Synod.

The movement was given a warmer reception at Westminster Abbey in January 1984 when a special Eucharist was held to mark the fortieth anniversary of the ordination in Hong Kong of Florence Li Tim Oi. Her ordination, deemed irregular and for many years rejected by the rest of the Anglican Communion, had taken place during the darkest days of the 1939–45 war as a desperate measure by the Bishop of Hong Kong. Now both he and Florence were present in Westminster Abbey to share in a celebration that worked wonders for the morale of MOW.

This was needed, since there were still difficult obstacles to be overcome. The presence in England of Florence Li Tim Oi and, from time to time, other women priests who had been ordained overseas, raised the question of whether or not they might be allowed to act as priests while in England. In spite of the fact that the deanery and diocesan synods favoured their acceptance, the General Synod decreed in 1986 that they were forbidden. A sense of outrage among their supporters followed, and soon it became common for visiting women priests to celebrate the Eucharist – usually, but not always, at private gatherings of MOW members and others.

9 A woman's place . . .

A warning to servers not to shun churches and priests where female severs are used is given in the current issue of *The Server*, the quarterly magazine of the Guild of Servants of the Sanctuary. The Revd. Arthur Whitehead, Warden of the Guild and Vicar of St. Mary Magdalene's, Munster Square, London, writes in the magazine: 'We see no reason to change the rules of the Guild in order to admit women and girls. This would be a far-reaching step, and, as yet, it has not become an issue of such importance as to make it either desirable or necessary.' He points out that there are very few places where women and girls do serve at the altar, and stresses that it would be very unwise for the Guild to panic into making a definite pronouncement.

Church Times

I deplore the C. of E.'s attitude towards women in the church, even on probation. Imagine a woman preaching a sermon. She wouldn't be able to stop. A woman's place is in the home, and this is even more true on Sundays, when we expect to get back from church to a nice hot lunch.

Letter in *Daily Sketch*

10 *Ten propositions for unity too many*

The failure of the Anglican–Methodist unity scheme led quite quickly to far more ambitious proposals for the uniting of all the main English churches. A Churches Unity Commission, representing all these churches, including the Roman Catholic, was formed in 1974 and two years later produced a plan consisting of Ten Propositions designed to bring them into a federal, rather than an organic relationship. These included mutual recognition of membership as being within the Body of Christ and of the ministries as being 'true ministries of word and sacraments in the Holy Catholic Church', with the Free Churches accepting episcopacy for the future. There would be mutually acceptable rites of initiation and all church members would be welcome to receive Holy Communion, without condition, in the participating churches.

A Churches Council for Covenanting submitted these proposals to the churches for comment in June 1980, but the responses were mixed. There was no possibility of the Roman Catholics accepting them and the Baptists also said no. The Methodists said they would accept provided the Church of England did so, and the United Reformed Church (recently inaugurated) said Yes, subject to the resolving of certain questions about the role of bishops.

The General Synod considered the matter in July 1982, aware that three of its leading members who had been on the Council for Covenanting had dissociated themselves from its proposals. There was also uncertainty expressed by Archbishop Runcie who declared that he would vote in favour but then voiced a number of serious criticisms. The interchangeability of ministries (these included women in some of the other churches) was his chief problem and he said later that this was 'the rock on which the covenant foundered'. And founder it did, but only just. All but two of the bishops voted for it, the laity produced the required two-thirds majority, leaving the clergy once again to scupper a unity scheme because of minority opposition within their ranks.

It has sometimes been said that had Runcie given a firmer lead the

General Synod might well have given its assent, but this seems doubtful as much opposition to it had been voiced in the dioceses and it was altogether too ambitious for the Church of England at that time to accept. The rejection signalled the end of serious unity negotiations for the remainder of the century.

11 *Did it really happen?*

The sight, on television, of the Pope and the Archbishop of Canterbury sharing in a service in Canterbury Cathedral in 1982 was so extraordinary as to be unbelievable. It was the first ever visit of a Pope to Britain and, notwithstanding that Roman Catholics had over several centuries affirmed their own status as the 'one, true church of Christ', there was John Paul II standing side by side with Archbishop Runcie in the mother church of the Anglican Communion. And, in the course of an imaginatively devised act of worship, he read the Gospel, following the reading of the Epistle by the Archbishop, and besides sharing in prayer embraced the other bishops present. Surely there was some mistake? Had the Vatican in its approval of the Pope's visit realized what the implications of his entry into Canterbury Cathedral might be? They were considerable and the event was easily the most memorable item in his programme.

A misunderstanding certainly occurred at a reception for the Pope held in Cardinal Hume's house in Westminster. I was among the large number invited to this and appropriately was allocated to a room reserved for members of other churches. In due course the Pope was ushered in and, having been handed a piece of paper, addressed us on the importance of money-raising. This seemed decidedly odd until we discovered that the room next door had been allocated to church treasurers and financiers. These had doubtless heard something edifying on the importance of church unity. All very amusing, but possibly less so for our hosts who were left by the papal visit with a debt of several million pounds and needed every penny they could lay their hands on.

12 *Wide vision at Liverpool*

During the early years of his ministry, Edward Patey was prominent among the young priests who declared further church building to be both undesirable and unnecessary. It was ironic therefore – though not without precedent in the Church of England – that he should have been appointed Dean of Liverpool in 1964 when two more bays and an entire west front were needed to complete Giles Gilbert Scott's massive cathedral.

After 60 years of building and constant fundraising, Liverpool had become weary in well-doing, but Patey, who had played an important part in the life of the rebuilt Coventry Cathedral, now recognized the importance of a cathedral's role and believed that faithfulness to those who had contributed so much over so many years to the building at Liverpool required the task to be completed. An appeal for £500,000 was then launched. The final stages of the building were beset by practical problems and when the Queen arrived for the service of dedication in 1978 it was still not fully completed. Three years later another appeal was needed to clear the debt.

All of which was a serious distraction from what Patey regarded as his 'real job'. This was to make Liverpool Cathedral a dynamic centre of worship and mission at a time when the image of the city itself had changed: from an important seaport to become the home of the Beatles and a heartland of football. He was a serious thinker with outstanding gifts as a communicator and a great flair for turning local and national concerns into major events centred on the cathedral. Far from being daunted by the vast nave, Patey used it to include in the centenary celebration of Liverpool's YMCA a wartime canteen and a football match – part of a dramatic presentation of the Association's history. A boxing ring was erected for a children's service on the theme 'Fight the good fight of faith', and various manifestations of evil were dealt knock-out blows by boxers representing faith. A congregation of chiropodists was surprised to be addressed by the Dean on the text, 'If your foot offends you, cut it off.'

In his final year at Liverpool (1982) he arranged a Festival of Peace, attended by 3,000 young people, in memory of Liverpool's most famous musician John Lennon; a memorial service for Bill Shankly, the celebrated manager of Liverpool Football Club; and a service to greet Pope John Paul II during his memorable visit to Britain.

13 *And an episcopal partnership*

David Sheppard's outstanding career as a cricketer – he was among the best of his generation – was more than matched by his achievements as Bishop of Liverpool from 1975 to 1997. He first played for England when he was an undergraduate at Trinity Hall, Cambridge, and during this time he also had a deep evangelical experience that led to ordination and a curacy at St Mary's, Islington in North London. This made him specially conscious of the wide gap between the church and the working class and of the injustice suffered by many in the inner cities. Success as warden of the Mayflower Family Centre in Canning Town, in London's East End, led Bishop Mervyn Stockwood to invite him to succeed John Robinson as Bishop of Woolwich, where he won the affection of the black community. He also wrote a substantial book, *Built as a City* (1974), and entered the realm of controversy by advocating the bringing together of all development land under public ownership and the absorption of public schools (he had himself been at Sherborne) into the state educational system.

When Stuart Blanch was translated to the Archbishopric of York in 1975 Sheppard was his obvious successor at Liverpool. Not long after his arrival, Merseyside found itself in an acute economic and social crisis. The decline of the port and its associated commerce led to widespread unemployment and the dislocation of community life. Racial tension became high and there were destructive riots at Toxteth and other deprived inner-city areas. Sheppard recognized immediately the need for all the churches to work together in their response to this situation and he established a close, remarkable partnership with Derek Worlock, the Roman Catholic Archbishop of Liverpool, whose appointment had quickly followed his own.

They spoke to each other on the telephone every evening and enjoyed such a close relationship that one Liverpool wag, seeing them walk down Hope Street, which links the city's two cathedrals, said, 'It's time you two got married.' Their partnership, shared with the Free Church leaders, brought about an astonishing change of atmosphere in what had previously been one of the most religiously divided communities in the United Kingdom. They devoted much time to social problems and tackled the city council for its partisan stance and lack of vision. They also identified themselves closely with the poorest sections of the region, which led Sheppard to develop an interest in the Latin American liberation theologians. He became chairman of the area board of the Manpower Services Commission for Merseyside and Cheshire and was vice-chairman of the Commission on Urban Priority Areas which produced the report *Faith in the City*.

His sharp criticism of some of the Thatcher government's economic and social policies may have cost him his chance to succeed Robert Runcie as Archbishop of Canterbury, but Tony Blair valued him and made him a life peer soon after his retirement from Liverpool. In this role he continued to speak in the House of Lords and was sometimes critical of the Labour government's policies, but soon after the turn of the century contracted cancer and died in March 2005.

14 House full at midnight

During the first half of the twentieth century the Christmas Midnight Mass was largely confined to Anglo-Catholic churches that took their cue from the customs of Roman Catholicism. The rest, the overwhelming majority, hardly gave it a thought, chiefly because the Eucharist had yet to recover its place as the central focus of Anglican worship, but there was also a feeling that the convivial celebration of Christmas Eve might not be the best way of preparing for the solemn reception of Holy Communion.

In Parish and People circles in the immediate post-war period there was the further point that if there was to be only one celebration of the Eucharist on Christmas Day, or any other day for that matter, at which the local church expressed its unity as 'one body', the choice of midnight would inevitably exclude the very young and the very old. Better, then, to have the service at 9 or 10 o'clock on Christmas morning.

All these reservations or objections were, however, swept away by a tide of popular demand, and within a couple of decades the Midnight Mass had become the best attended act of worship in the church's year. In cathedrals and other large churches in major centres of population the attendance runs in thousands, making it necessary, for safety reasons, to restrict the number admitted to some buildings. The faithful few who maintain a village church's worship and witness Sunday by Sunday find themselves searching out little-used hymn books or wondering if there will be enough copies of the order of service to meet the large but temporary demand. In many places the Free Churches have, unexpectedly, been drawn to midnight eucharistic worship and secured an equally encouraging response.

The explanation of this dramatic development awaits careful analysis. In the cathedrals and large town churches the number of communicants at midnight never seems to exceed about 50 per cent of the whole congregation, no matter what steps may be taken to get the hesitant to the altar. This suggests that the service may be meeting the needs of a significant section of the population who retain a residual Christian belief which falls some way short of full commitment.

15 *A bad prime ministerial decision*

From the moment Gerald Ellison announced his intention to retire from the bishopric of London at Easter 1981 an intense struggle developed over the succession. The conservative Anglo-Catholic supporters of Graham Leonard, who were particularly strong in the London diocese, had been disappointed when their man failed to be appointed to the see in 1973 and gone instead to distant Truro. They were determined not to fail again and the Crown Appointments Commission was bound to regard Leonard as a serious candidate. But many London church people were against his appointment, as were the four suffragan bishops of the diocese. Among those outside the diocese who were consulted about a post which has national as well as metropolitan responsibilities there was a strongly held view that it would be wrong to appoint so divisively conservative a bishop to such a senior position in the Church of England.

The Bishop of Durham, John Habgood, emerged as the liberal candidate who, although somewhat shy, was known to have the backing of the Archbishop of Canterbury, as well as most of the other bishops, and was believed to be favoured by the Queen herself. In due course the Crown Appointments Commission settled on Habgood as its first choice, but not by so large a majority as to indicate that no one else should be seriously considered. The name of Leonard was therefore on the list despatched to 10 Downing Street.

Notwithstanding the pledge of secrecy made by all the members of the Commission, this situation was leaked and the Anglo-Catholic lobby, having obtained the support of several politicians, including Michael Foot, the agnostic leader of the Labour Party, put pressure on the Prime Minister, Margaret Thatcher, to select Leonard. This accorded with her personal preference, so Leonard was appointed, but the Anglo-Catholics, who generally argue for the autonomy of the church, were challenged to justify their use of the machinery of the state to overthrow the declared wish of the church in the choice of a bishop.

Leonard appeared to have been quite unmoved by the controversy, but when, soon after his retirement, he became a Roman Catholic this occasioned neither surprise nor regret in his own church.

16 *Manx sensation*

The diocese of Sodor and Man rarely hits the headlines. In spite of their isolation, the bishop, the 2 archdeacons and the 11 parochial clergy, serving 45 churches in 27 benefices are not usually given to excess. But in 1990 the tranquillity of a former bishop, Vernon Nicholls, was disturbed when it was revealed that in 1982 he had, not long before his retirement, removed a personal deposit of £100,000 from the Savings and Investment Bank of the Isle of Man. A few days later the bank crashed, and thousands of small investors suffered losses totalling £42 million. A Manx MP wondered if the bishop had received 'divine guidance' or simply a tip-off from privileged sources. Nicholls denied any foreknowledge and said it was pure coincidence that he had withdrawn his money to buy a retirement home.

He had been a strong bishop who, with a good pastoral record in tough West Midlands parishes, had sorted out the diocese's administration and finances and, in strict accordance with the conservative tradition of the island, used his position in the Upper House of the Manx Parliament to vote against a Bill designed to curb birching.

17 No Falklands war triumphalism

The Falklands Islands war in the spring of 1982 was not a controversial event, at least not in Britain. I conducted prayers in the House of Commons at the beginning of the emergency session at which the Prime Minister announced that a task force was on the way to the South Pacific and, although there was broad agreement that the Foreign Office had seriously mishandled the events that led to the conflict, there was near unanimity that the brutal Argentine regime could not be allowed to seize this territory. Neither could any British government relinquish responsibility for it against the wishes of its inhabitants. Francis Pym, who had taken over from Lord Carrington as Foreign Secretary, and some other government ministers came to services at St Margaret's during the three weeks of the war and I preached about the issues two or three times.

The controversy arose when it was over and the government requested a special service at St Paul's – the traditional place for marking the end of military campaigns. What form should the service take? It had to be ecumenical, so the Dean of St Paul's immediately convened a meeting of representatives of the major churches as well as officials who needed to be involved in the organization. There was unanimous agreement among those present, and this reflected the views of the churches' leadership, that the service should contain no note of triumphalism. It was not to be a Victory Service with swords and guards of honour:

thanksgiving for the ending of the conflict certainly, but also penitence and remembrance of those on both sides, about one thousand in all, who had been killed and many others who had been wounded; and a commitment to reconciliation.

When word of this reached the public there was an outcry from those on the Conservative Right and some retired military people who accused the churches in general and Alan Webster in particular of betraying 'our brave soldiers, sailors and airmen'. The tabloid press weighed in with lurid headlines – 'Insulting the Troops', 'Insulting the Queen'. But St Paul's stood its ground and the service was in the end considered by most people, not least those who had lost relatives in the war, to be just right. A memorable sermon by Archbishop Runcie, who spoke with more authority than most, having won a Military Cross in the 1939–45 war, did much to articulate the feelings of those who were in the cathedral or became involved through television and radio. It was a good moment for the Church of England.

18 *First things first*

The Revd. B. Crockett, Vicar of All Saints, Mickleover, today appealed in his parish magazine for parishioners not to book weddings for Saturday afternoons because he does not wish to miss Derby County football matches.

The Times

19 *Arrival of unpaid reinforcements*

Although the concept of the worker-priest failed to win much support in the 1950s and 1960s, or to attract many vocations, the development of an ordained ministry financed by secular employment rather than by a stipend paid by the church gathered pace during the 1970s. By the end of the century there would be 2,000 of these, constituting one-fifth of the total ordained parochial ministry.

It is impossible to generalize about the factors that influence vocation, but there is ample evidence that a growing shortage of traditional full-time priests, causing acute difficulties over the provision of regular services in parish churches, especially in rural areas, was the main reason for this development. Readers were, in increasing numbers, already filling more and more gaps, but they were unable to preside at the Eucharist – a serious disability in a church where this was becoming in most parishes the chief act of Sunday worship. There remained moreover a great deal of heretical belief that the only authentic ministry is that of the ordained.

By 1982 there were about 770 priests who were described as nonstipendiary ministers (NSMs) – an unfortunate title inasmuch as it defines their status negatively and only in terms of money. It still awaits replacement: why not simply 'priest' except for bureaucratic purposes in the diocesan office? From the outset these priests have been drawn almost exclusively from the ranks of schoolteachers and other professional groups – managers, administrators and the like – which is hardly surprising since congregations largely consist of such people. A significant number were retired and, to distinguish them even further from the worker-priest concept, the overwhelming majority have always seen their ministry in terms of service to a parish, rather than of identification with a secular environment. Which is not to say that most of those in employment are insensitive to pastoral opportunities in their workplace, but their preaching rarely suggests constant grappling with the tension between the sacred and the secular.

As their number increased, decisions concerning their training became urgent and it was decided that this should be no less rigorous than that required of the stipendiary ministry. They must be educated at least to the standard of the then General Ordination Examination. This seemed laudable enough but concealed a number of problems, the first of which was that some of the candidates had not had overmuch previous education and this had ended many years earlier. Another was that the training had, of necessity, to be given on part-time courses – weekends, evenings and summer schools – which could never really match the full-time college curriculum. Perhaps most serious of all, the standard of the GOE, and this applied to all candidates, full as well as part time, was not sufficiently high in a society where educational standards were rising quickly and congregations contained an increasing number of able members. Among the new priests, however, were some of outstanding ability and all would make an important contribution to maintaining the parochial system in something like its traditional form. But their appearance offered no long-term solution to the church's fundamental pastoral and mission problems.

20 *A baronet in the back streets*

The baronets are I think the most interesting members of the aristocracy, often combining a deep commitment to public service with a degree of charming eccentricity. James Roll was a 26-year-old curate in Bethnal Green when he succeeded to the baronetcy created for his grandfather at the end of his term of office as Lord Mayor of London in 1921. With the baronetcy went a share, with two brothers, in an estate valued in 1939 at £465,000 – about £20 million in today's values.

But neither the title nor the money made a scrap of difference to the way of life embraced by a young man who, from the age of 16, had felt called to Holy Orders and to work among the poor. He spent the Second World War years as a curate in the most heavily bombed areas of East London, and when in 1958 he was with some difficulty persuaded to become a vicar he went to a tough parish in Dagenham where he remained until his retirement 25 years later. In this parish there was no official vicarage, so he lived in a small rented house similar to the council houses occupied by his parishioners, most of whom had moved to Dagenham from the slums of East London. He was a greatly loved priest who could be seen every morning and in the late afternoon, at precisely the same times, walking to church to conduct the daily services.

The press made Dagenham aware of his wealth, but without this and the evidence of his great generosity, no one would ever have guessed that their priest was rich. He accepted no stipend, spent next to nothing on himself and sometimes needed to be reminded that his shoes would benefit from repair. Most of his time was spent wearing them out on the streets of the parish, and his heavy responsibilities increased when three huge blocks of flats were built on a green-belt site. Children were his special delight and, besides his substantial support of children's charities, he established a holiday home at Westcliff-on-Sea for Sunday school pupils from his own and other Dagenham parishes.

When he inherited the baronetcy and the fortune he was asked if he intended to continue his work for the church. 'Why not?' was his response. 'I came here 18 months ago and I was a priest before I became a baronet. It isn't my fault that I happen to become a baronet as well as a curate. There is important work to be done here in Bethnal Green and I have found more kind hearts in these East End streets than I ever did before.'

21 *March for the unemployed*

By the early 1980s the number of unemployed in Britain had reached 2.5 million – about 9.5 per cent of the nation's total workforce – and every week another 25,000 people were joining the queue of those looking for jobs. When account was taken of people who had not troubled to register as unemployed, or were on retraining schemes, or were out of work only temporarily, the total was nearly 3.5 million. In some areas unemployment was as high as 30, sometimes 40, per cent, with young people, especially young blacks, affected worst of all.

This was a problem which had been unknown in Britain since the 1930s and which most people had believed would never recur. It blew up in the space of only just over two years and was due to a combination of factors – a world economic recession, the automation of many industrial and commercial processes, the consequence of an abnormally high birth rate in the early 1960s. Above all, however, it was the result of Margaret Thatcher's new Conservative government's attempt to control inflation by the pursuit of strict monetarist aims, and at the same time try to squeeze out of industry and commerce all waste. Hence a massive reduction in jobs and what turned out to be the destruction of Britain's industrial base.

A report produced by the Church of England's Board for Social Responsibility offered no solution to this problem, though it pointed out the catastrophic effects unemployment was having on the lives of individuals and communities, and made about thirty suggestions as to what local churches were and ought to be doing in the worst affected areas. These included the opening of counselling centres for the unemployed, starting funds to help pay the travel fares for those going in search of work, the sponsoring of community work projects, the encouragement of young people to remain in education, rather than swell the number of those hanging about the streets without work, the appointment of more industrial chaplains to work among the unemployed, and the convening of meetings and conferences to spread knowledge of the facts and increase concern.

Most unusual in an official church document in Britain was the suggestion that local churches should 'join an unemployment protest march; take your church banner with you; write to your Member of Parliament and to the Prime Minister'. This proved to be just the beginning of a conflict between church and government on social matters that would occupy most of the following decade.

22 The Kingdom of God in North-East England

North-East England, visited famously by a Conservative government minister, Lord Hailsham, wearing a cloth cap to demonstrate his solidarity with the workers, bore the brunt of the severe unemployment experienced during the 1980s and early 1990s. One-quarter of the employable population was without work, the rest fought for overtime. Church leaders, notably Bishop David Jenkins, offered prophetic analyses of the situation along with sharp criticism of the government policy that was largely responsible for the disaster.

On Teesside the Industrial Mission, still under the inspired leadership of Bill Wright, carried out a sustained programme of education and practical assistance. Groups were formed to consider whether the problem was the result of a deep recession or permanent de-industrialization, and the results were communicated to the government. Educationists, employers and trade unionists were brought together to consider what forms of education might be appropriate for young people who would no longer have traditional types of work waiting for them when they left school. Manpower Services Commission finance was used to develop youth training schemes, community programmes and voluntary projects. Collaboration with companies pursued early retirement schemes and split or shared jobs, especially for the young.

A long-term plan to develop self-employment among young people and immediate effort to help people working in the black economy to get the business skills necessary for setting up legitimate businesses were among other projects. Centres were established where older people who were unlikely to benefit from these experiments could determine their own future without paid work creatively and without stigma. The approach was entirely professional and said to be a response by the church to the teaching of Jesus about the Kingdom of God. Theologians from Durham University were deeply involved and a short book of biblical reflections and descriptions of experimental work in many parts of the North-East was published.

23 The church and the city

In 1983 Archbishop Runcie, prompted by Canon Eric James, at that time Director of Christian Action, appointed a commission to:

examine the strengths, insights, problems and needs of the church's life and mission in Urban Priority Areas (these comprising inner-city districts, many large Corporation estates and other areas of social deprivation) and, as a result, to reflect on the challenge which God may be making to the church and nation: and to make recommendations to appropriate bodies.

The Commission, which met under the chairmanship of Sir Richard O'Brien, who had considerable industrial experience and had only recently retired from the chairmanship of the Manpower Services Commission, included bishops and other clergy from deprived areas, together with specialist laity from a variety of social work fields. It consulted widely, its members went in sub-groups to some 40 different towns, cities and boroughs, where public consultations were held and, after 2 years of intensive work, produced a 398-page report, *The Church and the City*, containing much information and analysis, with 38 specific recommendations addressed to the church and another 23 addressed to the government and the nation.

It was the latter that hit the headlines and, since they advocated stronger action by the government in many areas of industrial and urban life, as well as increases in child benefits and unemployment benefit, the report was regarded by government ministers as hostile to Conservative policies. A few days before its publication a number of ministers sought to undermine its competence and one even went so far as denouncing it as 'Marxist'. In the brouhaha that followed it was scarcely noticed that most of the recommendations were for radical change in the church's work in the Urban Priority Areas, not least in the transfer of funds from richer to poorer dioceses.

Eric James, who had been released from his normal Christian Action responsibilities to serve the Commission, devoted further time to promoting the report, which was widely discussed. As with most reports of this sort, its chief effect was to widen awareness of the problems, rather than to energize their solution, though a Church Urban Fund raised over £20 million for projects in Urban Priority Areas.

24 The wit and wisdom of a Bishop of Peterborough

Douglas Feaver, an arch-conservative and said to be the rudest man in the Church of England, was at Peterborough from 1972 to 1984:

Of new ideas: 'Nothing is so tedious and ephemeral as the neurotic quest for novelty.'

Of women members of the General Synod: 'They have seething bosoms but nothing above.'

Of the General Synod itself: 'I wonder when I sit there why church-people should be asked for money to keep this cuckoo growing.'

Of suffragan bishops: 'They are consecrated nannies to look after the clergy.'

Of the new Alternative Services Book: 'Taste it and spit it out.'

Many more examples in *Purple Feaver*, compiled by John Kelly.

25 Religious orders in transition

During my teens I sometimes spent a day and a night in the Society of the Sacred Mission's mother house and theological college at Kelham, not far from my home in Nottinghamshire. It was never my intention to go there for ordination training, but it was good to have 36 hours or so for reflection and prayer, and the community was always welcoming. Father Kelly, the founder, was still alive, just, and walked in the grounds aided by a tall branch of a tree; Father Gabriel Hebert, a distinguished liturgist and Old Testament scholar, was there, as was Brother George Every, a lay theologian, poet and authority on the Orthodox churches. The theological college was full and, run like a Roman Catholic seminary, offered a long and thorough training under a tough regime. In a Compline address during one of my stays the Warden complained that the water pipes running through his room had felt warm that morning, which could mean only one thing – that some students were breaking rules by having hot showers.

The chapel was remarkable and one of the most numinous buildings I have ever known. It provided a huge space for a near-central altar, with four massive arches supporting a magnificent dome. On the sanctuary arch were figures of the crucified Christ, with Mary and John, sculpted in the late 1920s by Sargeant Jagger who contrived to make the eyes of Christ apparently follow those who gazed on him from below. The highly polished floor was jet black and only a small proportion of it was occupied by stalls and other necessary furnishings. It is still impossible to believe that this chapel is no more and that the space is now used for meetings of the local district council and, marketed as 'The Dome', is hired out for social functions.

The Society left Kelham in 1973. The theological college, which for almost seventy years had specialized in the training of young men of little education from High-Church parishes, was closed in a general reorganization of theological education. This removed one of the Society's chief functions and, with its own numbers also falling, it was decided to disperse and establish mission houses in Milton Keynes (where the Kelham rood stands in the garden), London, Durham and Middlesbrough, and also to have mixed communities.

The Benedictines of Nashdom Abbey were also driven by reduced numbers to move to much smaller premises near Newbury and nearly all of the Church of England's religious orders went into decline. This was not, however, on the catastrophic scale experienced by the Roman Catholics, neither was it characterized by a rush of monks and nuns leaving to get married. Shortage of novices was the problem, though the Franciscans bucked the trend during the 1950s and 1960s and continue to serve the poor and underprivileged in cities. Their Third Order, made up of men and women, single and married, lay and ordained, seeking to live according to Franciscan ideals in the ordinary walks of life, still flourishes and has over two thousand Tertians in its European province. The Community of the Resurrection at Mirfield managed to retain its theological college and some of the women's contemplative orders continued to attract a sufficient supply of novices. By the end of the century about twelve hundred Anglican men and women were living the religious life in the United Kingdom.

26 A failed attempt to defuse the Bomb

The Church and the Bomb (1982), a report by a working party of the General Synod's Board for Social Responsibility, aroused considerable interest and much hostility. But its proposals drew little support even from its parent Board or from the General Synod. The chairman of the working party, John Austin Baker, was one of my colleagues at Westminster and we sometimes discussed the subject before he left for the bishopric of Salisbury, but we never approached agreement.

The greater part of the report consisted of a valuable assembly of facts about modern warfare and a careful analysis of the moral and theological principles to be applied to them. Certain conclusions were then drawn and these were, in essence, first, nuclear weapons are in themselves so intrinsically evil that Christians can have no dealings with them; second, Britain must disband its own nuclear weaponry and thus encourage other nuclear powers to do the same. This, said the report, was the only hope for the future.

The stance was that of the Campaign for Nuclear Disarmament, and ran contrary to British defence policy since 1945. It drew a swift and sharp response from the Foreign Office which described its arguments as perverse and its proposals as completely mistaken, adding, 'Giving a moral lead may be good for conscience, but it is not a valid proposition in the real world. The Soviet Union is not interested in moral considerations.'

There was, it seemed to me, a further, related point, which the lack of a top-class moral theologian on the working party had caused to be neglected. In the final resort, decisions about nuclear weapons cannot be determined directly by compelling moral or theological principles. Given that an agreed objective is the avoidance of nuclear war, the decision as to whether this might at a particular moment in history be best achieved by maintaining a 'balance of terror' or by one side in the potential conflict abandoning its nuclear weapons, can only be a matter for the finest political judgement. There is nothing in either ethics or theology that will assist a political leader to reach an infallible decision in such a desperate crisis.

Although the report aroused a good, albeit often over-heated, discussion, most informed opinion judged that it had failed to make the case for a change in national defence policy – a policy that was maintained for the rest of the century, even beyond the collapse of the Soviet empire.

27 A Marine in war and peace

Donald Leyton Jones, a Royal Marine officer who had a hectic war and won a DSC for his courageous action while serving in an anti-aircraft cruiser off Tobruk in 1942, was ordained in 1959 and, after spending ten years as Vicar of Salcombe Regis, became Vicar of the North Devon fishing village of Appledore. In both parishes his salty and down-to-earth approach to belief and life went unchecked. He wore a green Marine beret, white cassock and sandals, and a splendid beard. He liked to do his parish visiting on horseback, often leaving hoof prints in gardens, and allowed his two cream labradors to enter his church immediately before and after services.

He was also an enthusiastic user of pubs where, he used to say, there was often more fellowship and more joy than in church. 'A pub is a sort of confessional,' he claimed. 'People communicate freely after a few drinks; they tell you their personal problems.' He advocated burial at sea, church blessings for divorcees and baptisms conducted in lighthouses. His success in getting Lundy Island incorporated into his parish reconciled his love of God with his need to be on the water. If bad weather broke the one telephone connection with the island, he used carrier pigeons to let his wife know that he was delayed, though the GPO warned him that he was infringing its monopoly.

At Salcombe Regis, PJ, as he liked to be called, had championed local hippies and won a seat on the council to advocate their cause. But this did not enhance his popularity with everyone: his congregation objected to open-air candlelit services that featured scanty dress and drug-smoking by the worshippers. He was, however, irrepressible. Despite the loss of his wife and two children, and the amputation of both legs during his retirement years, his mischievous sparkle never dimmed and he drove himself in his electric wheelchair to the pub, before retiring to the care of Nazareth House nuns.

28 *Those unneeded church buildings*

Among its many other provisions, the Pastoral Measure (1983) made it possible for church buildings to be declared pastorally redundant and wise decisions to be made about the future of these buildings. The options were deemed to be alternative use, demolition or, in the case of buildings of historic or architectural importance, preservation. The Church Commissioners were made responsible for determining, after wide local consultation, which of these choices was most appropriate.

Since the 1980s, therefore, many churches, usually of little or no architectural merit, have been demolished – mainly in overchurched towns and cities. Many, many more, some of considerable architectural importance, have been turned to alternative use – libraries, museums, concert halls and the like. A large number of the smaller buildings have been converted into private houses.

The remainder, about 300 at the end of the century, are maintained by the Church Conservation Trust which receives 30 per cent of its statutory funding from the Church Commissioners and 70 per cent from the Department of Culture, Media and Sport. They retain some basic church furnishings, are open daily to visitors (sometimes through a keyholder), and are available for concerts, exhibitions and lectures. Occasional services are also held, but not so many as to suggest that the parish has the use of a building at someone else's expense.

Until comparatively recently these churches would have been allowed to fall into ruin but now, besides their historic and artistic interest, they are often visited by those who, while rarely attending a church service anywhere, are drawn to them for spiritual refreshment when passing by.

29 *Prayers and more in the House of Commons*

A unique office in the Church of England is that of Speaker's Chaplain, dating back to 1661 and requiring its holder to conduct prayers at the opening of every daily session of the House of Commons. The black robes indicate the influence of the Reformation era and during my years in the office, 1982–87, the form of the prayers remained unchanged from those of the seventeenth century.

Until the latter years of the nineteenth century the office was held for a few years as a single appointment, at the end of which the House of Commons petitioned the Crown for an appropriate post, usually a cathedral canonry, for the outgoing priest. During the twentieth century, however, it was generally, but not always, more convenient to combine the office with that of Rector of St Margaret's – the parish church of the House of Commons – who is always also a canon of Westminster. As the two churches became increasingly busy it was impossible for the chaplain to do much more for the House of Commons than conduct the daily prayers and arrange occasional services in St Margaret's.

I attempted to remedy this by devoting about one-third of my time to pastoral work in the House, of which a good deal accumulated, there being 2,500 on the staff as well as 650 MPs; giving lectures and talks; and making myself generally available to the Speaker and anyone else who might need my services. This was greatly appreciated but proved to be too heavy a responsibility to be combined with the other roles. My successors continued and developed the House of Commons ministry and were provided with additional support to sustain a reduced ministry at St Margaret's.

30 *Another neglected strategy*

When he had completed five years as Chief Secretary of the General Synod's Advisory Council for the Church's Ministry, Canon John Tiller was asked to take time off to produce a report on a ministerial strategy, this to take account of previous Council discussions of the subject but to include wider consultations and his own personal judgements. The report, *A Strategy for the Church's Ministry*, appeared in 1983 and was nothing if not radical in its recommendations.

Tiller explained that he was not offering a quick fix for the church's serious problems, but rather a possible strategy to be developed over the next 40 years. A thorough survey and acute analysis of the present pattern of ministry led him to the conclusion that the day of the 'general practitioner' priest was over. No longer could one person discharge the varied tasks required in a local church – leader of worship, prophet, evangelist, teacher, pastor, spiritual director and so on. The priest must therefore become a specialist and the ministry of the parish be assumed by a group of its lay members, possibly with one of their number ordained to the priesthood in order to preside over the administration of the sacraments.

The new pattern of ministry would therefore require most of the stipendiary clergy and some of those in secular employment to consti- tute a 'task force', detached from parishes and under the direction of the bishop. All would be specialists and their role would be to foster the church's mission and to provide resources – preaching, teaching and pastoral, for example – that might be lacking in high quality in local churches. They would work in teams, always related to groups or cells of laypeople. The current trained lay ministers would be incorporated into the order of deacon.

Parish ministry, under this strategy, would therefore be the responsi- bility of the local church, with its locally chosen, unpaid priest, and supported by the diocesan specialists. Some of these specialists would be allocated to non-parochial work appropriate to their skills and voca- tions. It was a bold plan – necessarily so, following the church's failure to grasp the nettles offered by the Paul and Morley reports in the 1960s – and Tiller was wise to have suggested a 40-year time scale. He could hardly have anticipated however that 20 years on his report would not even have been seriously considered.

31 *Evangelical fervour in Brompton and Bishopsgate*

Evangelicalism thrives on success and the revival of this movement in the Church of England during the second half of the twentieth century was based on impressively large churches established in London and eventually in all the main centres of population. These churches had certain affinities of scale and style with long-established American models. During the early days of the revival, when Evangelicals appeared to be no more than a beleaguered minority, All Souls, Langham Place, in London's West End, not only kept the lamp burning but also extended its rays by rebuilding the war-damaged church to accommodate an ever-increasing congregation, converted the crypt into a multipurpose centre for educational and other serious purposes, and established chaplaincies in the major Oxford and Regent Street stores. John Stott, the presiding genius of all this, gathered together what became a large group of dynamic young clergymen who learned a great deal from him and showed themselves open to new styles of worship and evangelism. Their influence spread far and wide.

With the arrival of the charismatic movement, however, the centre of evangelical gravity shifted to Holy Trinity, Brompton. A liberal evangelical approach to Christianity had for several decades suited this fashionable area of Kensington but profound social change created a vacancy for something different that would attract many more people, especially young professionals, from every part of Central London and beyond. Under the inspired leadership of Sandy Millar, who started as a layman in the congregation, then became a curate and finally the Vicar in 1985, HTB (as it came to be called) was transformed into a church of international repute, albeit barely recognizable as part of the Church of England.

The scale of the operation became remarkable. Besides seven curates there was a large lay staff and an organization of impressive efficiency – all financed by the offerings of an ever-increasing congregation. At the Sunday evening service Millar simply wore trousers and a sweater, no clerical collar, and led a long session of hymn-singing with seemingly endless choruses, followed by a lengthy sermon and then the so-called 'Toronto Blessing'. This phenomenon, so named for its place of origin, consisted of prayer for the healing of sick people who came forward and was often accompanied by unusual happenings in the congregation – speaking in tongues, rolling on the floor and sometimes, it was said, barking. Within the life of the congregation there developed a warmth of friendship that was of particular importance to lonely people working in London.

In the City of London another Evangelical, Dick Lucas, was exercising a large-scale ministry at St Helen's, Bishopsgate. He went there in 1980 and during the next 18 years developed a lunchtime service that attracted many hundreds of City workers. This was accompanied by chaplaincies to major finance houses, requiring the employment of six to eight curates and a strong organization, all financed, as at HTB, by the generous offerings of the congregation. In both churches, as in other strong evangelical churches throughout the country, there was offered a deeply personal interpretation of the Christian faith, certainty and friendship – a combination that some found irresistible – enough in large centres of population to create, against current churchgoing trends, remarkably large and dynamic congregations. These were, however, often achieved at the expense of other churches, of all denominations, and there is no evidence that overall church attendance in their neighbourhoods increased significantly.

32 HTB spreads far and wide

The evangelistic spirit engendered at Holy Trinity, Brompton could not be confined to fashionable Kensington and the influence of this church expanded through two significant developments. The first of these came to be known as the 'church plant'. Aware that the church was struggling in a particular area of the Home Counties, often a place where one or more HTB members lived, an offer would be made to send a group, including a priest, for a longish period to help revivify its life. This was done, naturally, with the agreement of the local church and had good results. But problems could, and did, arise when the influence of the missionaries extended through house churches and other activities across parish boundaries. In these instances bishops were required to regularize the arrangements.

After a modest start, however, the concept of the 'church plant' as an agency of evangelism spread to other parts of the country and by 1990 they were growing at the rate of about forty per year. At the end of the decade there were 370 of them nationwide and the House of Bishops had concluded that the structures of the Church of England were flexible enough to cope with the new development. 'Plants' were by now extending beyond the parishes into specialized areas – youth centres, vocational groups – and coming to be regarded not so much as an outreach from an already established church but rather a parallel church with its own authority. There was potential in this provided that personal evangelism did not remain the sole aim.

The other significant HTB initiative was the development of the Alpha course. Devised by Nicky Gumbel, who went to the church as a curate in 1986 and stayed on to succeed Sandy Millar as Vicar in 2005, it was intended to be no more than a ten-week study course, plus a study weekend for new converts. The study material was biblically based and used, under lay leadership, with small groups, meeting in homes and starting always with a supper party. This formula proved to be attractive and the need for something of its kind so widely recognized that the Alpha course spread like wildfire throughout Britain – mainly, but not exclusively, in evangelical circles, and finding a place in some Roman Catholic parishes. Initial criticisms that the course lacked social concern were accepted and the material amplified in this direction. By the end of the century 14,250 churches in England (38 per cent) had run the course and worldwide the number was 17,000, with an estimated total attendance of 2.7 million – both figures still rapidly rising. A large supporting organization, based on HTB, provided handbooks, DVDs, conferences and a quarterly tabloid newspaper.

33 Excitement at Durham

Every so often a fuss is created concerning a bishop's beliefs in the virginal conception of Mary and the bodily resurrection of Jesus. Both remain part of the Church of England's official teaching and both are therefore possible beliefs, but neither is essential to faith. In other words, belief in the divinity of Jesus and his victory over death do not depend upon them.

This was the line taken by Professor David Jenkins in a television interview not long after his appointment as Bishop of Durham had been announced in 1984. I was at the time an adviser to London Weekend Television which was running a short series on *Who was Jesus?*, though I was not present at the interview which took place in a London hotel. The broadcast led to a storm of protest both inside and outside the church and the Archbishop of York was called upon to refuse Dr Jenkins consecration as a bishop. A petition organized by a cathedral school chaplain attracted 14,000 signatures and tagged him as 'Bishop of Blasphemy'. A *Daily Telegraph* editorial advised him to withdraw in the interests of pastoral unity.

The consecration nonetheless took place in York Minster as planned, but three days later the building was struck by lightning and a large section of its roof was destroyed by the consequent fire. Some of the new bishop's opponents declared this to be a clear sign of Divine disapproval, conveniently overlooking the fact that if this were the normal method by which God showed his displeasure with bishops there would hardly be a cathedral in the country left standing.

Part of the problem arose from Jenkins's characteristically arresting language – 'I wouldn't put it past God to arrange a virgin birth if he wanted, but I very much doubt if he would'; 'The resurrection of Jesus is not concerned with a miracle over a bag of bones' – and he did not immediately recognize that, while his gadfly approach to questions of religious sensitivity might well be stimulating for young undergraduates, they were not always appreciated by others in a senior bishop.

He proved to be, however, a highly regarded, deeply caring bishop who had pertinent things to say about social as well as religious issues. Teach-ins held at various parts of Durham diocese attracted hundreds of participants and during his ten years as its bishop this was the only Church of England diocese in which church electoral roll numbers actually increased.

34 Beyond ambiguity

David Jenkins was enthroned in Durham Cathedral in September 1984, not long after the beginning of the most serious miners' strike since the 1920s. The subject of his sermon was 'The Cost of Hope' and included a brief personal confession of faith:

> I face you as an ambiguous, compromised and questioning person entering upon an ambiguous office in an uncertain church in the midst of a threatened and threatening world. I dare to do this, and I, even with fear and trembling, rejoice to do this because this is where God is to be found. In the midst, that is, of the ambiguities, the compromises, the uncertainties, the questions and the threats of our daily ordinary world. For the church exists, despite all its failings and all its historically acquired clutter, because the disturbing, provocative, impractical, loving and utterly God-centred Jesus got himself crucified. Then God vindicated this God-centred way of life, loving and being by raising Jesus up.

He went on to discuss the strike and said:

> The miners must not be defeated, and this must be the first priority. But there must be no victory for them on present terms because these include negotiations on their terms alone. Yet equally there must be no victory for the Government . . . Therefore a negotiated settlement which is a compromise and demands of us all further work on the problem both of the miners and of society at large is the only hopeful thing. But how might this come about?

Might it be by Mr. MacGregor [the chairman of the National Coal Board] withdrawing from his chairmanship and Mr. Scargill [the leader of the National Union of Miners] climbing down from his absolute demands? The withdrawal of an elderly, imported American [Mr. McGregor was in fact of Scottish origin] to leave a reconciliation opportunity for some local product is surely neither dishonourable nor improper.

The sermon was greeted with prolonged applause by the congregation but most of the media expressed fury. The Bishop of Peterborough commented to the *Daily Mirror*, 'I thought the man had no sense of time or place', and the following March the Prime Minister, Margaret Thatcher, addressing a meeting of the Conservative Central Council in Newcastle, said: 'You may have noticed that recently the voices of some reverend and right-reverend prelates have been heard in the land. I make no complaint about that. After all, it wouldn't be spring, would it, without the voice of the occasional cuckoo!'

35 *No confidence in the bishops*

The Church Union, a creation of the nineteenth-century Oxford Movement and once-powerful instrument of Anglo-Catholicism, was by the mid-1980s a mere shadow of its former self, though it still supported a full-time General Secretary and an acerbic journal. It could also bark loudly, as it did in a resolution passed by its General Council in November 1984:

(a) The Council believes that theological questions underlying the issue of the ordination of women to the priesthood and episcopate can only be answered conclusively by a consensus among those parts of Christendom which have retained the faith and order of the undivided Church. The Council holds that the Church of England, being and professing to be only a part of the Church, has no authority to act in this matter without a consensus.

(b) The Council regrets that the House of Bishops in its recent vote on Thursday, 15 November, appears to show so little concern about causing in England the kind of division and possibly even schism which has occurred in other provinces of the Anglican Communion. It further regrets that the House of Bishops is also prepared to place a major obstacle in the way of Christian unity.

(c) The Council believes that the handling of the marriage issue and the vote for the ordination of women indicates that the House of Bishops is unrepresentative of the Church of England and defective in the guardianship of its faith and unity.

Fortunately, the Union's lack of teeth precluded episcopal injury.

36 Boys for bishops

The ceremony of the Boy Bishop was revived in Hereford Cathedral in 1983 and Salisbury soon followed suit. Of medieval origin, a boy – nowadays normally elected from among the senior choristers – is robed as a bishop on St Nicholas Day (6 December), placed on the bishop's throne, handed, by the real bishop, his episcopal staff, then preaches a sermon and gives a blessing. He (how long will it be before a girl chorister is elected?) holds office until Holy Innocent's Day (28 December).

Common in English monasteries and village churches during the medieval centuries, the ceremony was banned by Henry VIII, reinstated by Mary Tudor and finally abolished – at least, she thought so – by Elizabeth I. The symbolism was intended to demonstrate the reverence for children shown in the Gospels, and the bishop says, when handing his staff to the boy, 'He has put down the might from their seat: and has exalted the humble and meek', but the modern mind finds it less easy to make the connection.

37 Protecting the churches

When, in the late 1970s, Britain began to recognize the scale of the wanton destruction wrought on its historic towns and cities during the previous decade, there arose a new concern for the preservation of ancient buildings. Eyes were soon turned on the Church of England with its responsibility for about twelve thousand buildings of architectural importance – all of them in regular use. Enquiry revealed that, unlike other 'listed' buildings, these were not subject to any Local Authority planning control, since the Church of England, long before these authorities became interested in such matters, had established its own means of control. Changes to the fabric of a church, including fixed internal furnishings, required permission, granted by means of a faculty from the bishop, administered by his consistory court. The existence of this procedure allowed the church to be exempted from secular planning control.

The question now arose as to whether the church's arrangements were sufficiently strict. Examples were cited of alterations to church interiors which had upset conservative conservationists and of instances where church councils had, deliberately or accidentally, ignored faculty regulations. There was the further point that if the Church of England intended to press a case for a degree of state funding for these national treasures, the state, through one or other of its agencies, might expect to have an influence over the proposed expenditure.

Alert to these issues, a high-powered Faculty Jurisdiction Commission was formed under the chairmanship of the Bishop of Exeter, Eric Kemp, and when this reported in 1984, it presented a very strong case for maintaining the existing arrangements. Nonetheless it produced 229 recommendations for their improvement, most of these of a technical character, but one strengthening the authority of archdeacons and one reducing the age of diocesan chancellors from 75 to 72. The report was not challenged by the state, the church's freedom remained, and the chancellors had three more retirement years.

38 Bringing the deans and chapters to heel

Among the Commissions' recommendations there were 25 that related to cathedrals and these were altogether more substantial. For, unlike parish churches, the cathedrals were subject to no control whatsoever. Deans and chapters were not required to obtain faculties, even for large-scale modifications to buildings that were among the most important in the land. Deans and chapters were free agents and, although shortage of funds had in recent years precluded overmuch change to their great churches, there were instances of alterations causing public disquiet, and the same shortage of funds had led to the sale of some important treasures.

A recently formed Cathedrals Advisory Commission showed signs of encouraging restraint in these areas, and was already being consulted by deans and chapters when alterations were contemplated. But the committee was purely advisory; it had no teeth, and it was now proposed that it should be given some. Instead of being purely advisory, it should be given statutory authority and deans and chapters henceforth required to submit to it for approval 'any significant work or works to preserve, alter or add to the building or its contents which would materially affect the architectural, artistic, historical or archaeological character of the cathedral'. This definition was to include the sale or removal of any objects of value. Moreover deans and chapters should be required to appoint a local Fabric Committee, consisting of architects, artists, historians, archaeologists and the like, to offer advice and to determine which of its proposals for alteration required submission to the national Commission.

The deans and chapters did not like such a radical change. But the *Mappa Mundi* affair at Hereford in 1988 spurred Parliament into action and the prospect of substantial government aid for cathedral repairs, provided deans and chapters submitted to the proposed controls, ensured that a new order would not long be delayed. It was inaugurated in 1990 and during the first ten years of its existence proved to be more of a help than a hindrance.

39 *A conscientious churchwarden*

T. S. Eliot, the greatest poet and critic of his generation, died on 17 January 1985. He was also a notable Christian spokesman and for many years a churchwarden of St Stephen's, Gloucester Road in Bayswater. W. H. Auden said of him: 'In Eliot the critic, as in Eliot the man, there is a lot, to be sure, of a conscientious churchwarden, but there is also a 12-year-old boy who likes to surprise over-solemn wigs by offering them explosive cigars.'

40 *A precious parrot*

How do canons of Westminster Abbey spend their time? In a variety of ways, of course, as my diary record of a meeting of the Dean and Chapter on 31 January 1985 indicates:

We have turned down a request from Chichester Museum for the loan of the Duchess of Richmond's parrot. They have an exhibition from June to September of items relating to the Richmond family, whose seat is at nearby Goodwood House, but the parrot is altogether too delicate and too precious for us to allow him to make the journey. In any case many visitors to our own museum would be disappointed were he to be away from his usual haunts during the height of the tourist season.

The wax effigy of Frances, Duchess of Richmond and Lennox, was made immediately after her death in 1702 and is really very fine. She was evidently a great beauty and was the model for the original figure of Britannia on the copper coinage. Her effigy is clothed with the robes she wore, a few months before her death, at the Coronation of Queen Anne. The West African grey parrot – her favourite parrot – died a few days after the Duchess and, having been stuffed, joined the company of her effigy. It is believed to be the oldest stuffed bird in England and cannot be spared.

41 Seeking a credible Gospel

For most of the second half of the twentieth century one of the best known and most influential Anglican theologians was John (Ian to his friends) Macquarrie, who occupied the Lady Margaret chair of Divinity at Oxford during 1970–86, having spent the previous 14 years as Professor of Systematic Theology at the prestigious Union Theological Seminary in New York.

His special interest for many years was the forging of a link between existentialist philosophy and Christian theology in the expectation that this would produce a credible expression of faith for the modern mind. How far he succeeded in this remains an open question but a common view is that he scored a highly commendable 'near miss'.

As a young scholar his fluency in German took him into the sphere of existentialism long before it entered the British theological scene, and he translated into English the most important books of the German philosopher Martin Heidegger and the German theologian Rudolf Bultmann. Like Bultmann, Macquarrie had served as an army chaplain – an experience that led both men to perceive that the church's traditional teaching was no longer credible to most of those who encountered it.

Macquarrie's own attempt to remedy this began with two major works, *Twentieth Century Religious Thought* (1963) and *Principles of Christian Theology* (1966), both of which ran to several editions and were widely read by clergy and students of all traditions. They were followed by upwards of another 20 books, which included more major works as well as many shorter volumes, such as *Paths in Spirituality* (1972), *The Faith of the People of God* (1977) and *Thinking About God* (1975), which were intended for non-professional readers.

He began life as a Scottish Presbyterian, and taught for some years at Glasgow University. It was during his time in New York that his eyes were opened to the riches of the Catholic tradition expressed by the American Episcopal Church, and he was ordained to the priesthood, but he retained the best traits of the Scottish parish minister and was revered by his pupils.

At Oxford, where he was also a Canon of Christ Church and built up a worldwide reputation, his homely and friendly style was unaffected and he was always ready to accept an invitation to preach in a village church or to give a paper to a group of parish clergymen. He continued to write until shortly before his death in 2007, aged 87.

42 *Talking to the Tories*

In a General Synod speech in 1987 David Edwards, then Provost of Southwark Cathedral, having grown weary of the slanging match between church leaders and Margaret Thatcher's Conservative government, pleaded for a dialogue between the Church of England and the Conservative Party. Archbishop Runcie reported this to Mrs Thatcher who was keen on the idea and asked her former Parliamentary Private Secretary, Michael Alison, and the Head of her Policy Unit, Professor Brian Griffiths – both of them card-carrying Evangelicals – to organize such a dialogue.

David Edwards was naturally drawn into the arrangements and in due course a fairly large group held a series of meetings and two residential conferences. These, by all accounts, were profitable encounters. They led to the publication of *Christianity and Conservatism* (1990), consisting of 17 essays, which conveyed the main fruit of the dialogue, augmented by a preface from Margaret Thatcher, who was shortly to be hustled out of office in a most unceremonious manner by her own party.

The essays, all of which were of high quality, expressed the usual division between those who believe that Conservatism is ideologically sound, inasmuch as it takes human nature seriously and seeks to maximize human freedom, and is moreover the most pragmatically effective in the creation and distribution of wealth, and those who believe that market forces alone will not effect a just distribution of the created wealth. The dialogue did not reconcile these opposing positions, but it did confirm that only just beneath the surface of some heated political debate there was, even then, a broad measure of agreement on social and economic policy among the main British parties.

43 *More than a storm in a teacup*

The so-called '*Crockford's* Affair' of 1987 was a storm in a teacup that became a cause célèbre and soon turned into a desperate personal tragedy. Gareth Bennett, a respected historian and a Fellow of New College, Oxford, had been commissioned to write the traditionally anonymous Preface to the latest *Crockford's Clerical Directory*. He had for several years been deeply involved in the General Synod and also had a sharp pen. Unfortunately he was a deeply embittered High Church-man, nursing a grudge against those he believed to have stood in the way of his preferment to a bishopric or a deanery.

When the Directory appeared it was immediately noted that the Preface contained a savage and hurtful attack on the Archbishop of Canterbury, Robert Runcie – who was actually one of the author's close friends. He was accused, among other things, of not knowing what he was doing, of having no clear basis for his policies other than maintaining the line of least resistance – 'He has the disadvantage of the intelligent pragmatist: the desire to put off all questions until someone else makes a decision.' A phrase of Frank Field MP was quoted with approval: 'The archbishop is usually to be found nailing his colours to the fence.' What is more, Runcie favoured his liberal friends, especially those with strong media experience, for senior church appointments.

Had the Preface appeared under Bennett's signature, its contents would have been treated as no more than the expression of a personal opinion. Had *Crockford's* still carried the imprint of the Oxford University Press, who owned it until 1981, the Preface would have been seen for what it was – an independent enterprise. But appearing in a General Synod publication it could be taken to carry some degree of official endorsement, akin to the appearance of an anonymous attack on the Prime Minister in a government document.

Massive media attention followed and when the search for the author of the controversial work was narrowed to Gareth Bennett, he took his own life rather than face the embarrassment of this disclosure. My own involvement in the affair was only very marginal, but I was among those members of the General Synod's Publishing Committee who sought, in company with its chairman Tom Christie, a canon of Peterborough, to wrest control of the Preface's commissioning from the unfettered hands of Derek Pattinson, the Synod's autocratic General Secretary. We lost that battle, as we did the attempt to call Pattinson to account for his failure to spot the explosive character of the Preface before passing it for publication.

It turned out later that the last straw for Bennett had been his failure to be appointed in 1987 to the Deanery of Winchester – a post he greatly coveted. He had in fact been strongly recommended for it by both Runcie and Graham Leonard, the Bishop of London. On the wisdom of the Prime Minister to choose otherwise it is not for me to comment, except to say that in the making of their recommendations Runcie and Leonard can only have been influenced by considerations other than the welfare of Winchester Cathedral.

44 A valuable mistake

In 1987 the General Synod agreed that women might be admitted to Holy Orders, but only as deacons. Bishop Graham Leonard of London and other opponents of women priests supported this move with some enthusiasm, since it indicated clearly that they were not opposed to women exercising an ordained ministry; it was simply that they should not become priests. As a diversionary tactic it might have potential.

This was, however, a fatal mistake on their part. Soon some 1,400 deaconesses and other trained women were ordained as deacons and returned to their parishes to continue ministries they had been exercising for several years. A few became deacons-in-charge of parishes, others went as new curates. They could not preside at the Eucharist or pronounce blessings, but in every other respect their ministries were indistinguishable from those of the male priests alongside whom they were working. They had the same titles, wore dog collars and the same robes. The result was that over the next few years a very large number of people experienced for themselves the ordained ministry of a woman and, in the process, not only lost any hesitations or even fear they might have had, but also identified many positive gains. This was to be an important factor when the final vote was taken in 1992.

45 A brilliant second choice

In 1987 the Crown Appointments Commission presented the then Prime Minister, Margaret Thatcher, with the names of two candidates for the vacant bishopric of Birmingham – Bishop Jim Thompson of Stepney and Bishop Mark Santer of Kensington – indicating a preference for the first. But the left-wing views of Thompson had been frequently voiced through the media and greatly irritated the Prime

Minister. So she chose Santer. What she did not realize, however, was that Santer's views, though more carefully stated, were if anything further to the Left than those of his London colleague. He was an avowed republican (a position he later modified), a member of the Campaign for Nuclear Disarmament, and strongly opposed to Thatcherite policies, which, he said in his enthronement sermon, 'turned selfishness into a publicly acceptable principle of social and personal policy'. He also believed the time had come for the Church of England to be disestablished.

In the event Santer proved to be a highly effective bishop of England's second city and many believed that he should have been translated to London in 1985. He combined a razor-sharp mind with a strong pastoral sense and was a good enough theologian to become co-chairman of the Anglican/Roman Catholic Theological Commission. This did not prevent him, however, from throwing his weight behind the move to get women ordained to the priesthood. Jim Thompson later became a highly popular Bishop of Bath and Wells.

46 Lambeth bishops opt for unity

The 1988 Lambeth Conference reached no earth-shattering conclusions, neither did it make any sensational pronouncements. It was, however, considered to have been a great success, partly because it was much better prepared for than its predecessor in 1978 had been, but overwhelmingly because of the content and style of Archbishop Runcie's presidency. For the first time the bishops from the developing world outnumbered the rest and in his invitations to the Conference Runcie asked all to bring their dioceses with them. By which he meant the deepest concerns of their dioceses, so that these might be aired and taken account of.

This proved to be an eminently satisfactory process and issues related to the possible consecration of women bishops did not divide the Conference, as the media had forecast, but were remitted for further consideration to a commission headed by the Primate of All Ireland, Robin Eames. The acknowledged highlight of the three weeks, spent residentially in Canterbury, was an address given by Runcie on the nature of church unity and the proper place of authority in the maintaining of that unity. He said that a choice had to be made between independence and interdependence, between unity or gradual fragmentation, and his presence and approach encouraged all present to believe that only one decision concerning this was possible. It would be a very different story at the next Lambeth Conference.

47 A wounded scholar

In February 1988 the Revd Bertrand Brasnett died in Oxford, aged 95. But hardly anyone noticed, even though he was in his day a distinguished theologian. His trilogy on the nature of God, published between 1928 and 1935, earned him an Oxford DD and he continued to illuminate and exercise the minds of serious scholars. Among them the renowned Professor Jürgen Moltmann of Tübingen, who acknowledged his indebtedness to Brasnett in a seminal book, *The Crucified God* (1973).

The trilogy was written during Brasnett's time as Principal of Edinburgh Theological College where he was something of a Victorian martinet in his strong sense of duty and obsessive attention to detail in the life of the College. This was tolerated throughout the 1930s but in 1942, with a different kind of student in residence and the strain of war requiring some change of priorities, he was asked to make way for a new Principal who would prepare the College for the post-war era.

He resigned under pressure and was deeply wounded psychologically by a sense of rejection. Thus he returned to his old haunts in Oxford where, sustained by a more than adequate private income, he lived for another 45 years as a recluse. At the same time every morning, until infirmity intervened, he was to be seen walking to a newsagent for his daily paper. He received no visitors, wrote no more books, sent Christmas cards to a few old friends. For a time he attended the Holy Communion in the local parish church, but otherwise remained quite isolated, though served by a devoted housekeeper. He never married.

48 Costly heroics in the Middle East

The saga of Terry Waite was extraordinary and claimed world attention in the late 1980s. Unusually tall, bearded, gifted, courageous, Waite joined Archbishop Runcie's staff in 1980 for a behind-the-scenes role. Expansion of activity in the worldwide Anglican Communion required the Archbishop to be kept informed of what was going on. There was need also for negotiations about his programmes when undertaking overseas visits. Waite, who as a Church Army officer had worked in

Uganda and for an international order of nuns in Rome, seemed ideally suited for this post and for several years did it well. But it did not require heroics and, since Waite was not by disposition a low-profile man, it was not altogether surprising to those in the know when it was announced in January 1987 that he had disappeared in Beirut while seeking the release of hostages held by a terrorist organization.

He had in fact undertaken two previous rescue missions, both of them successful. The first had been to Iran and involved three British mission-aries and four Iranian clergy who had been held in prison since the 1979 Iranian revolution. When efforts by the Foreign Office to secure their release failed, the Bishop in Iran asked Runcie if he could help, so Waite was sent to Teheran as an emissary. He persuaded the authorities that they were no threat to the new regime and returned to London with the three Britons to great media acclaim.

Lambeth Palace now began to receive requests for assistance with the release of other prisoners and hostages, not all of which could be met. But in 1984–85 Waite went to Libya where he got on well with Colonel Gaddafi and returned with four British hostages. He now appeared to be a significant figure on the stage of international politics, with a taste for adventure and danger, but his next mission, to Beirut, proved to be his last.

He simply disappeared, and for a long time it was not known whether he was still alive, but eventually it was disclosed that he was being held with other British hostages. This lasted four years and during this time he displayed remarkable faith and courage, enduring long periods of solitary confinement and sometimes the threat of death. Back in England he seemed to many to combine the dashing hero and the godly saint. Candles were lit for him in churches and cathedrals, prayers were said in parishes throughout the land and far beyond, international efforts were made to get him freed. When at last these succeeded, he returned to a hero's welcome, was appointed CBE and over the next few years accumulated many honorary degrees and other awards.

None of which had the remotest connection with Waite's responsibil-ities at Lambeth and, besides the acute personal anxiety suffered by Runcie over the event, it was inevitable that serious questions should be asked about his readiness to allow a member of his staff to engage in such highly dangerous enterprises. The truth was that Runcie had no choice in the matter. Although he urged Waite not to go to Beirut, he disregarded this request and later admitted that, had he been absolutely forbidden to go, he would have resigned from Runcie's staff and gone as an unadorned individual.

Runcie was at the airport to greet him when, in the spotlight of the world's media, he returned, but the four-year-long nightmare, together with the *Crockford's* affair, clouded the final phase of his Primacy and seemed to add years to his life.

49 Hereford's map saved

A national outcry followed the Dean and Chapter of Hereford's announcement in 1988 that it proposed to sell the cathedral's copy of the thirteenth-century *Mappa Mundi*. The cathedral was at that time on the verge of bankruptcy. Lacking the support of industrialists and financiers, and off any of the main tourist routes, it found it impossible not only to meet daily running costs but also to embark on the urgent task of conserving and rehousing a unique library of chained books. Although the decision to sell had been taken after deep heartsearching by the chapter as a whole, the Dean and the Treasurer were subjected to much unfair criticism. During the storm of protest, however, the National Heritage Memorial Fund stepped in with a substantial grant which saved the map, and John Paul Getty, an American philanthropist, paid for the library to be rehoused. The incident also alerted Parliament to the inability of the cathedrals to protect national treasures without assistance, and the result was that English Heritage grants were eventually made to them all.

50 Square pegs and round holes

The Christian priesthood, and not least that of the Church of England, has always attracted individualists and often provided scope for the exercising of his, and now her, particular gifts. This proved to be the case even for Paul Kingdom whose checkered ministry ended with his death in June 1989. He was essentially a scholar and having gone from Oxford to Tübingen gained an unrivalled knowledge of German theology. This enabled him to write a history of the church in Germany and to edit and translate into English two extracts from Kittel's monumental *Theological Word Book of the New Testament*. But at Exeter College, Oxford, where he was a Fellow from 1933 to 1945, he proved to have no teaching gifts. He was relentless in the pursuit of arcane detail and lectured in terms so obscure that few of his undergraduates could understand him.

When the war ended in 1945 the College solved its problem by presenting him to the living of Somerford in Wiltshire – a parish of some 700 souls. But he found it difficult to get on with people and sought fulfilment in the further pursuit of his studies. After six years he returned to teaching, but King Alfred's College, Winchester, with its two-year course for school teachers, was hardly suitable for a specialist scholar of his sort and unsurprisingly he was not a success.

He then became Vicar of Chewton Mendip near Bath, a post he combined with that of a lecturer at nearby Wells Theological College. But he was quite unfitted for either post and left the second after a mere fortnight. Relief from the first was longer in coming – eight years, in fact – but then he inherited enough money to retire and became an honorary curate of Almondsbury in Bristol where, freed of responsibilities, he exercised a much valued pastoral ministry and, I gather, lived happily ever after.

51 *The very model of a Secretary General*

The first twenty years of the life of the General Synod were inextricably bound up with the career of its Secretary General, Derek Pattinson. Speaking in the Synod when Pattinson retired in 1990, Archbishop Runcie said: 'Where the Synod is, there is Derek; where Derek is, there is the Synod. It is not too much to say that Derek has been married to the Synod, and has loved and cherished it even in its most unpopular moments.' Further speeches of appreciation were interrupted by an ad hoc choir which sang a variation on a song from *The Pirates of Penzance,* each verse ending with 'He was the very model of a Secretary General'.

Some outside commentators were less complimentary, one describing him as 'a pin-striped *eminence grise*', another remarking that he was 'almost a caricature of the discreetly powerful civil servant'. He had in fact moved across to Church House, Westminster from the Treasury when the General Synod came into being in 1970 and had been in the Home Civil Service since coming down from Oxford. For the first two years he was deputy to Sir John Guillam Scott, who had for many years been Secretary of the former Church Assembly, but it was understood that Pattinson would succeed him once the Synod was launched.

Pattinson brought to the task a huge competence and a genuine commitment to the Church of England's work. He was at heart a reformer, though his position always precluded any expression of reformist views in public. Nonetheless, he was highly skilled in facilitating proposals for such matters as church unity and parochial reform. Besides the supervision of the Church House administrative machine, his most important role was that of advising and briefing successive Archbishops of Canterbury. He got on very well with Michael Ramsey, who relied on his advice, less well with Donald Coggan, who did not wish to be advised, and resumed strong relations with Robert Runcie.

The one serious blemish on Pattinson's career was the misjudgement that led to the so-called '*Crockford's* Affair', which was damaging to the church and led to the death of Gareth Bennett, his close friend. Coming close to the end of his time at Church House, it was possible to see this event as further evidence that he had been there too long and accumulated too much power for his own office and for the Synod generally. Nonetheless, he soldiered on until he was 60, secured a knighthood and was then ordained to the priesthood for a retirement ministry.

52 *Openness, struggle, laughter and prayer on Piccadilly*

One of the few churches where the spirit of the radical 1960s was not only kept alive but developed along imaginative lines was, improbably, St James's, Piccadilly, in London's West End. By 1980 this once fashionable church which had numbered five archbishops, including William Temple, two bishops and three deans among its previous rectors was in low water. The congregation had fallen to a handful and it was difficult to see how revival might be achieved.

The Bishop of London, Gerald Ellison, was a conservative Establishment churchman, but he believed strongly that the Church of England should embrace a wide variety of traditions. So he persuaded Donald Reeves, who had spent the previous 11 years as Vicar of St Helier, Morden – a housing estate parish of over 30,000 people and one of the most demanding assignments in South London – to move to Piccadilly. Before going to St Helier, Reeves had been Chaplain to Bishop Mervyn Stockwood of Southwark and his commitment to 'South Bank religion' had been reinforced by a lengthy stay at an urban housing centre in Chicago.

Ellison told him, 'I don't care what you do, but keep the church open. You have a big job.' And he offered his full support of anything he might attempt. Reeves did more than keep the church open: before long it was attracting upwards of 250 of all ages from all parts of London, and increasingly from many different countries, to the Sunday morning services. A radically different approach to worship was on offer – 'dignified informality', it was said to be – and Reeves declared the church to be an inclusive community that welcomed and celebrated diversity, including spirituality, ethnicity, gender and sexual orientation. It should 'create a space where people of any faith or none can question and discover sacred life through openness, struggle, laughter and prayer'. It should also have a commitment to be in solidarity with poor and marginalized people and to cherish Creation.

Weekday activities included New Age spirituality and meetings of lesbian and gay Christians. There was a daily market in the churchyard and a much used coffee shop; Reeves undertook pastoral work in the nearby Ritz Hotel and the Royal Academy across the road. All of which, and much more, occupied him for 18 years and when he officially retired in 1998 he launched, with his friend Peter Pelz, 'Soul of Europe', a group that had considerable success in encouraging Christians, Muslims and others to work together in the reconstruction of war-torn Bosnia.

53 Still fighting the good fight

The Editor
The *Daily Telegraph*

Sir – Following recent letters on the Bishop of Manchester's ban on the singing of 'O Valiant Hearts' at an ecumenical Remembrance Service next month, can I say that the hymn will be sung at the Trafalgar and Remembrance Day services in St. Peter's Church, Pimperne, Dorset.

The following hymns, all from *Hymns Ancient and Modern Revised* will also be sung: 351 ('I heard the voice of Jesus say'), 487 ('Eternal Father, Strong to save'), 488 ('Holy Father in Thy Mercy'), 629 ('Onward Christian Soldiers'), 579 ('I vow to Thee My Country') and the whole of 577 including the second verse: 'Our Lord, O God, arise,/Scatter our enemies,/And make them fall;/Confound their politics,/Frustrate their knavish tricks,/On thee our hopes we fix:/God save us all'). The church will be full on both occasions, and the collection at the latter for the Poppy Appeal will be the largest in Dorset.

Rev. Capt. D. A. FARQUHARSON-ROBERTS
Blandford Forum, Dorset

5

The Dispiriting Nineties

The ignominious rejection of Margaret Thatcher in 1990 set the Conservative government on a downward path from which it never recovered during the remaining years of the century. Her successor, John Major – a self-made man in the George Carey mould – failed to inspire, and a serious financial crisis on 'Black Wednesday' 1992 undermined the long-standing belief that only the Conservatives could be trusted with the economy. The steps taken to deal with this crisis led to a speedy recovery, but it was too late and a disenchanted electorate inflicted a savage defeat on the government in 1997 and welcomed Tony Blair, the leader of 'New Labour'.

The Church of England's one sign of hope in an otherwise dispiriting decade came earlier with the General Synod decision in 1992 that women might be ordained to the priesthood. This was a historic moment and a matter for profound rejoicing, though the cheering was distinctly muted, except at the first ordinations of women. The introduction of 'flying bishops' to pacify the dissentients brought a foreign element into the Anglican tradition.

By the end of the decade there were about 2,000 women priests, which did something, but not enough, to stem the serious decline in the number of parish clergy which had been a feature of the previous 50 years. In 1951 there were 18,196 of these and by 2,000 only 8,872 – plus 2,000 non-stipendiaries. The general decline in church attendance continued unchecked and, although the 1990s were declared to be a Decade of Evangelism, next to no resources were allocated to this project, at the end of which the total number of people in the pews was actually fewer than at its beginning. A survey revealed that 40 per cent of the population had never ever set foot in a church except for the weddings and funerals of family and friends.

In seeking to assess the quality of leadership exercised by a modern Archbishop of Canterbury it is necessary to recognize the peculiar difficulties that beset any holder of this office. Success, as commonly understood, is always to be attempted, but is virtually impossible to achieve in the present state of the Church of England. That said, it has to be admitted that George Carey's Primacy was less than inspiring and also that the leadership of many of his episcopal colleagues lacked lustre. Most of them were recruited to be pastoral managers, rather than visionary leaders, and, in their desperate attempts to improve the morale of the clergy and keep the parishes cheerful, they seemed unwilling to face the stark facts concerning the church's continuing decline and its dwindling financial resources. Thus no attention was given to the formulation of new strategic approaches to the church's mission.

Instead, the church became involved in an unedifying quarrel about an element in its own life. The place of homosexuals aroused high emotions, turned into an obsession and distracted attention from life-or-death challenges. This was an outrageously unsatisfactory way of celebrating the opening of a new millennium and, as its predecessor ended, the Church of England's traditional espousal of tolerance seemed distressingly precarious.

1 New ideas for country parishes

The report *Faith in the Countryside*, published in 1990 as a companion to *Faith in the City* (1985), was no less thorough than its predecessor but proved to be much less controversial and therefore attracted much less attention. Once again a distinguished commission, representing wide interests and considerable expertise, had been recruited and the chair was taken by Lord Prior, a former Cabinet minister and himself a substantial landowner. Four of the first six chapters were devoted to social and economic matters and raised important questions about government policies in some areas, but criticism was muted and recommendations dealt with the need for more affordable (i.e. council housing), the future of post offices and the importance of resisting some EEC policies. Although rural policy was identified as a serious problem in certain places, there was no broad assault on government policies. Given the presence of Lord Prior this was perhaps unsurprising.

The rest of the 400-page report included a careful, informed analysis of the problems and opportunities in the countryside and offered a multitude of examples of good practice in rural parishes, as well as many stimulating suggestions as to how new opportunities might be seized. Serious criticism was, however, voiced about the methods employed in the grouping of several parishes under the care of a single incumbent: 'Often new benefices have been formed when convenient vacancies have occurred and parishes have been bundled together without proper planning . . . There is lack of awareness among church leaders of the subtleties of rural society and the way it differs from urban situations.'

The need for rural experiments to be monitored, in order that lessons might be learned and shared, was stressed, as was the urgent need for clergy to be better trained for ministry in country parishes. Clergy should lead no more than two major services, in addition to an early said service, on any Sunday morning, and lay leadership of worship should be encouraged. Existing youth work in the community needed support, as should new initiatives taken to explore and promote the place of teenagers in the life of the church. And so on – all very constructive, but ten years on it was far from clear whether the response had been equally so.

2 *Revolution*

Within the lifetime of some of the people in this place, the vicar has changed from being the person who distributed money to those who were the chief charge on the community, to now being the chief charge on the community himself.

Evidence submitted to the Archbishops' Commission on
Rural Areas (1990)

3 *The machinations of the Crown Appointments Commission*

The 1990s brought unwelcome evidence that the most senior appointments in the Church of England had, through the machinations of the Crown Appointments Commission, become pawns in the game of church politics. This was always the fear when the new selection system gave greater influence to the General Synod and the dioceses. The translation of the virtually unknown George Carey to Canterbury in 1991 after fewer than three years at Bath and Wells was explicable only in terms of his evangelical credentials. Likewise, the translation of David Hope to York in 1995 after only four years in London – a post that cried out for a much longer stay – appeared to have more to do with his reservations about women priests than his ability to become a national church leader. Again, his replacement at London by Richard Chartres, an able Suffragan Bishop of Stepney, was related more to partisan pressure from within that diocese than to his potential for leadership in the wider life of the capital.

Among the 34 other appointments to dioceses there were, however, some good choices. Stephen Sykes bravely left the Regius Chair of Divinity at Cambridge in 1990 to give nine good years to Ely before returning to academic work in Durham. Kenneth Stevenson, a church historian, took his scholarship to Portsmouth in 1995 and the size of this diocese enabled him to continue to write books. Peter Forster, an Evangelical and another scholar, went to Chester in 1996, and in the following year Peter Selby left a professorial Fellowship in Applied Christian Theology at Durham to become, at Worcester, one of the church's most radical and outspoken social commentators.

At Salisbury, to which he was appointed in 1993, David Stancliffe exercised an innovative episcopate in the increasingly challenging rural areas of Wiltshire and Dorset and, as chairman of the church's Liturgical Commission, was a key figure in the completing of *Common Worship*. Michael Nazir-Ali's move from the General Secretaryship of the Church Missionary Society to the bishopric of Rochester in 1994 was an overdue recognition of the multi-racial character of late twentieth-century Britain. He combined a conservative theological and ethical stance with the vision of a missionary strategist and had at one time been Bishop of Rawind in Pakistan.

The appointment of Michael Ball to Truro in 1990 and of his twin brother to Gloucester two years later must have been a unique coincidence. They had been joint founders of a small religious order, the Community of the Glorious Ascension, and both had been suffragan bishops – one at Jarrow, the other at Lewes. They were as alike as peas in a pod and both became much loved diocesan bishops, but Peter's ministry at Gloucester ended tragically when his exploitation by a young man led to a police investigation and a court appearance. After an interval of several years he was permitted to conduct services in Bath and Wells diocese, remaining as always a guide and inspiration to many.

4 *A damp evangelism squib*

Back in the 1920s Bishop Henson of Durham advised one of his clergy that evangelistic missions were unnecessary in well-run parishes and mischievous in those that were ill run. Doubtless he would have said something similar had he been present at the 1988 Lambeth Conference where it was declared that the 1990s would be a Decade of Evangelism. The idea, which reached the conference via the US Episcopal Church, was not entirely original. The previous year the Pope had called for a decade of evangelization that would win a billion new Christians by the end of the century 'as a present for Jesus on his two-thousandth birthday'.

Anglicans should have known better than this and even George Carey felt uneasy about the decision, but the Decade was deemed to have started in 1990. There was no discussion of what was meant by 'evangelism', neither was there any consideration of what changes might be required in the organization of the different provinces, witnessing in a multitude of different circumstances. As far as the Church of England was concerned, nothing much happened. The Bishop of Wakefield declared in 1993 that God was 'doing great things' in his diocese and twelve months earlier Carey commissioned two evangelists in St Paul's

Cathedral to run a 'Springboard' campaign designed to stir dioceses and parishes to greater missionary zeal. Their influence was limited.

5 *Supermarkets of religion*

There were a few signs of much needed cathedral reform during the latter decades of the nineteenth century, and during the 1920s Frank Bennett at Chester became the first dean to show how cathedrals could be transformed into dynamic centres of Christian mission. But it was not until the 1960s that Bill Williams, at the rebuilt Coventry Cathedral, set in motion a movement that would by the end of the century enable the English cathedrals to be described as 'Flagships of the Spirit', 'Shopwindows of the Church of England', 'Supermarkets of religion'. That this transformation should have taken place when the rest of the church was in serious numerical and financial decline made it all the more astonishing. There was nothing comparable in any other part of Western Europe.

Williams saw clearly that if the leadership of the cathedrals could be changed from the elderly and the scholarly to the dynamic and the outward-looking, and if the staff could be enlarged to include specialists in education, youth work and social work, and if the worship could be offered in a variety of forms, the great churches would be in a position to offer a Christian witness complementary to that of the parish churches and attractive to many who would not normally set foot in their local church.

This proved to be true, not only in Coventry where new beginnings offered new opportunities, but also in every cathedral where there was vision and energy. Ease of travel helped, as did a massive increase in international tourism, so that by the mid-1990s the number of visitors to English cathedrals was of the order of 14.5 million annually; Canterbury and York shared 4.5 million of these, while St Paul's claimed 1.4 million, Chester 1 million, Salisbury and Norwich each half a million, and 11 others each 300,000–400,000. Donations from visitors and, in a few instances, admission charges (sadly reintroduced) exceeded £4.5 million, while profits from shops and refectories, both seen as essential tools, brought in another £1 million.

Friends organizations, started by Dean George Bell at Canterbury in 1927 and adopted by most of the other large cathedrals in the 1930s, also expanded to a total membership of about 55,000, providing finance to the tune of well over £1 million per annum and much voluntary labour as welcoming stewards, guides, cleaners, library, shop and refectory assistants. The total number of volunteers reached about 10,000 and if to this figure is added about 190 salaried clergy, and about 1,800 full- and part-time paid lay staff (musicians, stonemasons, administrators and the like) it becomes apparent that an average of 300 people are involved in the running of every cathedral.

I was fortunate enough to be involved in the ministry of both Westminster Abbey and Winchester Cathedral during this period of development and found it to be as stimulating and rewarding a form of ministry as could be found anywhere in the church. But it became increasingly evident that the historic structures of these ancient institutions were not suited to the changed demands being made of them. Reform became essential.

6 A dean's gardener

The size of my Winchester garden was deemed, mercifully, to entitle me to the services of a full-time gardener. But this did not always solve the problem, as my diary entry for 2 January 1990 records:

The New Year finds us without a Deanery gardener, the last incumbent of this office having officially retired on the last day of 1989. In fact he had done nothing in the garden for quite a long time and it would be more unkind than untrue to say that he retired some years ago. He always arrived in good time in the morning but the lighting of his pipe was attended with great difficulty and the surveying of three and a half acres occupied much time. Indeed before he could turn over more than a few spadefuls of soil the mid-morning break demanded attention. This accomplished and the spade prepared once again for action, the call of the betting shop necessitated a stroll in to the city.

A gardener thus exercised requires a hearty lunch, and afterwards another pipe of tobacco, carefully packed and patiently coaxed alight. There was barely time for a tea-break before the fading light of the winter afternoon made it impossible for the keenest of gardeners to distinguish between a prize-plant and a weed. And there was the pressing matter of which horse had won the 3.30 at Newbury. Inevitably, the weeds won the race for occupation of the Deanery garden and they gained a further advantage when the gardener was accused by a neighbour of having an affair with his wife and was so injured in the ensuring assault that he needed six weeks' sick leave –

this coinciding exactly with the spring season of sowing and planting.

The recovery of the gardener, and also of the garden, was protracted and the injuries to the lower part of his body were succeeded by acute breathing problems, induced surely by the pungent fumes generated by his pipe, rather than by excessive exertion. The hot summer came and went, autumn turned out to be a season of mellow fruitlessness and the garden, like the gardener, had lain fallow for a year. Never has a gardener entered into retirement better prepared.

7 *George Carey*

The appointment of George Carey to the archbishopric of Canterbury in 1991 occasioned very considerable surprise and could not easily be explained. When the Bishop of Winchester's lay assistant, Colin Peterson, telephoned me with advance warning of the announcement, I found this incredible. Carey had been the vicar of a vibrant evangelical church in Durham marketplace, brought a new breadth of outlook to the evangelical Trinity College, Bristol, where he was principal from 1982 to 1987, and for the last 30 months had been a popular Bishop of Bath and Wells. Unless he possessed outstanding qualities that had gone unnoticed, this seemed hardly sufficient equipment for the leadership of the Church of England and the Anglican Communion during a time of particular difficulty and challenge.

The Ladbroke's betting stakes had offered odds of 25–1 against Carey and he was himself astonished when the offer came. But a decision which had taken his predecessor an agonized six weeks to make took him no more than ten minutes. Evangelical access to the Divine will often appears to be uncomplicated and speedy. The Crown Appointments Commission may perhaps have fallen into the trap of supposing that it was the 'turn' of an Evangelical, this being the one growing area of the church's life. Or it may have seemed attractive to have a younger and different style of archbishop – not public school, not Oxbridge, self-made rather than privileged. Possibly there was an awareness that the social commitment of John Habgood (York) and David Sheppard (Liverpool) would not make either of their names attractive to Prime Minister Margaret Thatcher. Maybe it was a combination of all these factors; it is hard to believe there could have been any other.

Nonetheless, Carey was off to a lively start. In a speech shortly before his enthronement he said, 'People know where I stand. If they want a wishy-washy archbishop who is just a flag blowing in the wind, then it's not me.' In an interview published in *Reader's Digest* he described the Church of England as 'an elderly lady who mutters away to herself in a corner, ignored most of the time . . . she sits muttering ancient platitudes through toothless gums.' Of the Authorized Version of the Bible and the Book of Common Prayer, he asked, 'Why should the church be expected to use the language of 300–400 years old just for sentiment's sake?' And in the same interview he said that those opposed to the ordination of women to the priesthood were guilty of 'a most serious heresy'. In the ensuing furore it was left to the scholarly Archbishop Habgood to rescue his colleague by explaining that heresy was a rather ambiguous subject.

But it proved to be a false start, for Carey turned out to be no more than an updated model of his predecessor but one, Donald Coggan. He was a godly archbishop, enthusiastic, bold – though often unwise – in his public utterances, and immensely industrious. It was reported in 1998 that during the previous 12 months, in addition to spending 3 weeks presiding over the Lambeth Conference, he had visited 30 countries, delivered 140 speeches, sermons and addresses, made more than 50 broadcasts, contributed 10 articles to journals and books, spent many hours in the House of Lords and on other state affairs, given innumerable interviews and dealt with a mountain of letters, e-mails and faxes. His car was equipped with a telephone and a computer to enable such work to continue uninterrupted on journeys, and it was also reported that he rose at 6.30 a.m. or earlier, rarely went to bed before midnight and took one weekend off every six weeks. He calculated that by not having coffee after meals he could save two hours a week for work.

To what purpose? His single great achievement – considerable and historic – was the General Synod's agreement in 1992 to the ordination of women to the priesthood. Without his strong endorsement it is most unlikely that the two-thirds majority required for this would have been achieved then. The long-term value of the Archbishop's Council, set up in 1999 following a Church Commissioners' debacle, is a good deal less certain, and David Hope, who became Archbishop of York in 1995, eventually complained that he was fed up with the bureaucratic approach.

Once the women priests issue was settled, the question of homosexuality took its place at the head of the agenda and remained there for the remainder of Carey's Primacy. His own position was never in doubt: homosexual behaviour is contrary to the teaching of the Bible, it is contrary to nature, it is always and in all circumstances sinful. There was no room for compromise in this belief and this left him helpless to mediate between those whose opposing views were tearing the church apart.

Although Carey did his best during his Lambeth years and did some good things, his style attracted much unfavourable media comment and his approach was not what the Church of England needed in the last, testing decade of the century.

8 Moral and pastoral chaos promoted

The debate about homosexuality and the place of homosexuals in the church began in the 1970s when, in response to a request from the principals of the theological colleges, the General Synod Board of Social Responsibility appointed a working party to prepare a study of 'the theological, social, pastoral and legal aspects of homosexuality'. The report, published in 1979 as 'a contribution to a discussion', was liberal enough to divide opinion among Board members as to the desirability of its publication and in the end it went out with an additional section of 'critical observations'. The Gay Christian Movement was disappointed by the working party's views, while many others, not exclusively Evangelicals, believed Christian moral standards had been betrayed.

Another working party on the same subject, chaired by June Osborne, at that time a parish deacon and a future Dean of Salisbury, reported in 1989 but the House of Bishops refused permission for publication. Instead, they produced their own, disastrous, statement, *Issues in Homosexuality* (1990). This decreed that lay Christians were free to follow their own consciences in regard to homosexual activity but the clergy 'cannot claim the liberty to enter into sexually active homophile relationships'. This was, they explained, because of their calling, status and consecration.

Few were pleased with the statement, many were appalled by it and for different reasons. Evangelicals could not accept the 'concessions' to the laity, whereas homosexual clergy felt exposed to possible witch-hunts, especially those living in a partnership relationship to which their bishop had previously turned a blind eye. Must such relationships be severed as the price of remaining in the ordained ministry? Would all future homosexual ordinands (a large number) be required to take a vow of chastity as a condition of their ordination? Great unhappiness broke out.

In the event, most bishops chose not to ask searching questions about the sex lives of their homosexual clergy, many of whom were numbered among the best in their dioceses. But some did and, although few clergy were actually driven from office, some decided on their own initiative to resign, and there were instances of preferment to a senior post or even to another parish being denied. Besides which there remained a fundamental questioning of an understanding of Christian ethics that permitted one section of the church to follow the dictates of conscience while another was forbidden to do so. Some years after his retirement from the bishopric of Salisbury, John Baker, who had been chairman of the working party responsible for the statement, confessed that this distinction had been a serious mistake, and added that homosexual clergy should enjoy the same freedom as the laity and be encouraged to 'marry'. Such was the moral and pastoral chaos into which the Church of England had now fallen – a chaos that would shortly engulf the entire Anglican Communion.

9 Bishop takes Church Commissioners to court

In October 1991 Richard Harries, the liberally minded Bishop of Oxford, who had a special interest and some expertise in ethical questions, took the Church Commissioners to the High Court for a judgement on its investment policy in South Africa. By this time opposition to apartheid was mounting rapidly in South Africa itself as well as worldwide. The legal and moral issue for the Church of England was whether the Commissioners' sole responsibility as trustees was to maximize its income for the benefit of clergy stipends or whether the statement in their constitution that they were to be responsible for 'the cure of souls' involved a wider concern for sustaining the church's mission to humanity. In other words, were they free to invest some of their assets in South African companies and thus tacitly lend support to apartheid, if this was highly profitable, or did 'the cure of souls' require them to disinvest in order to undermine, if only in a small way, the South African government's detestable policy?

The Church Commissioners, with strong legal support, robustly defended the first option; Bishop Harries, who was acting not only for himself but for wider Christian anti-apartheid interests, also had strong legal support and the case aroused much public interest. In the end the court found in favour of the Church Commissioners and the question then arose as to responsibility for the costs, those of the Commissioners amounting to over £100,000. The judge made an order for payment, but not beyond the £30,000 that Harries had secured for a guarantee fund, and in the end the Church Commissioners, well satisfied with the outcome of the case, decided not to pursue him for the rest.

10 *Holy festivities in dockland*

Deptford, in South London, was a place where a traditional Anglo-Catholic approach to worship and parish ministry could still be made to work, though it needed an outstanding priest of unusual qualities to provide the leadership. David Diamond was only 33 when in 1968 the Bishop of Southwark, Mervyn Stockwood, took a chance and made him Rector of St Paul's, Deptford – a huge church of flamboyant baroque architecture set in a large former dockland parish where the problems of inner-city alienation were all too evident.

The church provided the perfect setting for the man and the method. His heroes were the great Anglo-Catholic slum priests of the nineteenth century, so the worship became extravagant and colourful, but arranged with great sensitivity and care. All who took part in it were made aware of life's spiritual dimension. It offered warmth without superficial mateyness and spoke powerfully to many who had previously been beyond the Church's range of influence – not least at baptisms, weddings and funerals. All of which was accompanied by intense pastoral work in the streets. Diamond mixed easily with people of all ages and backgrounds – most especially the young – and developed a special rapport with the criminal classes. He spoke up for them in the courts, visited them in prison and cared for their families while they were away – even though his Rectory was burgled on 40 occasions.

This was serious ministry, but not without its fun. Celebrations within the church soon spread to the streets of the parish in the form of the annual Deptford Festival, of which Diamond was the founder and chief impresario. It included a wide variety of parties and festivities, which engaged virtually the entire population of the area, and at one time was visited frequently by Princess Margaret who took a special interest in the parish and offered encouragement. Solemn celebrations of Mass were made an integral part of the programme, since Diamond saw the whole of life in sacramental terms.

He was in Deptford for nearly a quarter of a century, exercising an unfashionable paternalistic ministry, but its heavy demands and sheer pace were too much for so devoted a priest, even with a strong team of curates to share the load. He suffered a heart attack and a slight stroke in 1982, made a good recovery and was soon in action again, but ten years later, aged 57, he died suddenly in Glasgow, soon after arriving on the night sleeper for a holiday. The local newspaper marked his death with a special edition devoted to his ministry.

11 *High on doctrine, low on practice*

In 1986 it was recognized that sooner or later the Church of England would need to consider whether or not women might be consecrated as bishops. Inasmuch as they had not yet been ordained to the priesthood in this country, this was looking ahead somewhat, but there were already rumours of women bishops soon to appear in other parts of the Anglican Communion and the point was also being made that once women were admitted to the priesthood there could be no case against them becoming bishops. The Archbishops therefore appointed a representative group under the chairmanship of Sheila Cameron, an ecclesiastical lawyer and soon to become the first woman Warden of Keble College, Oxford, to look into the matter.

At its initial meeting the group decided that it could only consider the position of women in relation to the episcopate by looking afresh at the episcopate as a whole, so permission was obtained for its remit to be enlarged. Almost immediately, however, news reached Lambeth that the Anglican Church in America was thinking of consecrating a woman bishop and that the comments of the other provinces would be welcomed. The group was therefore asked to produce for the English House of Bishops a memorandum on the subject by May 1987. They rebelled against this, partly because they wanted to take a long look at the issues involved, but also because they were sharply divided and there was no possibility of producing an agreed memorandum. In the end, George Carey, at that time Bishop of Bath and Wells and a member of the group, submitted a personal document outlining the differences of opinion. The chairman later reported that 'heated exchanges had taken place'.

When the atmosphere cooled, the group set to work and in 1990 published a 354-page report, *Episcopal Ministry*, which amounted to a treatise on the theology and history of the ministry of bishops in the church. No stone had been left unturned and its doctrine of church order could not have been higher:

It is a way of being in which the relationships of the persons united in Christ, and of the local churches to which they belong, are enabled to reflect, even though in a limited, creatively way, the relationship of the Persons of the Trinity.

The task of relating this to such mundane matters as the General Synod, bishops' meetings and the appointment of bishops via the machinery of 10 Downing Street proved to be beyond the group's capacity. And on the matter of women bishops, over which the doctrine of the Trinity might have indicated difficulties over their exclusion, the members remained as sharply divided as ever. Even more seriously, they quite failed to tackle the question of what kind of leadership the Church of England required in the urgent missionary situation with which it was now confronted and how the office of a bishop might fulfil this role. It had been four years of wasted time – and doubtless money.

12 *Translating the Good Book*

When I was ordained deacon in 1951, during the service the bishop handed me a copy of the New Testament in the Greek text. Forty years later, when involved in ordinations at Winchester, I noted with some surprise that the new deacons were handed a variety of versions – New English, Revised Standard, Jerusalem, even that of the Good News Bible, which is more akin to a paraphrase. I learned that ordinands were permitted a personal choice. This was a clear sign that those entering Holy Orders could no longer be assumed to have a working knowledge of New Testament Greek and also evidence of the variety of new translations that appeared in the 1960s and 1970s.

All were, in varying degrees, welcomed as products of the latest biblical scholarship and as serious attempts to bring out the vividness of the original narrative by skilled translation into modern English. Many millions of copies were sold and the new versions came quickly into use in church services, though those who still valued the beauty and familiarity of the 1611 Authorized Version were naturally unhappy. And it was perhaps the quality of its language, as well as that of the scholarship, which made the American Revised Standard Version the most popular for public use, and by the end of the century its editors had responded to a call for more inclusive language. Greater intelligibility of language did not, however, lead to wider understanding of the Bible's meaning and significance.

13 *Church music out of tune*

The 1992 report of an Archbishop's Commission on Church Music, *In Tune with Heaven*, concluded that the state of music in parish churches is 'generally unsatisfactory'. It noted, however, a very wide variation in standards, and this continues. In some large town parishes the choir is good enough to be invited to sing in a cathedral when its own choir is away. Market towns often have choirs of a good standard and occasionally a country parish will produce surprisingly good music. In every case all depends on the skill and commitment of the organist and the support he or she receives from the clergy and congregation. Few are paid more than a modest honorarium. In many evangelical parishes, however, there is less dependence on a choir and, although the result is not to everyone's taste, groups of instrumentalists and chorus-singing congregations produce powerful acts of corporate worship.

A survey carried out for the Archbishop's Commission among 680 representative parishes, two-thirds of them rural, found that 63 per cent had a choir, most of them robed, and another 21 per cent had separate singing groups. Among the rural parishes only just over half had choirs and only half had organists, one-third of whom described themselves as 'reluctant'. The average size of choirs was about 15 and a dramatic decline in the number of boy choristers was noted, their places being taken by girls and women. In three-quarters of all churches Anglican chant was still used for canticles and psalms, but the traditional Merbecke setting of the Eucharist had been replaced by modern settings (few of high quality) for the new rites.

The general standard of music would certainly be even less satisfactory were it not for the sustained efforts of the Royal School of Church Music with its training programmes, handbooks, diocesan festivals and other attempts to improve the quality of worship. In marked contrast to parish churches, the standard of music in the cathedrals has never been higher and, although the style is still appreciated by only a minority of regular churchgoers, an increasing number of these are forsaking their local church because they 'cannot stand the music'.

14 *Church Commissioners run into deep trouble*

For more than thirty years Archbishop Fisher's decision to get the Church Commissioners to raise their income by the movement of a significant proportion of their assets from rural land to equities paid off. The clergy did not become rich, but their stipends were improved and adjustments in deployment enabled the parochial system to be maintained in a more or less traditional pattern. Whenever the Commissioners' affairs were mentioned in the Church Assembly or its successor, the General Synod, it was customary for the First Church Estates Commissioner to be congratulated and thanked for great achievement. He could do no wrong.

But all this changed dramatically in July 1992. While attending a meeting of the General Synod in York and not long before he was due to make a speech – ironically on the subject of Christian stewardship – George Carey was handed a cutting from the *Financial Times*. This consisted of a carefully researched article which showed conclusively that during the past two years the Church Commissioners had, by mismanagement, lost £500 million – a figure which, on deeper investigation, turned out to be nearer £800 million. Carey was dumbfounded. Only a few weeks earlier he had chaired the Commissioners' Annual General Meeting, in the course of which the chairman of the Southwark Diocesan Board of Finance had severely questioned the First Estates Commissioner, Sir Douglas Lovelock, and been assured that there were no major problems; indeed they had done better than many of their competitors. Lovelock recognized, however, that there was, as he put it, 'a tension between the increasing expenditure commitments of the Commissioners and the yield on income-producing assets'. The AGM consisted of too large and inexpert a gathering of dignitaries for him to be cornered on what must have seemed to some at least of those present to be a rather important admission. At the York General Synod, following the *FT* revelations, Lovelock assured the members, 'This is not a crisis; it is a manageable problem, though serious . . . We have not lost £500 million – valuation rises and falls.' It would nonetheless be necessary to restrict clergy stipend increases, while personal giving by church people would need to be increased so that it constituted at least 5 per cent of take-home pay. For the rest, await the recovery.

An enquiry conducted by a leading accountancy firm indicated serious problems and the need for more radical solutions. The losses could not be explained solely by the ups and downs of the marketplace. Some serious errors had been made as a result of a decision to move substantially into speculative property development in Britain and the USA. In particular the purchase for £3 million of three fields at Ashford in Kent, but without planning permission for development, had led to a loss of nearly £90 million. It was also revealed that the investment in development, some of which had been highly successful, was financed, not by use of the Commissioners' own capital, but by borrowings that eventually reached £500 million – an unusual and undesirable policy for an organization needing regular, reliable income to pay clergy stipends. Then there was the little matter of the willing response to requests from the General Synod and the Pensions Board for clergy pension increases (an additional £5 million a year), the payment of the clergy's community charges (£8 million to start with), a £1 million annual grant to the Church Urban Fund and increased grants to poorer dioceses – all worthwhile but in the end dependent upon increased income.

The crisis, for no other description would really do, came on the eve of Sir Douglas Lovelock's retirement and marked the beginning of the end of the Church Commissioners' power. Other factors hastened the process, but this was the turning point.

15 Christian–Jewish friendship upheld

The refusal of Archbishop Carey to become Patron of the Church's Ministry among the Jews (CMJ) when he took office caused a great deal of fuss in evangelical circles. Every Archbishop of Canterbury since 1849 had been Patron and the organization, although not large, had enjoyed wide support, often benefiting from collections taken at Good Friday services. Tony Higton, at that time a fanatical evangelical vicar of a parish in Chelmsford diocese and later to become general director of CMJ, described Carey's decision as 'a shameful betrayal' and 'a grave undermining of the cause of the gospel'.

It was in fact a small but significant sign that the Church of England was beginning to take inter-faith relations seriously. Until quite recently the organization had been known by its original name, 'Church Mission to the Jews', and saw its task as that of converting Jews to the Christian faith. A change of name to 'The Church's Ministry Among the Jews' suggested a modification of this objective, but the more aggressive image remained – especially for the Jewish community – and was reinforced by the support of Higton and others of his kin.

Carey saw clearly that his patronage was incompatible with his developing friendship with the Chief Rabbi, his joint presidency of the Council for Christians and Jews, which existed to promote dialogue between adherents of the two faiths, and his recognition that inter-faith collaboration, rather than competition, would become increasingly important during his Primacy. This did not discourage Bishop John B. Taylor, the evangelical Bishop of St Albans, from accepting the presidency of CMJ when he retired in 1996.

16 *Women priests – at long last*

November 11 1992 was a historic day in the life of the Church of England. The General Synod vote in favour of the ordination of women to the priesthood rolled back centuries of fervent belief and unbroken practice. The debate in Church House, Westminster was full of drama, witnessed worldwide through television and by crowded galleries. Hundreds, excluded for want of room, waited outside. The Bishop of Guildford, Michael Adie, who proposed the motion, chose wisely to eschew rhetoric and emotion and spoke quietly, low key almost. The Bishop of London, David Hope, who was opposed, said nonetheless that whatever decision was reached at the end of the day he would respect it 'with as good and generous grace as I can'. The strong support of the Archbishops of Canterbury and York was important, less so were the words of Father Peter Geldard, a leading opponent, who likened the Church of England to a village oak tree that was about to be cut down, and went on to plead with the Synod to 'put down your axe'.

In the period immediately before the debate it was by no means certain that the outcome would be favourable to women priests. In the diocesan synods, 68 per cent of the clergy and 66 per cent of the laity had voted in favour, which was much too close for comfort for a General Synod decision requiring two-thirds majorities in each of the three Houses – laity, clergy and bishops. During the week preceding the debate, however, there was a growing belief among the supporters that the tide had turned and that the required majorities would be achieved. And so it turned out – just. The narrowness led some opponents to question the validity of so momentous a decision, but for a coalition church, holding together a variety of beliefs, a majority in excess of two-thirds was very substantial. There was every reason for the members of MOW to spend that evening rejoicing.

17 *'Flying bishops' launched*

Once the decision had been made, it might have been supposed that the bishops would return to their dioceses also rejoicing and ready to lead celebrations marking a historic development in the church's ministry. Not at all: most returned puzzled and worried men. For them the result had been totally unexpected and some had set aside days for counselling and consoling frustrated, angry and distressed women deacons. There had been an often-repeated threat by the opponents of women priests to create schism or to become Roman Catholics – figures between 1,000 and 5,000 were talked of, though in the event only 383 working priests left, and of these 40 soon returned. A significant number of those who had no intention of leaving said they would no longer accept the ministrations of their bishop once he had ordained a woman, since they did not wish to be 'tainted' (their word) by his action. There was also a sordid financial problem: clergy who left because of the decision had been promised up to £30,000 severance pay, which if multiplied by (say) 2,000 would leave the church with a destructive bill of £60 million.

There was therefore no bishop-led celebration. Instead the bishops concocted a scheme, later to become an Act of Synod, that would provide alternative episcopal oversight for those dissidents who rejected their own diocesan bishops. In some instances a suffragan bishop, who refused to ordain women, would conveniently serve this purpose. But since there would be insufficient of these it was proposed to consecrate three Provincial Episcopal Visitors who would have a roving commission to minister to dissident priests and parishes. This would, it was claimed, meet a pastoral need and at the same time recognize the existence in the Church of England of what they called 'two integrities', that is to say, those who accepted and those who did not accept women priests. In spite of some fierce opposition in the General Synod, the proposal was accepted, with the Archbishop of York, John Habgood, leading the way. Three PEVs (soon to be known as 'flying bishops') were consecrated – two for service of about a hundred parishes in Canterbury province, the other for many fewer in York province. It was understood that they would function with the good will and ultimately under the jurisdiction of the bishops of the dioceses into which they 'flew'.

18 *A dangerous compromise*

This development was advertised as 'a sensible Anglican compromise', with an underlying, but unstated, belief that with the passage of time opposition to women priests would fade and the 'flying bishops' would be grounded. Among the new women priests and their many supporters, however, the Act of Synod (renamed by them Act of Folly) was massively offensive, even though its practical operation in a parish-centred church went largely unobserved.

It called into question the authority of their own priesthood, since its rejection by a minority, albeit one recognized by the appointment of its own bishops, left them in a position inferior to that of their male colleagues and unrecognized within their own dioceses. The recognition of 'two integrities' moreover suggested that the arguments of those in favour of and those opposed to women priests carried equal weight, whereas, in truth, the Church of England, having prayed for the guidance of the Holy Spirit, had decided by very large majorities in its Diocesan and General Synods that women should be ordained. There was the further, important, theological point that if Catholic order requires the church's unity to be centred not only on union with Christ but also with the bishop of a diocese, then the existence within a diocese of priests and parishes who do not recognize the bishop, and elect to receive the ministry of another, can only be destructive of true unity. It soon became evident also that the 'flying bishops', far from being a temporary expedient, were becoming the focus for long-term continuation, and possibly expansion, of schism, with ever-threatening noises and threats about the consequence of making women bishops.

Vigorous opposition to all this was mounted by GRAS (Group for Rescinding the Act of Synod), but its support and influence was limited and before long even more sinister schismatic developments would engulf the entire Anglican Communion.

19 The disappearing dog collar

The rapid abandoning of riding dress by dignitaries, following Michael Ramsey's translation to Canterbury, was not altogether surprising. But the decline in the wearing of the clerical collar by the parish clergy and others during the 1960s was less expected. The probable explanation was the desire of priests to identify more closely with their parishioners, or maybe, in an increasingly secularized society, a certain embarrassment over a distinctive sign of a holy calling. One benefit of wearing the collar was said to be the certainty of ample space when using public transport, though, more seriously, there was evidence of clergy offering pastoral care to strangers who identified them and sought instant counsel.

The clerical collar was in fact unknown in Britain until the second half of the nineteenth century when the influence of the Oxford Movement led to its importation from the Roman Catholic continent. Before then, gentlemen in Holy Orders were content with a cravat or sometimes a small white bow tie. A black shirt and white tie was made fashionable by Canon Alec Vidler in the Cambridge of the 1960s and continued to be worn by Cambridge-influenced priests for several more decades. Others, usually High Churchmen, followed a post-Vatican II fashion with collars of modest proportions – no more than a small piece of white plastic inserted into the designed slit of a black shirt – while Evangelicals boldly adopted shirts of varied hue, often pale blue. The ordination of women to the priesthood promised much wider variety of fashion, but sadly most adopted something close to the male model and seemed more than ready to wear it.

20 *Church and Crown*

The Queen's advancing years and the sequence of unfortunate happenings in the Royal Family and other aspects of her life that led her to describe 1992 as her *annus horribilis* inevitably caused some discussion about the future of the monarchy. In a television interview the Prince of Wales expressed the wish to be regarded as 'defender of faith', rather than 'defender of *the* faith', and this was seen by some as a desire to dismantle the historic Church/Crown nexus and replace it with some sort of religious mish-mash. But it was in fact no more than an off-the-cuff remark in which he was indicating his readiness to protect the spiritual space in the nation of all religious believers.

In a lecture in Westminster Abbey on 'Spirituality, Shakespeare and Royalty', Canon Eric James called for the setting up of a commission on church and nation to consider the future of the monarchy. He believed the time had come for 'a profound reflection upon and reconsideration of the role of monarch', and suggested that there is not a lot to be said for the lottery element in the hereditary principle because, as he put it, 'you can never tell what you are to get'. The audience was reminded that in England until 1213 the monarch was elected and, although James emphasized that he did not wish to see immediate changes, he wondered 'if the time is returning for election to the task and the role'. That such a possibility had been even as much as hinted at in Westminster Abbey of all places, and by a royal chaplain of all people, was sufficient to send the media wild for a day or two but James denied emphatically that he was advocating a future change in the direction of an elected monarchy.

21 *Divine respect*

On Sunday morning I went to divine service – 11 o'clock Mattins and Sermon. After the surpliced choir had performed a beautiful anthem, and the 17th century ritual had been got through, a clergyman in collar, hood and scarf emerged from behind a rood screen (19th century wrought iron) and delivered the message – 'The barrier between the sacred and the secular has been broken down.' He then ducked back behind the screen and waited for the end of the service and processed out behind the choir and clerics while we stood 'as a sign of respect.'

Peter G. Morris

22 *High church, low church, short church?*

During his retirement years in Bath, Bishop Mervyn Stockwood was asked by a parishioner of its noble Abbey, 'Bishop, are you high church or low church?' The reply was immediate, 'I used to be high church, now I am short church.' This sentiment is undoubtedly shared by many retired clergy, not so much because they are no longer 'performers' and therefore oblivious to the passage of time, but chiefly because in recent years the length of services has increased considerably. As the size of congregations has become smaller, so the services have become longer – or is it the other way round?

Liturgical revision is the true explanation. Digging deep into the history of early Christian worship has led to the unearthing of previously discarded patterns and material that were entirely suitable for the less-hurried times in which they were devised and are now returned to use in the cause of liturgical 'correctness'. This has certainly led to an enrichment of the Church of England's worship, but at the cost of an 'expert' in liturgy throwing into the cauldron of worship everything he or she has to hand, notwithstanding its effect of extending a service by 10, 15 or even 30 minutes. Special events, confirmation, installation of parish clergy, deans and bishops, and the like, may now take two hours or more and become tests of physical stamina. Of spiritual stamina, too, since the 'overtime' has the effect of reducing the impact of what has gone before, leaving a weary worshipper thankful when the service is ended rather than inspired to move from the worship of God to the furtherance of his Kingdom in daily life.

23 *The Christian atheist*

Don Cupitt, who taught at Cambridge for over thirty years, worked on the frontier between religion and philosophy and his approach was primarily that of a philosopher rather than of a theologian. He came to believe that religion is essentially a human invention and that the word 'God' has no objective reality. It is, he said, 'a necessary myth', and his position was best described as a form of Christian atheism. His attacks on the church and theologians were often savage. In *Taking Leave of God* (1980), he accused the church of exercising 'psychological terrorism' and saw his own role that of 'rescuing Jesus from dogmatic captivity and God from metaphysical captivity'. None of this won him many friends among church leaders or indeed among his fellow academics and in 1996, after 23 years as a lecturer in the Cambridge Divinity School, he resigned because he felt that his colleagues were not taking him sufficiently seriously. He was, however, revered by successive generations of undergraduates at Emmanuel College, where he was Dean from 1966 to 1991. They enjoyed his revolutionary thinking, and at the same time greatly valued his high-quality pastoral care. Curiously, as it seemed to some, he was very conservative on liturgical matters.

The development of Cupitt's thinking could be charted in his books, which appeared at regular 12-month intervals (30 by the end of the decade) and of which *The Long-Legged Fly* (1987) was specially important. These often seemed more akin to work in progress than to substantial summas, and they tended to be somewhat repetitive, but they constituted an important challenge to theologians, since they asked important questions which few of them appeared willing to face.

At various times it was suggested that Cupitt's beliefs were incompatible with his position as a priest in the Church of England, but he never accepted this and believed it to be the task of the clergy to encourage exploration of the unknown. His own faith was summed up in *After all: Religion without Alienation* (1994): 'We should live as the Sun does. The process by which it lives and the process by which it dies are one and the same. It hasn't a care. It simply expends itself gloriously, and in so doing gives life to us all.'

24 *Sea of Faith*

Although Don Cupitt's books were not easy reading for those of non-philosophical mind, he was a brilliant oral communicator. This was recognized in 1977 when he presented a television documentary *Who was Jesus?* Encouraged by its success, the BBC engaged him for an expensive series of programmes with the title *Sea of Faith*, in which all the world's main religions were brought under critical scrutiny. Large numbers watched the series and, following the publication of a book based on it, a 'Sea of Faith Movement' came into being. An annual national conference attracted 200–250 people, about 800 joined local groups and a magazine had over 1,000 subscribers. Some were keen on promoting church reform, others were content simply to be non-dogmatic religious people in a context where they could speak freely, a few were trying to remake religion entirely.

Members tended to be treated with considerable suspicion in church circles, especially if they were clergy, and, according to Cupitt, even more so in the academic world. In 1992 the Revd Anthony Freeman, who combined the posts of Adviser on Continuing Education and Assistant Director of Ordinands in Chichester diocese, with responsibility for a small Sussex parish, published a book *God in Us*. He was a disciple of Cupitt and the book raised serious questions about the reality and existence of God. This troubled the Bishop of Chichester who consulted various people, including Professor John Macquarne and Professor Charles Moule, and reached the conclusion that Freeman should be relieved of his diocesan posts. But the parish of which he was the priest-in-charge was much too small for him to be allowed to remain there and the Bishop was unwilling to appoint him to another.

25 Two talented women priests and a deacon

Among the women ordained in the 1980s and 1990s were some of unusual talent and experience. Susan Cole-King, born in 1934 and a daughter of Leonard Wilson, the legendary Bishop of Singapore, then of Birmingham, trained as a doctor, spent nine years in Malawi on primary health care in rural villages, studied Third World Development at Sussex University, and in 1981 became chief health adviser to UNICEF. Based in New York, she travelled extensively, advising on health care as an integral part of social and economic development. But she came to recognize the importance of the spiritual factor in healing and felt called to be a priest. After two years at the General Theological Seminary in New York, she was ordained and joined the staff of the Church of All Angels on 80th Street, off Broadway, combining her medical skill and spiritual insights in the service of the poor.

Returning to England in 1989 to join those women struggling to be accepted as priests, she was unable at that time to minister in this country as a priest but served as a deacon at Dorchester Abbey in Oxfordshire, then spent two years as deacon-in-charge of St Peter's, Drayton. In both parishes her work was greatly valued and she also addressed meetings in other places and conducted retreats. Following the authorization of women priests by the General Synod in 1994 she was able to share more fully in the life of the church and came top of the Oxford diocese poll in an election for the General Synod. Her experience soon led to her being made vice-chairman of its Board of Social Responsibility's international and development committee. She also became an honorary canon of Christ Church Cathedral. On her official retirement in 1987, concern for the poor and suffering often drew her back to Malawi to try to persuade its leaders to tackle AIDS more effectively, and she preached a memorable sermon on suffering at the 1998 Lambeth Conference.

Joyce Caine, born in 1921, taught in Lancashire schools before volunteering for service with the evangelical China Inland Mission. She went to China in 1949, but her missionary efforts were severely restricted when the People's Liberation Army took control and she returned to England two years later. Further theological training led to appointment as a lecturer at Dalton House, Bristol, where women were trained for overseas mission and parish work in England. Subsequently she was vice-principal and then principal, and when Dalton House was merged with Tyndale Hall and Clifton theological colleges to form Trinity College, Bristol in 1971, she became Dean of Women.

Her concern for the ordination of women had been aroused by her acquaintance with women bearing heavy missionary responsibilities in China, as well as by her experience of male domination in evangelical circles. Thus she played an important part, as a biblical scholar, in persuading many Evangelicals that, contrary to their previously held beliefs, there was nothing in the Bible to preclude women from being ordained. Nor, she argued, did the doctrine of the headship of Christ exclude women from positions of leadership in the church. She trained women for ordination but, having herself been made deacon in 1987, decided not to proceed to the priesthood when this became possible, since her vocation remained that of a scholar.

Margaret Kane, born in 1915, had never intended to seek Holy Orders, but when the ordination of women became possible she offered herself, primarily to support the other women priests. After training at St Christopher's College, Blackheath, she became what was then known as 'an accredited lay worker'. Ministry in a tough London/Essex border parish was followed by service as a chaplain's assistant with women in the Forces, both reinforcing her awareness of the detachment of the church from the working classes. Further study, at William Temple College, Rugby, and the influence of the French worker-priests, took her to specialist work in the Yorkshire coal-mining parish of Maltby. During the next seven years she went down one of the pits every week to engage in pastoral work among the miners, but chiefly to get them together to discuss in a biblical context the various issues arising from their work.

In 1959 she joined the Sheffield Industrial Mission and soon made her mark in the steel works, but her arrival coincided more or less with a change in the Mission's leadership and friction over the recent change of policy. She went therefore to Hong Kong to advise on industrial mission there and on her return spent the next 12 years as a consultant on industrial and social affairs to successive Bishops of Durham – Ian Ramsey, John Habgood and David Jenkins. She also wrote three books on themes related to the gospel in an industrial society. Many believed that, although she had not intended to become a priest, the final stage of her ministry was enriched by her ordination.

26 A bishop's lament

When Prime Minister Margaret Thatcher sought to solve Lincoln Cathedral's problems with the appointment in 1989 of a new Dean, the cabal of Evangelicals then working in 10 Downing Street advised her to choose Brandon Jackson, the abrasive Provost of Bradford whose theological credentials were accompanied by a law degree. She ordered him to 'sort things out', but the effect of his arrival in Lincoln was akin to that of pouring petrol on fire. The immediate cause of the resulting conflagration was an investigation of the circumstances in which the Sub-Dean, Rex Davis, had taken the cathedral's copy of the Magna Carta to an exhibition in Australia and sustained a loss of about £80,000. Clash of personality was also unfortunate but a public struggle for power between Dean and Sub-Dean was nothing short of disastrous and engaged the attention of the national media on and off for seven years.

The Bishop of Lincoln, Robert Hardy, had no power to intervene but in the report of an official Visitation of the cathedral he delivered one of the most devastating attacks ever made by a bishop on the Dean and Chapter of his cathedral:

The plain fact is that the Dean and Residentiary Canons have been at odds with each other, and the intemperate language and indiscretions on both sides have simply added to the sense of conflict. There does not seem the will to change. I consider the attitude of the Residentiary Canons to me to have been on occasion reprehensible and that they and the Dean have conducted themselves shamefully in the media. As far as I am concerned, the past eight months have been the saddest period of my ministry. The whole Chapter seems to have little perception as to how all this comes across to the general public. It all seems a very long way from Jesus of Nazareth.

His call to the canons to 'consider their position', later reinforced by the Archbishop of Canterbury, who added the Dean to his call, went unheeded. Jackson eventually resigned in 1997 but Davis went on until his retirement in 2003.

27 Cathedral reform and reorganization

The damaging publicity attending problems at Hereford and Lincoln Cathedrals, as well as lesser difficulties at Exeter and St Paul's, brought to light the fact that the statutes given to the English cathedrals in the early part of the seventeenth century and hardly modified since were no longer adequate for the governing of institutions whose activities had changed almost beyond recognition. Deans lacked the authority necessary to effective leadership. Canons were uncertain of their role, and chapters often lacked the expertise to administer what were in effect medium-sized companies with budgets of £1 million or more. By the early 1990s there was broad agreement among the deans and provosts that corporate action was needed, if only to forestall unwelcome intervention by the General Synod, which was known to have limited sympathy for cathedrals and might well seize the opportunity created by scandal to bring them under centralized control.

The result was the setting up, at the request of the cathedrals, of an Archbishop's commission to examine their life and make recommendations for improvement in their governance. Meeting under the robust leadership of Lady Howe of Aberavon, the 13-member commission completed its work in two years, having despatched some of its members to every cathedral and received submissions from nearly 400 bodies and individuals. The 262-page report, *Heritage and Renewal*, published in October 1994, paid tribute to the impressive life of the cathedrals and their ability and openness to change. They were, it said, not in crisis and any problems were capable of being resolved within the evolving tradition that had marked them for centuries.

Nonetheless, 104 recommendations followed, ranging from evangelism to trading, and including 33 related to governance and management. Most of them were of a general kind and concerned with good practice in matters such as Friends organizations, shops, education and accountancy and required no structural changes. But some related to accountability and required the setting up of a council to act as a watchdog over the cathedral's life, including its finances. Up to three lay people, each with particular expertise, should be appointed to the chapter and a qualified administrator employed to deal with day-to-day management. Deans should continue to be appointed by the Crown and although canons would still be appointed by the bishop this would be only after full consultation with the chapter. Canons should no longer hold office until they reached the age of 70 but for a term of years or until it was considered desirable for them to leave.

The report was met, initially, with hostility by a large proportion of the deans and provosts who appeared to have forgotten that it was they who had asked for the commission to be appointed and that the recommendations were not therefore to be regarded as something imposed from on high. Eventually, after some further huffing and puffing, most of the recommendations were accepted, some in modified form, and passed into law in 1999. The value of a lay element in the chapter was quickly recognized, but an increase in bureaucracy became an unwelcome problem for some cathedrals. The remainder of the changes will take a decade or more to evaluate.

28 Rape and murder at the vicarage

The incidence of physical assault on the clergy, and sometimes members of their families, became so high in the 1990s that a number of dioceses felt driven to arrange for parish priests to attend special courses on self-defence. The explanation was to be found in the general rise in drug-related crime and violence in British society as a whole, but the clergy were at particular risk because of their believed readiness to aid the needy. It was often when a parish priest refused to give money to a drop-out drug addict that violence flared.

This was not the case, however, in March 1986 when the Vicar of St Mary's, Ealing in West London, Michael Saward, who later became a canon of St Paul's, answered the doorbell of his vicarage on an otherwise quiet afternoon and was confronted by three men who knocked him unconscious with a cricket bat and went on to rape one of his twin daughters. Saward required a spell in hospital for recovery but he and his daughter, who subsequently wrote a book, *Rape's My Story*, declared themselves ready to forgive their assailants.

Worse was to follow. In August 1996 the priest-in-charge of St Margaret's, Anfield in Liverpool was murdered outside his vicarage by a man he had for some time been trying to help. Christopher Gray was 32 and described by the Bishop of Liverpool as 'one of the brightest hopes of his generation'. He had won a county scholarship to Winchester, gone on to gain a congratulatory double first in classics at Oxford, and, after taking a first in theology at Leeds University, was described by Professor Adrian Hastings as 'quite the most brilliant student I have had the pleasure of teaching'. He spoke nine languages.

Disdaining an academic career, Gray chose instead to devote himself to the service of the poorest of the poor in Liverpool. In this he drew his strength and commitment from beliefs in the nature of God, the incarnation, the church and the sacraments, and in a contribution to a book, *The Fire and the Clay* (1993), he wrote: 'The supreme act of the shepherd is to lay down his life for the sheep . . . Priests are called to be people who grow to be like Christ in the faithful service of their flocks, even to the point of sacrificing their own lives.'

29 *The honorary consul*

The General Synod has never failed to attract to its membership a good many unusual laymen and -women. The Lay House of its predecessor, the Church Assembly, was said to be populated by 'the squires from the shires and the spinsters from the spas', but this tradition was diluted when Maurice Chandler, having failed to win election to Parliament, was returned to the Assembly in 1955 by the electors of Birmingham diocese.

He became a familiar figure in Church House, Westminster, in clothes that might have come from Oxfam, and was a prominent Anglo-Catholic churchman who over the course of 35 years, until 1990, was at the centre of church politics. He was a thorn in the side of those who proposed Anglican–Methodist unity, revision of the Book of Common Prayer or the ordination of women to the priesthood, and, being a sharp political operator, knew how to exploit the General Synod's procedures.

More constructively, he was chairman of a committee that created a new Anglican diocese in Europe and was said by Archbishop John Habgood of York to be the only man ever to have created a diocese single-handed.

He had, however, many other interests, some of them mysterious. He worked as a public relations consultant and evidently derived income from this source. He found his way into diplomatic circles as honorary consul of the tiny Commonwealth state of Kiribati in the Pacific, an office he exercised from a room above a High Church bookshop in Westminster. Following his appointment as CBE 'for political and public services' in 1984, he was asked jokingly by Archbishop Runcie if this was a reward for his services to MI5. He replied, 'Not to MI5' with heavy emphasis on the '5'. This was the nearest he got to lowering his guard. His reputation as a 'fixer' aroused constant suspicion, as did his ability to turn up in unexpected places, in, for example, the royal box at the VJ celebrations a few months before his death in 1996.

30 *The role of the Reader*

The unsung heroes of the Church of England during the second half of the twentieth century were its Readers – men and women who, after two years or more of part-time training, were licensed by their bishop to conduct non-sacramental services. They were responsible for leading Mattins and Evensong in those churches, an ever-increasing number, where no priest was available, and many of them undertook teaching and other responsibilities in their own parishes. Eventually there were about 10,000 Readers, drawn, like the Church of England itself, almost exclusively from the professional classes.

In spite of their gifts and commitment, however, they tended for a long time to be regarded as second-XI substitutes for the clergy. A lay-man recounted to me how on one occasion when attending a service conducted by a Reader he switched off at the time of the sermon, only to discover that he had missed an important pastoral letter from the diocesan bishop. The development of the Parish Communion provided further opportunities for Readers to assist with the Bible readings and the administration of the chalice, though these roles were more widely shared among parishioners.

The advent of non-stipendiary priests raised in the minds of many Readers serious questions about the future of their office. Men and woman, often with scarcely more training than theirs, were ordained to a full sacramental ministry and also appeared, as clergy, on territory previously occupied by Readers, thus relegating them to a lower place on the liturgical hierarchy – and making some feel even less valued. A suggestion that Readers should be ordained to the permanent diaconate was offered as a solution to this problem, but required much further consideration of the true place of the diaconate in the modern church and, even more importantly, the true role of the laity. The clericalization of 10,000 of their number would hardly seem an advance in the church's mission in the secular world.

31 Correction

A vicar promised tonight to apologise for using the word 'wog' in his parish magazine. He said: 'I am sorry I used the word. I did not really mean to suggest colour prejudice. What I really meant to say was "Continental gentlemen". I intend to apologise in the next issue.'

The Times

32 Victorian values in the East End

Not every priest striving to solve the seemingly intractable church problems in London's East End turned to new methods. Donald Pateman, who spent 42 years as Vicar of St Mark's, Dalston, until ill health forced him to retire just a month before his death in 1998, moved in the opposite direction. A banner strung to the church announced, 'A Victorian Church with Victorian Values'.

A man of surprising and strong views, he once described Britain as a scrounger's paradise. 'Money is handed out', he said, 'on a lavish scale. As soon as you arrive from Zambia or Botswana or Timbuctoo your first question is, "Where is the nearest Social Security Office?" Arrived there you receive your first handout, the first of many hundred. There are a million abusers in this country, a million cuts waiting to be made, a million scroungers to be given the proverbial kick in the backside.' This led to his being reported to the Race Relations Board and to the Archbishop of Canterbury, but no action was taken and he had in any case deputed one of his curates to welcome specially the many West Indians who were settling in the parish in the 1970s. A significant number of these were attracted to the church by Pateman's forthright personality and remained staunchly loyal – probably because they shared his values.

In 1965 he called the Home Secretary a 'purring old pussy' for closing down Britain's largest approved school and phasing out corporal punishment for misbehaved youths. Returning to this subject in 1978 he accused local councillors of wasting rate-payers' money on a 'cosy home for nasty little female muggers' and wanted the law to be changed so that those found guilty of mugging, football hooliganism or robbery with violence could be flogged. A referendum on this subject conducted among 5,000 of his parishioners won overwhelming approval.

When Pateman was appointed Vicar of St Mark's in 1956 he had already spent some years as a curate in Bethnal Green. His new responsibilities were considerable. The cathedral-like church, which was a listed building, would obviously need constant attention, but it was poorly attended and apparently unloved. Being of the conservative evangelical tradition (he had been trained by Donald Coggan when he was Principal of the London College of Divinity), he decided the task required the combination of the Book of Common Prayer, the King James Bible and intensive pastoral work in the streets of the parish.

Over the next 42 years he never deviated. His sermons were short and down to earth; he hated pomposity. In spite of his fulminations against delinquent young people he was fond of children. Irrespective of race or religious background, he encouraged them to use the Vicarage for their games. When in 1962, the choristers asked that they might wear Eton suits, including the traditional collars, he advertised for second-hand items and a local store also supplied six complete outfits. The choristers were not, however, exempt from corporal punishment if they stepped out of line, and this was administered by the Vicar who claimed that parents thanked him for taking their errant sons in hand. The punishment for brides arriving late for their weddings was different. In 1992 he introduced a sliding scale, details of which were handed to couples at wedding rehearsals. Ten minutes late meant the cutting of one of the hymns, twenty minutes the loss of two hymns and the dismissal from the church of the photographer, twenty-five minutes the dropping of a hymn and the dismissal of the choir, and thirty minutes late would cause the wedding to be cancelled.

Twenty years earlier when postmen were on strike, Pateman had announced that any of them seeking marriage in St Mark's would be given a 'work-to-rule' service – no choir, no bells, no heating, no lighting, no music, no photographs, no confetti. He added, 'Postmen earn the same money as me. I spent three years at university and am expected to live on £21 a week. Why can't they?' It is not known whether any postmen entered into the holy estate of matrimony in this austere environment. What is known, however, is that the congregation grew and that large sums were raised to maintain the building. Pateman, who was unmarried, was delighted to be exempt from the regulation requiring clergy to retire at 70 and was in fact 83 when ill health gave him no choice. Over a thousand people of all races and faiths attended his funeral and thanked God for his ministry.

33 A 'free' election

Towards the end of my time at Winchester – 25 September 1995, to be precise – I presided over the election of a bishop. It was the sort of election that used to be normal in the Soviet Union and other parts of Eastern Europe. The form was barely different from that of 1173 when King Henry II despatched the following missive to Winchester:

> Henry, King of the English, and Duke of the Normans and Aquitanians and Count of the Angevins, to his faithful monks of the Church of Winchester: greetings.
>
> I order you to hold a free election, and I forbid you, however, to accept anyone save Richard my clerk, Archdeacon of Poitiers.

In 1995 there came from London a *congé d'élire* granted by Queen Elizabeth II under the Great Seal authorizing the Chapter to hold an election. With it was a Letter Missive indicating the Crown's nomination of Michael Scott-Joynt, Bishop Suffragan of Stafford, expressed again in flowering legalese, but signed, disappointingly, by Virginia Bottomley, the Heritage Minister, the Queen having, it seemed, delegated church matters to the Department for the National Heritage. Absent from the document was any threat of horrific punishment in the event of the Chapter refusing to elect, the Statutes of Praemunire having being repealed in 1967.

An attempt by the General Synod to have the election of bishops replaced by the granting of Letters Patent was rejected by traditionalists in the House of Commons. So we assembled in the Lady Chapel of the cathedral, wearing our cassocks, at 10.30 a.m. and the Chapter Clerk called the names of the Chapter (myself, the canons residentiary and the honorary canons) to ascertain who was present, or rather who was absent. There were two – one serving in Zimbabwe, the other detained by the death of his mother-in-law that morning – but I ignored the law requiring them, by means of a ferocious statement, to be declared contumacious. One of the honorary canons present announced his intention to abstain, on the grounds that the procedure was an outdated nonsense, but I took the line that the quaint occasion provided an opportunity for the diocese to indicate its acceptance of a nomination which had involved much consultation, the church having had the decisive voice. So we elected our new bishop and, more importantly, prayed for him and his future ministry among us.

34 A bishop on pilgrimage

Peter Knott, who was a stimulating and popular Bishop of Norwich from 1985 to 1999, marked in 1996 the nine-hundredth anniversary of the building of Norwich Cathedral and the transfer of the bishopric from Thetford to Norwich by devoting 20 weeks to a carefully planned pilgrimage to every part of his diocese. He visited the churches, conducted services, had meetings with the clergy (all of whom he knew pretty well), went into schools and retirement homes, visited the sick, talked with farmers and local authorities, and occasionally took time off to employ his considerable gifts as a water colourist – the delightful results of which alone make his published diary of the year, *Bishop Peter's Pilgrimage* (1996), a worthwhile investment.

On the whole, he found the parishes in good heart. Attendances at services and meetings were quite small – around the 20–30 mark – but such a turnout usually represented a high proportion of the village populations. He came to believe that the church buildings were in a better state of preservation than at any other time since the Middle Ages and was particularly impressed by the quality of the churchwardens and other lay leaders. Quite often the Bible studies he attended were conducted by a lay person, as were the sermons in many of the churches. He saw his own primary role as that of leading the groups he met in prayer, though he also gave a good deal of time to helping the clergy to recognize their changed role in the modern world and the need for some to specialize. The strength of the lay leadership was obviously not unrelated to the fact that Norfolk has become a favoured retirement area for the ex-military and well-heeled professionals.

On his pilgrimage, Bishop Knott offered badges and prayer cards to all whom he met and these were declined only once – by a child who informed him that her mother had told her never to accept gifts from strange men.

35 *The death of a princess*

The events following the tragic death of Diana, Princess of Wales in August 1997 were, I thought, disturbing. I met her formally on several occasions and we once had a longish conversation. She had serious personal problems but offered an example of love and care that was attractive. Yet, although I deplored the circumstances of her death, I could not begin to feel the intensity of grief evidently experienced by millions who had never met her personally. The extraordinary scenes in London at the time of the funeral were far too close to mass hysteria for my liking.

The Westminster Abbey service also left me uneasy. I had been closely involved in the funeral that followed the assassination of Lord Mount-batten in 1979 and this, because of the circumstances, was a profoundly moving event. It was not to be expected that 18 years later the funeral of a young princess would take exactly the same form. But once a decision has been made to depart from the church's appointed liturgy and to sub-stitute for a preacher, who might be expected to place the occasion in some sort of eternal context, a relative or friend, who will simply pay tribute to the deceased, considerable care needs to be taken to ensure that the Christian message of penitence, hope and consolation gets through.

In the event, the mixture of material, including the scarcely veiled attack on the Royal Family by the Princess's brother, which drew applause from inside and outside the Abbey, failed to do this. It prob-ably expressed well the emotions of the hour, but the church is called to do more than this. The simplest and best comment by a churchman was, I thought, made on the day following the tragedy when the Bishop of Ely, Stephen Sykes, said, 'Diana is in heaven, not because she did good things, but because God loves her.'

36 *The do-it-yourself funeral*

An unanticipated consequence of this extraordinary funeral was soon to be observed in the services arranged for other funerals, especially those of non-churchgoers. The provisions of the Alternative Services Book offered a degree of flexibility absent from the Book of Common Prayer rite and sensitive pastors already took pains to meet personal requests so that the service might be helpful to those most deeply affected by the death. But now came requests, often demands, for all manner of secular material – readings, sentimental songs and the like – together with tributes from tearful members of the family or friends. The result was to concentrate attention entirely on the deceased and, in many instances, to lose touch with that other realm where true comfort is alone to be experienced. Secularization is insidious in its expansion.

37 *Unhappy* Daily Telegraph *readers*

Sir – How dare Mrs Blair appear in Westminster Abbey without a hat?

Angela Ellis
Murcott, Oxon

Sir – Until the past 20 years or so, the church-going section of the nation prayed collectively for the Queen, the Prince of Wales, and all the Royal Family every week at Matins, Evensong or Holy Communion. Now, almost invariably, these prayers are omitted from the traditional services, and some of the new services such as the Rite A Communion Service do not include an appropriate prayer at all.

As someone who believes in the power of prayer, I am sure the omission has made much more difficult the Royal Family's task of creating successful relationships and setting a moral example.

That section of the nation who are practising Christians have a duty to pray for all our leaders. If that duty is disregarded, we cannot reasonably expect the Royal Family, with the pressures they face today, to be able to set the example they once did.

(Miss) Vanla Oxley
Queen Carmel, Som.

38 *Priest, pathologist and guru*

One of the most unusual of the Church of England's priests during the last quarter of the century was Martin Israel who was also a pathologist and a mystic. As a spiritual counsellor, a conductor of retreats and the author of many books, notably *Precious Living* (1976), *The Dark Face of Reality* (1989) and *Angels – Messengers of Grace* (1995), his influence was considerable.

He was born in Johannesburg in 1927, nurtured in the Jewish faith, and at the age of three felt called to 'a lonely life to discover life's meaning'. In his family's African servants he found what he called later 'an authenticity of character absent from Europeans'. One of the servant girls gave him an evangelical Christian tract in which the image of the crucified Christ made a deep impression on him, but it was another 35 years before he became a Christian.

Meanwhile he pursued a brilliant medical career and, after spending three years with the British RAMC, returned to civilian life in 1958 to become Lecturer, then Senior Lecturer in Pathology at the Royal College of Surgeons. He co-authored what became the standard textbook on histopathology. He was, however, always a loner and for a period of 16 years suffered periods of acute depression, but he was released from this through the help of a woman psychologist, broke with Judaism and began to exercise a ministry of spiritual healing and counselling.

Israel became an Anglican largely through the influence of a number of monastic communities – he had the style and appearance of a monk – and was encouraged to seek Holy Orders in 1974 by the then Bishop of London, Graham Leonard. After serving as an honorary priest at St Michael's, Cornhill in the City of London he became Vicar of Holy Trinity Church, Prince Consort Road in Kensington where he remained for 20 years until 1997. This large church had fallen on hard times but under his leadership and aided by a large number of devotees, for whom he was a spiritual guru, it soon began to flourish. He conducted some 15–20 retreats every year, spoke at many meetings and saw hundreds of people for personal counselling. He was president of the Guild of Health and of the Church's Fellowship for Psychical and Spiritual Studies, and although he officially retired from the Royal College of Surgeons in 1982 he continued to lecture there ten times a year until his parish and national commitments made this impossible. His ministry as spiritual guru was extended into the present century.

39 *The artists return*

Although Walter Hussey worked ceaselessly to re-establish contact between the church and the artist, with remarkable results at St Matthew's, Northampton and Chichester Cathedral, and even though Coventry Cathedral came to be admired more for its artistic content than for its design, the church remained reluctant to introduce the work of contemporary artists into its buildings. Towards the end of the century, however, this began to change and cathedrals and churches, willing to be a little more adventurous, found a ready response from artists who were sensitive to the sacred and generous in their recognition of limited church budgets.

In 1979 my predecessor at Winchester, Michael Stancliffe, commissioned Thetis Blacker, a leading batik artist, to create for the nave of the cathedral 16 large banners on the themes of creation and redemption. The result was spectacular – a vivid yellow-orange background for a multitude of figures, some of them mythological and symbolic, all reflecting something of her Peruvian family background and time spent in South East Asia, as well as her own exuberant personality. Stancliffe said at the time, 'They will do for people's spirits what a fanfare of trumpets does for them through their ears.' And they did, though not everyone liked the sound. Examples of her work, often with a Phoenix as a resurrection symbol, can now be found in Westminster Abbey, St George's Chapel, Windsor, St Albans, Aberdeen and Durham Cathedrals as well as in numerous other churches – everywhere illuminating and inspiring.

Peter Eugene Ball's contributions, as a sculptor, to Winchester Cathedral started by accident. In the early stages of his career he sent to an art exhibition in the cathedral a *Christus* that had been rejected by the church for which it was commissioned. We hung it high in the Norman north transept where it seemed immediately at home, so much so that it has remained there ever since, paid for by a member of the congregation. Other work was subsequently commissioned from him – a moving *pietà* for the Lady Chapel, which portrays Mary as an older, peasant-like woman in deep sorrow, a delightful Christmas crib in technicolour, an unusual altar reflecting a rippling stream and fishes, with two standing candlesticks (the Apostles Andrew and Peter) – all appropriate to a chapel where Izaac Walton, father of English anglers, is buried.

Ball works with driftwood and other discarded materials, including beaten metal, and makes extensive use of gold leaf and colour. His style owes much to the Romanesque, yet has a timeless quality that speaks powerfully to the modern age. Other examples of his work are to be found in Birmingham, Worcester, Southwark, Southwell and Portsmouth Cathedrals, as well as in many parish churches.

Antony Gormley, Britain's leading sculptor, provided as a gift a life-size human figure in lead – Sound 2 – which relates to the element of water and makes a dramatic and moving sight in the cathedral crypt, especially in winter months when this is partly flooded.

40 *Discarding a bishop*

On 7 October 1997 two leading members of Forward in Faith – an organization of Anglo-Catholics formed to continue the opposition to women priests, and perhaps better called 'Backward in Doubt', were interviewed on the BBC's *File on Four* programme. Father Chris Collins and Father Beresford Skelton, both priests in Durham diocese, were questioned about their attitude to the Bishop of Durham – Michael Turnbull – and their replies were unequivocal.

Father Collins said:

> There's no doubt that the Bishop of Beverley [the flying bishop for the Province of York] is my bishop. He is the bishop that I pray for daily. He is the bishop I look to for spiritual direction. He is the bishop I look to as my Father in God . . . The Bishop of Durham is bishop in juridical terms. I'm not actually in sacramental communion with him because of the action he has taken over the ordination of women and so I find it very difficult even to contemplate receiving communion at his hands.

Father Skelton, asked if he would welcome the Bishop of Durham to celebrate the Eucharist in his parish, replied, 'No, he wouldn't be welcome – not for a Eucharist. He would be welcome to attend non-eucharistic worship, but would not be allowed to celebrate at the altar.'

41 *'Outrage' in the pulpit at Canterbury*

On Easter Day 1998 Archbishop Carey entered the pulpit of Canterbury Cathedral at the morning service, thus continuing a custom observed by most of his predecessors. Unlike them, however, he was followed by six young men carrying banners and shouting slogans. They were members of 'Outrage', an organization fighting for homosexual rights, and their leader, Peter Tatchell, seized the pulpit microphone and spoke to the congregation about the wickedness of the church's attitude to homosexuals and, in particular, Carey's opposition to the lowering of the age of consent and his attitude to homosexuality generally. None of the cathedral vergers was sharp enough to turn the microphone off, but eventually the police removed the protesters from the pulpit and peace and order were restored. Carey assured the congregation that the incident was not important when compared with the Easter theme, but it gained worldwide publicity.

Twelve months earlier, also on a Sunday, Tatchell and his supporters had gatecrashed an informal gathering in the garden of Lambeth Palace of the Archbishop and ten other Anglican leaders from different parts of the world who had travelled to London to plan the 1998 Lambeth Conference. Banners were waved, slogans were screamed and Tatchell accused Carey of being a moral coward, of hating homosexuals and of refusing to talk to them. Much publicity resulted from this and, taken together, with the prospect of more to come, the two incidents ensured that the church could no longer hope to get away with general statements about 'compassion' and 'concern for you', but must face the homosexual issue head on.

42 The Lambeth rift

The 1998 Lambeth Conference was said by the Archbishop of Canterbury to have been successful and even made money, but for many of the 750 bishops who were present it turned into something of a nightmare. The programme was harmless enough. There were discussions on familiar themes – the Bible, the World and the Church, Third World debt and relations with Muslims. Rowan Williams, then Bishop of Monmouth, gave a profound presentation on the 'Making of Moral Decisions', which a good few failed to understand, and there was an embarrassing moment when an address by the President of the World Bank on world poverty was preceded by a Christian Aid film highly critical of the World Bank. This was remedied by a standing ovation for the speaker.

Throughout the three weeks, however, there simmered a painfully divisive conflict over the issue of homosexuality and right at the end of the conference this boiled over and did much harm. The signs of its danger were evident long before the bishops convened. A gathering of Third World bishops and laity at Kuala Lumpur had issued a strong statement attacking the provinces of the Northern hemisphere for their toleration of 'sinful' homosexual practices and their disregard of the authority of the Bible. Bishop Jack Spong led some American bishops in a response that not only attacked the statement but included George Carey and the General Synod in its condemnation and went on to present a new and more liberal form of Christianity.

With all this, and more, being exchanged, Carey and the conference organizers made the fatal mistake of delegating the subject of homosexuality to just one of its sections, with the request that an appropriate resolution should be submitted to a final plenary session of the conference. This meant that a very large number of bishops who had strong views on the matter had no opportunity to ventilate them until one afternoon shortly before they were due to depart. The resolution, when it came, offered a compromise so weak that it satisfied none of the protagonists. An ugly debate ensued, during which things were said that ought never to be said at any Christian assembly, and Carey, seeking to calm the situation, proposed an eight-word addition to the resolution – 'While rejecting homosexual practice as incompatible with scripture' – and explained, 'I have long been persuaded that the entire Bible and Christian tradition gives us no permission to condone sexual practices of any sort outside the relationship of husband and wife in holy matrimony.' A vote on the amended resolution was called almost immediately, and this was passed by 526 to 70, with 45 abstentions. The conference had declared its mind but in the process deepened the rift between Anglicans who had, not only a passionate disagreement about a particular sexual issue, but also about the nature of Christianity itself. More than a majority vote was going to be needed to resolve this.

43 Rallying the young

It seemed curious that by the 1990s only Evangelicals devoted substantial resources to work among young people. During my years at Winchester an annual 'Rave in the Nave' organized by the diocesan youth department filled the cathedral for a long Saturday evening, but by and large it was only the evangelical churches that undertook large-scale youth work. They had a special ability to attract students. Archbishop Carey, aware of the serious lack of young people in the pews, made two major efforts to rally those already attached to the church and in the process discovered more about the bleakness of the scene. He decided to lead 1,000 of them on a pilgrimage to Taizé, in Burgundy, and asked each of the dioceses to nominate 20 young people between the ages of 16 and 23 to accompany him. Many of the dioceses told him that they could not raise 20 such young people, but in the end he managed to get his 1,000 from the rest and a very profitable week was spent with the world-famous community.

His next initiative was to organize in 1998 a Spring bank holiday weekend rally in London, under the title 'Time of Our Lives', to which the dioceses were asked to send 100 young people. Five thousand were hoped for, but again many dioceses could not raise their quota and fewer than four thousand were recruited. Young people from London churches helped to fill the gap and a varied programme of services, seminars and jazz concerts was a great success, though the whole week-end cost £400,000.

Later that year the General Synod applauded the Archbishop's initia-tive and urged him to organize a similar rally a few years hence. He agreed to do this provided that each diocese was prepared to contribute £5,000 to its cost (he had himself raised the money for his first venture), but more than half the dioceses responded that they could not afford this, even though payment might be made in two instalments spread over a few years. Carey was not surprised by this but his reaction was candid: 'Once more, vision was blunted by shortsightedness.'

44 Two dames and a doctor

The General Synod, and the Church Assembly before it, provided a forum for three outstandingly able women, two of whom were re-warded for their contributions by being appointed DBE, the other earned a PhD in sociology at the London School of Economics.

Betty Ridley, a daughter of Bishop Henry Mosley of Southwell who confirmed me, and the widow of a priest who died young, was elected to the Church Assembly in 1945 when she was only 36 and gave 36 years to the church's central government. She and a few like-minded friends founded the Anglican Group for the Ordination of Women some 40 years before the legislation that allowed women priests was passed, and for most of this time battled against a mixture of prejudice and ridicule. But her concerns were not confined to this issue. She was deeply involved in ecumenical affairs with the British and the World Councils of Churches, served on commissions dealing with theological colleges, clergy deployment, redundant churches and synodical government. In 1972 she became the first woman to be appointed Third Church Estates Commissioner, with special responsibility for clergy housing.

In all these and many other spheres her grasp of essential points, directness of speech and a delightful sense of humour brought her great influence. Indeed there developed an unwillingness to reach a decision in committee until 'Betty's mind' on the matter had become known. Her retirement years were spent in Winchester from where she made a memorable television programme on the glories of Evensong, based on a Hampshire village church she had once attended. When she became dangerously ill, following a major operation, I ministered the church's last rites to her and bade her farewell, but she lived on for another three years and died aged 95. She wept with joy when she heard on the radio news of the decision that women could become priests.

Christian Howard was elected to the Church Assembly by York diocese in 1960 and brought to its debates an acute mind, a mature political sense (she was also active in the Liberal Party) and formidable skill as a debater. There was no mistaking her origins in the great aristocratic house where much of her life was spent and, following the early deaths of both her parents in the 1930s, she found herself, when only 19, more or less in charge of running Castle Howard.

She had a natural authority and soon made her presence felt in any company. But her robust style was tempered by a deep compassion, an unswerving commitment to liberal values in both church and state, and a warm sense of humour. She seemed quite indifferent to her appearance and evidently spent little on new clothes. Her chief concerns in the Church Assembly, then in the General Synod, were church unity and the ordination of women. The first took her into involvement in the World and the British Councils of Churches and the second into the vice-moderatorship of the Movement for the Ordination of Women. She was also responsible for the compilation, in 1972, of a magisterial report on the present state of opinion in the church on this subject. Like Betty Ridley, she never felt drawn to ordination herself, but both would have made excellent bishops had that ever been possible.

Margaret Hewitt's approach to the church's life was totally different. Elected to the Church Assembly by Exeter diocese in 1961, she was a leading member of the Anglo-Catholic traditionalist element and a founder-member of Women Against the Ordination of Women, the membership of which eventually rose to 5,500. Many found this inexplicable, since she specialized in teaching women's studies, was president of the Exeter branch of the National Council for Women and chairman of the Reid Trust for the Education of Women. She chaired an Ecumenical Decade for Women. But she professed a distinction between priesthood and ministry, and between Holy Orders and secular employment.

Her studies as a sociologist – she was Reader in Social Institutions at Exeter University – convinced her, she said, of the importance of tradition. Thus she was a strong supporter of the Prayer Book Society, chaired a committee responsible for reconsidering the Act of Settlement at a time when it was thought possible that the Prince of Wales might marry a Roman Catholic, and conducted a controversial investigation into Freemasonry. In the General Synod she relished her reputation as a grande dame, and rendered her presence all the more conspicuous through her penchant for large hats. Holding forth, incisively, from beneath this magnificent millinery, she appeared an almost insuperable opponent. But, although she was robustly dismissive of anything she classed as humbug, she also possessed warm sympathies, which enabled her to mix happily with everyone, including those with whom she most disagreed.

45 Old and new school ties

At the end of the century the social and educational backgrounds of the church's leaders had changed considerably. As late as 1958 no fewer than 38 of the 43 diocesan bishops had been to either Oxford or Cambridge. Eighteen of these had been to the leading public schools – Eton, Winchester, St Paul's, Rugby, Repton and the like – while the remainder had been to minor public schools and well-known grammar schools. Virtually all were from privileged backgrounds, thus reinforcing the general perception that the Church of England was to be identified with the prosperous and usually conservative minority in society. By 2000, however, the number of diocesan bishops who had attended major public schools was reduced from eighteen to four, with none from Eton, Winchester and Rugby. Twenty-eight had been to grammar schools and one, none other than the Archbishop of Canterbury, had been to a humble secondary modern school – at the time the lowest form of educational life. Twenty-six went on to Oxford or Cambridge, matriculating before these and other leading universities were flooded with top-class applicants, five to London University, four to Leeds, two to Lampeter and one each to Exeter, Lancaster, Edinburgh, Nottingham, Belfast and Karachi. It was not evident, however, that the calibre of the episcopal bench as a whole had been strengthened, but the explanation of this involved other factors.

46 Paying the cathedral bills

Multi-million-pound appeals for the repair of cathedral fabrics became normal from the 1970s onwards – ever increasing with the scourge of inflation and with heightened ambition. York Minster astonished most people and secured a knighthood for its Dean, Alan Richardson, by raising £2 million (worth £25 million in modern money) in the 1960s – a huge sum for those days, made possible by the 'patriotism' of

Yorkshire local authorities. Westminster Abbey was aiming for £10 million during my time there but this was later raised to £25 million and achieved – again because of its power to attract corporate money.

Elsewhere a new concern for ancient buildings enabled deans and chapters to draw a generous response from the counties and regions. Ely raised £4 million in the 1980s, Worcester and Salisbury then raised £5 million, Winchester topped £7 million, Norwich and Southwark asked for £10 million (some of which was required for ancillary buildings) and at the turn of the century St Paul's set out to raise £33 million for a massive programme of restoration and refurbishment to mark the three-hundredth anniversary of the completion of Wren's great building in 1708. Proximity to the finance houses of the City of London made this a realistic target. Another significant factor in all the appeals was a change of attitude by the government, and state funding, offered in return for self-help, led to the allocation of about £20 million over a period of 15 years.

I was, inevitably, deeply involved in the raising of Winchester's £7 million in 1990–92 and although this was a time of severe economic recession, when many Hampshire companies were laying off staff rather than giving money away, the achieving of what was then the highest cathedral appeal in a mere 18 months was not difficult. Much hard work by a large team of dedicated and generous laypeople, led by the Lord Lieutenant, and advised by a professional consultant, was the secret of the success and an invaluable spin-off benefit came from the need for me to devote about 12 months to visiting every part of the diocese and making new links with the parishes. I explained that, as a younger man, I had left a money-orientated career at the Westminster Bank in order to serve people, but had in the end spent most of my ministry dealing with money, including five years as Treasurer of Westminster Abbey, a £900,000 appeal for St Margaret's, Westminster, and now £7 million for 'our cathedral'.

Many cathedrals nonetheless ran into serious financial problems during the closing years of the century when the number of visitors went into sharp decline. This cut off the source of income on which the expansion of activity during the previous two decades had been based and was followed by a reduction in the Church Commissioners' grants. In 1994 the Howe Commission reported that 19 cathedrals were in deficit and that if legacies and appeals were excluded this figure would rise to 30. The largest annual deficit was then £486,000 and another seven cathedrals had deficits in excess of £180,000. The office of dean suddenly became much less attractive.

47 *The cost of clergy retirement*

By the end of this decade, the number of retired clergy (6,000) was approaching that of parish clergy in the full-time service of the church (8,872). There were several reasons for this. A continuing excess of retirements over ordinations was obviously the prime explanation, but there were a number of contributory factors, of which the inability of dioceses to pay more than a certain number of priests was becoming increasingly significant. This in turn was related to the high cost of pensions provisions, which were by then claiming a major proportion of the Church Commission's resources.

At the time of my own ordination in 1951 there were still some parishes in which the retired parson could lay claim to one-third of the benefice income as his pension. Unless this income was unusually high his successor would need a private income or take on additional responsibility until death ended the pension commitment. Most clergy continued to minister well into their seventies and often into their eighties and nineties, and this, not simply because pension provisions were small, but chiefly because there was little retirement housing available. Stipends provided no opportunity to accumulate capital for the purchase of even a small house on retirement.

All this began to change radically when a compulsory retirement age of 70 for all clergy was introduced in 1975. Pensions had to be substantially improved and shared-equity schemes and affordable rents were made available – these together making an increasingly heavy demand on the Church Commissioners. The effects of this were not felt immediately since the new retirement age did not apply to present office-holders. But gradually the pensions and housing accounts were plundered and the increasing strains and stresses of parish life pushed most of the clergy into retirement when they became 65. The effect was to make the Church Commissioners no longer the primary paymaster of the clergy but, instead, the administrators of their pension fund, with dramatic consequences for the finances of parishes and dioceses. When in 1998 responsibility for new pensions was transferred to the parishes and a subsequent actuarial review indicated a deficit of £11 million, the crisis deepened and it was noted that transfer of financial responsibility normally leads to transfer of power.

48 *Another tier of government*

The Archbishop's Council, which came into being in 1999, owed its existence to the debacle over the Church Commissioners' heavy financial losses in 1992. It was evident that the church as a whole exercised no effective control over a massive amount of its resources and George Carey was aware from the moment he became Archbishop that the church had no machinery for the co-ordination of the activities of its central departments. A commission was therefore appointed, under the chairmanship of the Bishop of Durham, Michael Turnbull, to investigate the situation and make proposals for reform. Its report, *Working as One Body*, appeared in 1995 and provided the most wide-ranging review ever of the Church of England's national structures.

The chief proposal was the setting up of a national council to take over the functions of the advisory Board of Ministry, the Central Board of Finance, the General Synod Standing and Policy Committees and to oversee the work of all the other national boards and councils. Many of the functions of the Church Commissioners were also to come under its oversight. The General Synod accepted most of the proposals but insisted on having ten of its own number, besides the two archbishops, on the Council, leaving only six to be nominated from outside its ranks. This was a disappointment to Carey who had hoped to infuse some new life and expertise into the machinery of government.

The function of the Council is to provide coherence, a scale of priorities and a sense of direction in Church House, Westminster, and to keep a close eye on finance. Since any significant proposals for change require the approval of the General Synod, its power is obviously limited, though its influence over the Synod's agenda and control of purse strings means that it is not toothless. Apparently the contribution of the nominated members has so far been considerable and refreshing. The Church of England is not, however, open to dramatic reformation and the insertion of an additional tier of government is rarely a recipe for renewal.

49 *Uncommon worship*

The Alternative Service Book, published in 1980, was the first authorized alternative to the 1662 Book of Common Prayer but was not intended to be the final word in liturgical revision, which had now come to be seen, at least by the Liturgical Commission, as an unending process. The General Synod authorized the new book for use until 1990 in order that its material might be tested further in the parishes and also to give time for the production of additional services. This authorization was subsequently extended to 2000.

The Liturgical Commission was therefore busy for another two decades and compiled volumes of material for the Advent and Christmas seasons and for Lent, Holy Week and Easter. Another book covered saints' days. The Commission was now conscious of the criticism that the ASB was too large to be easily manageable in congregational worship and the *Faith in the City* report had commented that the placing of a volume of 1,300 pages in the hands of a worshipper was a symptom of the gulf between the church and ordinary people in Urban Priority Areas.

It was decided therefore to abandon the idea of a single book in favour of a library of books, this to include *Common Worship*, published in 2000 and containing most of the material required for Sunday services, *Pastoral Services*, also published in 2000 and providing for Marriage, Funerals, Emergency Baptisms, Thanksgiving for the Gift of a Child, and Healing. These to be followed by volumes of Initiation Services, Daily Services, Seasonal Services and Ordination Services – six in all, and a treasury of rich liturgical material.

Such a library could hardly be said to be manageable in the hands of worshippers, and cost alone precluded investment in copies for congregational use. In any event, *Common Worship*, though elegantly printed, contained so many variants that its use required a considerable degree of liturgical dexterity. The two problems were solved by the printing of booklets for use at particular services, though even this proved to be an expensive option if seasonal variations were accommodated. Those wishing to stay with the Book of Common Prayer – a considerable number in Hereford and other rural dioceses – were spared any expense for as long as their old prayer books remained usable. No other church on earth ever elected to have wider variety or greater complexity in its forms of worship – not even those without liturgical texts.

50 *Chaplain to the Gastronomes*

When William (Bill) Atkins left a minor canonry of St Paul's Cathedral in 1955 to become Rector of St George's, Hanover Square, his Mayfair church, once attended by Handel and the place where Emma Hamilton, Shelley, Disraeli, George Eliot, Theodore Roosevelt and Asquith were married, was still busy with fashionable weddings. This soon changed, however, when the wealthy moved to the country at weekends, reducing also the size of Sunday congregations. Nonetheless, Atkins found plenty of other duties and, as a clubman, became a well-known figure in Mayfair. His appointment as chaplain to the Reunion des Gastronomes reflected his love of good food and wine. He displayed his flair for business by selling the church's old burial ground to solve an acute financial problem and provide a long-term income for the parish, and, although he was deeply attached to Anglican traditional forms of worship, he was one of the first in the West End to replace Sunday morning Mattins with a Sung Eucharist. He also played a major part, with Dean W. R. Matthews, in the co-editing of an acclaimed *History of St Paul's* (1957). On his completion of 40 years at St George's, the Bishop of London asked him gently if he had ever contemplated retirement. He replied immediately, 'No, I have never regarded this as a temporary appointment.' He stayed on for a further five years, retiring only when his eyesight failed him, by which time he was aged 89.

51 *'A friend to all on board'*

Although the Channel Islands come under the jurisdiction of the Bishop of Winchester (they were once in the nearby French diocese of Coutances), they constitute a world of their own where church attendance is significantly higher than in mainland Britain. Jersey is an island of no more than 50 square miles and a resident population of about 65,000. Yet, in common with Guernsey, it has most of the external apparatus of a great nation-state expressed in miniature. The Lieutenant-Governor represents the Queen, the Bailiff combines the offices of Lord Chancellor, Prime Minister and Speaker of the States – the equivalent of the Westminster Parliament. It also has its own legal system, more akin to the French than the English. And, being a tax haven, it has many citizens with extraordinary wealth. Attending a lunch after the annual service to mark the opening of the legal year, at which I had preached, it turned out that the Bailiff and myself were the only ones at the table who did not own his own aircraft.

The social and political role of the Anglican clergy is interesting. Until 1939 the 12 Crown-appointed rectors, of whom the Dean is one, had seats in the States and exercised considerable power. This arrangement did not survive the war, when all the islands came under German occupation, but the Dean still has a seat in the States (non-voting) and serves on a number of its committees. The rectors have retained a similar role on their secular parish councils. For a period of about 250 years until the nineteenth century, no Bishop of Winchester visited the Channel Islands, so the Deans of Jersey and Guernsey acquired a good deal of delegated authority, including that of collating new rectors and, being 100 miles from the mainland, they also have an important pastoral role among the clergy and in the parishes.

The Dean of Jersey, during the whole of my time at Winchester, was Basil O'Ferrall who, like several of his predecessors, had been a senior chaplain in the armed forces. The gifts of personality, pastoral skill and leadership that took him to the post of Chaplain of the Fleet were ideal for Jersey. He treated the island as if it were a very large naval vessel at sea, with himself in the traditional chaplain's role of 'a friend to all on board'. He took his position in the States very seriously and was known and admired by all social classes ranging from the Lieutenant-Governor to the migrant workers in the hotels. He was often able to defuse the potentially explosive conflicts that can arise in small, introverted societies, and did a great deal to strengthen relations between Anglicans, Methodists and Roman Catholics. O'Ferrall proved to be the last of the ex-service chaplains to be appointed Dean and the post now tends to be filled from among the existing rectors, thus returning to the normal pre-1939 practice.

52 Back to rural Hampshire

When Bruce Kington succeeded Samuel Boothman as Rector of the Hampshire parishes of Farley Chamberlayne, Braishfield, Michelmersh and Timsbury in 1981 (see pages 15–17), he became responsible for four parishes, whereas there had previously been two. In 1998 a fifth, Awbridge, was added, extending his territory to an area 5 miles long, 9 miles across. A countryman by birth and style, he was nonetheless struck by the amount of travelling involved, both for the Sunday services and for general pastoral work, as well as involvement in church and other community organizations. His arrival coincided with the retirement of the village schoolmistress after decades of service and the opening of a new village hall, so times were changing.

Whereas Farley Chamberlayne and Braishfield had normally had two, sometimes three, services every Sunday, this was no longer possible and the proposed reduction was not welcomed by the parishioners. But Rector and churchwardens devised a new pattern that would provide one service in each church, and this was eventually accepted. Social change, already noticed by Boothman during his final years, also helped.

The villages became attractive to medical consultants, barristers and the like. The gentry in the great houses were replaced by media and sports personalities – David Frost occupies the magnificent eighteenth-century former Rectory at Michelmersh, while David Gower, the former England cricket captain and now a television commentator, lives in a large new house at Braishfield – and the parishes have become very expensive places for housing. Even so, the population has increased to about 2,000.

Diligent though he undoubtedly is, and an ideal country priest, Kington can no longer offer the kind of ministry possible to his predecessors. He conducts three or four Sunday services, I usually undertake responsibility for another, and there are other retired clergy in the area ready to help. Awbridge frequently has laity-led services, it being a strong outpost of Evangelicalism, with impressive Sunday school and youth work. A typical 8-day Christmas diary included 12 services. Fifty per cent of all services are those of the BCP, 50 per cent modern forms. Besides the services, most months there are as many as a dozen other events and activities – Bible study and prayer groups, lunch clubs, worship committees, wives' groups, Alpha courses and money-raising for developing-world churches – as well as church council meetings. Couples are prepared for marriage, the sick are visited and the bereaved comforted, but it is impossible for the Rector to undertake indiscriminate house-to-house visiting or to be a constant presence in every village. A well-produced monthly magazine and weekly information sheets at services are a vital means of communication of which he makes good use.

Strikingly different from 50 years ago is the involvement of the laity in both the worship and mission, and the Rector, being an Evangelical, ensures that evangelism is not overlooked. The financial affairs of this united benefice are handled entirely by the laity, and the diocesan quota of £36,000, rising annually, suggests a different church world from that of 1950 when the five parishes were asked to contribute no more than about £50 between them.

For a fairly recent arrival from the cathedral world such as myself, church attendances seem small – forty or so at Braishfield and Awbridge, about a dozen each at Farley Chamberlayne, Michelmersh and Timsbury. But these figures increase significantly when mid-week services and non-weekly attendance are taken into account and all the churches are still used for weddings, baptisms and funerals by many others. As a proportion of the population, attendance is much higher than in urban churches and influence greater. This is not unrelated to the class structure.

In spite of the many difficulties and disappointments in the life of the Church of England, experienced in the second half of the twentieth century, the country churches continue to provide in most regions a basically traditional and much valued ministry. The united benefice in which I lend a hand has had just two Rectors in sixty years.

53 All's well that ends well – or does it?

Archbishop Carey recalled in his autobiography *Know the Truth* (2004) his feeling on the day he left Lambeth Palace for the last time, having gone into retirement at the end of October 2002:

> We drove out of the darkened Palace into the brightly-lit and noisy Lambeth Palace Road, and across the bridge to the Embankment. We were on our way home, with no regrets and no looking back – simply profoundly thankful to God for his guidance over the years.
>
> Much had been achieved by so many people working together. There was a deeper unity in the House of Bishops, and, more importantly, no one could now point the finger at so-called 'unbelieving Bishops'. The ordination of women to the priesthood was now a fact, and women were visible at practically every level of church life. Indeed I was sure that the ordination of women to the episcopate, although a contentious issue, would happen one day. The financial crisis created by the Church Commissioners' problems in the early nineties had resulted in reformed and clearer structures. Mission and evangelism were priorities in church life, and 'Springboard' was truly a 'gift' to the wider church. Ecumenical relations were firmly on track and beginning to bear fruit. Inter-faith co-operation and dialogue were significant realities in the church and the nation, with the Archbishop of Canterbury taking a leading role. Relations with the monarchy and the government were also very healthy. The Anglican Communion was in good heart, and the Lambeth Conference of 1998 had revealed the strength of the church in the developing world. As we drove away we felt confident about handing on to my successor, Rowan Williams, a national church that was in good heart, even if, like other great institutions, it faces many challenges in the years ahead.

It seems fair to assume that Rowan Williams, faced with crisis after crisis, including the possible dismemberment of the Anglican Communion itself, would have judged his inheritance differently.

An Epilogue

1 *The inconvenience of new ideas*

By the end of the century the church was in many ways very different from the church into whose ministry I was ordained in 1951, as indeed was the wider world to which it belonged. Yet in all but a few places it was still recognizable as the Church of England and if it were possible to relive my life I would unhesitatingly seek to develop my Christian discipleship within its borders. There were many surprises on my 50-year journey and hardly a dull moment. This because it was my good fortune to meet, among a large number of fellow-travellers, men and women of deep faith, considerable gifts and immense courage.

My heroes remain the parish priests whose dedicated ministries have helped to keep the faith alive, led the offering of worship and provided constant pastoral care in a great variety of circumstances, many of these difficult and discouraging. I have a special admiration for those lay-people, priests and bishops whose faith has driven them to pioneer new approaches to mission and ministry. Within the Church of England there has always been ample freedom to strike out in new directions and I am sad that this freedom was not more fully exploited and that when it was the results were not often incorporated into diocesan and other structures.

Equally, I regret that although many of the best minds in the church were appointed to examine specific problems and opportunities that arose in a particularly turbulent half-century few of their findings and recommendations were taken seriously. The attempts of theologians to present the faith in terms appropriate to the modern age were also given a dusty reception, and the retreat of university teachers into the realm of technical scholarship unrelated to living faith deprived the church of a vital source of inspiration. The parish clergy, for the most part, no longer read serious books.

A totally unexpected development was the serious decline in the church's numerical strength in every part of its life. By the end of the century this had halved. I belonged to the post-war generation of new priests who believed that if certain elements in the church's life were to be reformed the erosion of its membership could be halted and possibly reversed. Even the sociologist Leslie Paul forecast conservatively, in his 1964 report, that the number of ordinations would rise annually to a peak of 831 in 1971. In fact, they never reached more than 592, then fell steadily to 393.

What we did not foresee was that the major obstacle to the church's revival, and possibly its survival, would come from the fragmentation of Western European society and a widespread rejection of most of the established institutions of social cohesion. The causes of this profound cultural change are still debated but its effect in most countries was the forsaking of churches, especially those with strong historical roots in society, along with political parties, trade unions, agencies of law and order, lifelong marriage and many voluntary organizations. Sport and entertainment, conveyed to homes by television, became the major preoccupation of the masses and the door was opened to creeping secularization.

Faced by such a cultural transformation, it is hardly surprising that long-established churches did not know which way to turn. But it was a constant source of frustration and disappointment to me that the leadership of the Church of England, and by this I do not mean simply the bishops, was unwilling to face challenging facts and to recognize the need for flexibility of structures and strategies essential to mission in an ever-changing society. There are of course few things more inconvenient than new ideas, but a community that claims to be an agency of God's free-ranging Holy Spirit in the world should be open to at least some of these – provided it is not lacking in faith and vision.

2 *Signs of hope*

Without faith and vision little can be achieved, yet the Church of England still has very considerable resources awaiting constructive use – over 16,000 places of worship, 8,700 full-time stipendiary clergy, 1,250 chaplains in hospitals, schools and colleges, the armed services and prisons, 2,000 non-stipendiary clergy, 6,000 retired clergy, of whom about half are assisting in parishes, 10,000 Readers, 400 authorized lay workers, 370 dignitaries in leadership roles. Church schools number 4,700, educating 925,000 pupils, and at the time of the 1992 crisis the assets of the Church Commissioners were valued at £3,000 million. This is not a church on its beam ends.

Church life as a whole is much healthier than it was when I entered its ordained ministry. The best of its worship is livelier and more attuned to contemporary needs, over 2,000 women are in the priesthood, the laity are more deeply involved, greater financial responsibility is accepted by the parishes and there is wider social concern. These are changes of considerable significance and I am thankful to have experienced their arrival.

The Church of England retains therefore the capacity to survive a little longer and indeed to expand its influence, if not its numerical strength, provided the leadership is bold enough to move resources in new directions. The need for change has become very urgent, since the parochial system on which the church's ministry has been almost exclusively based for 13 centuries or more is on the verge of collapse. There is no possibility, within the foreseeable future, of recruiting men and women in numbers sufficient to continue this system under the traditional leadership of full-time priests. Even if there were, it is very doubtful if the money necessary for the adequate remuneration of such priests would become available. What is more, the point has now been reached at which the effectiveness of local church life will not tolerate further increases in the size of multi-parish benefices. The maintenance of a significant presence, with the prospect of growth, in every community requires a different strategy.

Fortunately the kind of new strategy needed has been considered over several years by some of the church's bolder spirits and there has been sufficient experiment to indicate a way forward. Theology and need combine to demand that local churches become more lay-orientated and lay-led. Yet a church order that is faithful to origins and tradition requires an ordained priesthood, though not necessarily, or even now desirably, one that is a salaried occupation.

Let the parishes therefore nominate their own priest to serve within a predominantly lay ministerial community. Such communities may well require, however, certain gifts that are not to be found within their own membership. These should be provided by a diocesan ministerial team, perhaps 100 strong, of full-time priests and lay specialists who, under the direction of the bishop, will be available to the parishes for tasks such as the ordering of worship, education, youth work and particular pastoral problems.

The responsibilities of the diocesan team should extend to the many other Christian communities that come into being whenever a few believers gather in the name of Christ – in workplaces, educational institutions, politics, the health service, recreational activity and other spheres of human activity. Such expressions of church life are not less important than the residential parishes and everywhere the involvement of other churches should be sought.

The Church of England's future depends therefore more on the development of a multitude of small influential cells than on the building of larger congregations, though there will always be a place for some of these in cathedrals and town churches. Whatever their size, it is essential that they be open, tolerant communities in which men and women who are at different stages of the Christian journey are accepted and valued. In the early years of the new millennium I am encouraged by clear signs that this fresh understanding of the nature of the church and its mission is becoming more widely recognized. So my journey ends with renewed hope.